Praise for A DIFFERENT SPIRIT

"Where was this book when my own children with disabilities approached their b'nai mitzvah? We had no road map and would have cherished the wisdom gathered here—the honest reflections, an abundance of practical tools, and generous stories from others who had walked this path before us. If you're a parent preparing for your child's b'nai mitzvah, or a clergy member or Hebrew school director or teacher seeking to understand what a child and their family need at this precious and sensitive time, this book is the companion you'll be grateful to have by your side."

—Rabbi Dianne Cohler-Esses, Romemu, New York City

"Howard Blas and Ilana Trachtman have given our Jewish community an extraordinary gift. *A Different Spirit* is a call to conscience, a wellspring of practical wisdom, and a celebration of every child's sacred worth. It opens our hearts and imaginations to what b'nai mitzvah can—and must—be when we honor every soul as *b'tzelem Elohim*, created in the image of God. I am inspired and deeply grateful for this indispensable resource."

—Rabbi Angela Buchdahl, Central Synagogue, New York City

"Children with disabilities have too often not been included in bar and bat mitzvahs, leaving them and their families excluded from the synagogue community. This pioneering book is transformative. It declares not just that we *can*, but that we *must* include these children; and it offers a wealth of practical advice on how to make meaningful ceremonies for these children. This book will change lives, families, and communities."

—Rabbi Chaim Steinmetz, Congregation Kehilath Jeshurun, New York City

"*A Different Spirit* is an unparallelled resource for individuals, families, and professionals. And well beyond its practical value, it opens unimagined paths toward full spiritual inclusion and communal membership."

—Andrés Martin, MD, PhD, Riva Ariella Ritvo Professor, Yale School of Medicine

"This immensely accessible, useful book is an invaluable resource in making the message of *b'tzelem Elohim* a reality. It will be read with gratitude by parents, rabbis, educators, and the children themselves."

—Mark Oppenheimer, author of *Thirteen and a Day: The Bar and Bat Mitzvah Across America*

"Invaluable information and advice for any parent of a child with a disability who is planning a b'nai mitzvah—and in fact for every Jewish parent planning one. There has never been a more comprehensive compilation of knowledge on the subject than this."

—Rabbi Mordechai Liebling, faculty emeritus at Reconstructionist Rabbinical College

"This wonderful book is guided by a passionately and uncompromisingly held principle: There is simply no physical, cognitive, or psychological challenge that cannot be met, indeed, that has not already been met. [Blas and Trachtman] challenge us to recall and help us to embody an elemental truth of Jewish life: the Torah belongs to all of us. This book is a significant contribution to Jewish life for which we should all be grateful."

—Rabbi Shai Held, president of the Hadar Institute and author of *Judaism Is About Love: Recovering the Heart of Jewish Life*

"An extraordinarily important book that should be essential reading for synagogue and community leaders, educators, and truly, for everyone. It offers valuable insights, guidance, and comprehensive information to support families with a member with a disability as they navigate Jewish communal life, and it also deepens our sensitivity to becoming more inclusive in all aspects of our community."

—Debbie Niderberg, co-founder and executive director of Hidden Sparks

"Finally! A definitive how-to guide that offers concrete advice and spiritual wisdom to make the b'nai mitzvah experience truly accessible to everyone. *A Different Spirit* should be on the shelf of every rabbi, synagogue staff-person, and Jewish educator.

—Jay Ruderman, Ruderman Family Foundation

"A vital resource for clergy, educators, parents, and individuals with disabilities. In the spirit of 'nothing about us without us,' *A Different Spirit* provides the powerful perspective of individuals with disabilities, whose reflections about their experiences add richness and depth to the conversation. Moreover, readers will discover that in considering the needs of individuals with disabilities, they will, in fact, be moving their congregations or schools to a more welcoming and inclusive stance for all members of the community. This book has my strongest recommendation as an educator and as a parent."

—Professor Jeffrey Kress, provost and Dr. Bernard Heller Professor of Jewish Education, Jewish Theological Seminary

"A wonderful book on many levels. . . .With many insights about the Jewish faith and a theological understanding of being created in the image of God, the book offers inclusion resources, accommodations, family supports, and most of all, hope that any child with a disability can be valued, included, and appreciated as a child of God."

—Rev. Tom Jones, executive director, Faith Inclusion Network

"[The authors] understand the value and the magic that the b'nai mitzvah ceremony and event mean to all Jewish youth and their families, regardless of their physical, mental, or financial status. Thank you for your deep commitment to supporting the next generation of Jews, in all our forms."

—Peter Shapiro, music entrepreneur, owner of Brooklyn Bowl and Capitol Theater, publisher of *Relix Magazine*

A Different Spirit

Creating Meaningful B'nai Mitzvah for Children with Disabilities

HOWARD BLAS AND ILANA TRACHTMAN

BEHRMAN HOUSE
www.behrmanhouse.com

To all of my students and their families, who have served as my most important teachers and sources of wisdom and strength throughout my b'nai mitzvah teaching career—H.B.

For Lior Liebling, who opened the door—I.T.

The Publisher gratefully acknowledges Deborah Bodin Cohen, Jessica Fein, and Ellen Seidman for their thoughtful comments on the manuscript during its development.

The ideas, suggestions, and advice in this book are not intended as a substitute for professional diagnosis, treatment, or therapy, nor to replace the services of qualified medical or mental health professionals.

Published by Behrman House, Inc.
Millburn, New Jersey 07041
www.behrmanhouse.com

ISBN 978-1-68115-099-4

Library of Congress Cataloging-in-Publication Data
Names: Blas, Howard, author. | Trachtman, Ilana, author.
Title: A different spirit : creating meaningful b'nai mitzvah for children with disabilities / Howard Blas and Ilana Trachtman.
Description: Millburn, New Jersey : Behrman House, Inc., [2026] | Includes bibliographical references and index. | Summary: "A comprehensive guide for clergy and families as they create meaningful and inclusive b'nai mitzvah celebrations for teens with special needs"-- Provided by publisher.
Identifiers: LCCN 2025015595 (print) | LCCN 2025015596 (ebook) | ISBN 9781681150994 (paperback) | ISBN 9781681151724 (ebook)
Subjects: LCSH: Bar mitzvah. | Bat mitzvah. | Teenagers with disabilities.
Classification: LCC BM707 .B545 2026 (print) | LCC BM707 (ebook) | DDC 296.4/424--dc23/eng/20250510
LC record available at https://lccn.loc.gov/2025015595
LC ebook record available at https://lccn.loc.gov/2025015596

Design by Zatar Creative
Edited by Aviva Lucas Gutnick

Cover art: *Hora*, 1957 (oil on canvas) by Baruch Agadati (1895–1976), Tel Aviv Museum of Art, Israel. Gift of Sir & Lady Sydney Lipworth/Bridgeman Images.
Cover art background: Adobe Stock.

Interior images: p139: George Studio, Shutterstock, and Canva: Seza, evegenybobrov, medzcreative; p142: AdobeStock; p157, 161: Marion Green and cantoreducator.com; p174 Mark Skitsky, Shutterstock; p160, 162, 164, 165, 235-243: Gateways.

Printed in China

9 8 7 6 5 4 3 2 1

CONTENTS

* INTRODUCTION *

Howard Blas and Ilana Trachtman

Yes, This Book Is for You

When I (Howard) first conceived of this book many years ago, I pictured a desperate parent searching the Judaica section of a large bookstore for a book that would help them with a seemingly insurmountable problem: how to imagine *b'nai mitzvah* for their child with disabilities. For years, their attempts to get advice and guidance from clergy were not adequately addressed. How would their child—who is deaf or blind or autistic, or who has mobility challenges, learning disabilities, or intellectual and developmental disabilities—meaningfully mark this important life-cycle event like other siblings or classmates did? Such a book didn't exist. Until now. Parents, this book is for you! You will hear from parents like you who have found the best way for their child, family, and community to mark b'nai mitzvah.

Perhaps you are a rabbi or cantor who felt unprepared, frustrated, at a loss, or even embarrassed when a family came to meet with you to discuss b'nai mitzvah for their child with disabilities and you had no idea what to offer. How in the world might a nonverbal child have an *aliyah*, a call to the Torah? Or how does a blind person coming up to the Torah fit in with your synagogue's established norms and practices? Clergy, this book is for you! We want to share with you real-life examples of ways synagogues of all denominations have marked b'nai mitzvah for people with disabilities—from Shabbat morning in the main synagogue, to celebrations on other days and in other venues. You will read personal stories of clergy who have disabilities themselves and children with disabilities who have celebrated their milestone.

If you are tasked with teaching sometimes very hard-to-teach students, this book is for you! For many, preparing for b'nai mitzvah means learning to read Torah or *Haftarah* (reading from the Prophets), lead prayers, and deliver a *d'var Torah* (Torah teaching), but preparation for students with disabilities involves so much more. We have included for you tools for working with many learning styles and disabilities.

And if you are a student with a disability who is nervous and unsure and wondering what your b'nai mitzvah preparation and milestone could look and feel like, this book is for you! Several contributors—some who celebrated their own b'nai mitzvah relatively recently—share how they started off very nervous or even negative (anti), then got through the process and felt good about it!

The Reason for This Book (Ilana's Story)

The bar mitzvah of a boy with Down syndrome changed my life.

This is not hyperbole.

In 2004 I was trying, unsuccessfully, to pray with intention at a Rosh Hashanah service. In fact, I felt unsuccessful at praying anywhere with intention. Connecting to God, the spirit—any spirit—eluded me. And so I found myself daydreaming, my usual synagogue activity.

Daydreaming didn't last long because of the piercing passion of someone behind me, someone who had no problem connecting. The voice was loud and off-key, and pronounced *reish* (the Hebrew "r" sound) like *weis*. After a few minutes, curiosity beat out manners, and I swiveled around. I was surprised, and then fascinated, by the source of that atonal devotion: a twelve-year-old boy with Down syndrome. To my knowledge, I had never seen anyone with a disability in synagogue before, let alone swaying and praying with the focused devotion of a Chasid. And so I stalked Lior Liebling, with the same idea as the restaurant customer in *When Harry Met Sally*, who witnesses Sally Albright's performance of ecstasy and announces, "I'll have what she's having."

How could Lior, a child with a cognitive disability, pray if I couldn't? When I heard that Lior would be having a bar mitzvah in eight months, I doggedly pursued this question in the way that I knew how: with a film crew. Lior, and the Liebling/Iser family, opened their lives to me and the crew. They were overwhelmingly generous and humble, sharing whole days, secrets, hopes, grief, and triumphs with us. And in the process, we discovered that there was much more to their story than the fact that their son and brother could pray like nobody's business.

Over eight months, we embedded with Lior's family, school, and community, and captured the journey to his bar mitzvah on film. *Praying with Lior* premiered in theaters in 2008, and the popularity and critical acclaim surprised everyone, especially me and my distributor. One critic called Lior's bar mitzvah "the most spiritual experience I ever had at the movies." Most people, it turned out, were like me and had never prayed with someone who has a disability, let alone attended his b'nai mitzvah. But they were eager to do so as voyeurs. Within a few years, *Praying with Lior* had been screened commercially in about fifty cities, played in more than a hundred film festivals, taken home numerous awards, and become a staple of synagogue programming across the country.

During my far-flung travels with the film, I was catapulted into the world of disability rights, faith inclusion, and families' personal experiences. After every screening, I was approached by families wanting to share their children's b'nai mitzvah stories. They came in one of two variations: proud tales accompanied by the suggestion that I make a film about *their* child (after four years making *Praying with Lior*, this was hardly an appealing prospect), or tearful stories of thwarted dreams for b'nai mitzvah for their child. Any number of factors were to blame: community rejection, prohibition on religious grounds, inability to imagine just how it could happen, lack of educational resources, lack of know-how. I was struck by how much progress the Americans with Disabilities Act, adopted in 1990, brought to public accessibility, and how little to religion. Striking, too, was the fact that for all the umbrella organizations that connect Jews regionally, politically, denominationally, and financially, when it came to disability inclusion and special education, each Jewish community seemed to be operating in a silo. Those that did create b'nai mitzvah ceremonies for children with disabilities seemed to be reinventing the wheel for each child.

At the same time, I was meeting people doing incredible work in Jewish special education. I was introduced to the trailblazers, the organizations, and the practitioners working in the trenches. I was invited to synagogues, churches, and mosques that made inclusion and accessibility a priority in ways I had never considered. I even attended a meeting of an organization for siblings of children with disabilities.

And so the idea for this book took root. After a screening of *Praying with Lior* at Camp Ramah in New England, I discovered that the very same thoughts were marinating in the heart of Howard Blas, then director of Ramah's Tikvah Program for campers with disabilities. We came at this project from very different places, but like those old Reese's commercials celebrating the union of chocolate and peanut butter, our collaboration yields something new: a best practices, go-to resource for families, clergy, and educators who seek to learn how to make "untraditional" b'nai mitzvah happen.

Lior Liebling is now firmly an adult, yet I still receive screening and speaking requests for the film about his bar mitzvah. I am delighted that Lior's story still contains gifts for the audience. Making the film gifted me with numerous lessons in filmmaking, the introduction to my husband, life in a new city, more filmmaking opportunities, and lifelong friends and colleagues. Watching it with students at the University of Kentucky recently, I was struck both by the ways the film holds up, and the ways it doesn't. While I believe that Lior Liebling, with his sense of humor, intelligence, and big love of life is one of the all-time greatest documentary subjects in history, the bar mitzvah of a boy with Down syndrome is no longer newsworthy. Welcoming synagogues now offer an Inclusion Committee, alongside Sisterhood and *tikun olam* (social action) initiatives. Today, families of children with cognitive or mobility disabilities, if they desire b'nai mitzvah, can expect, or actually insist on, the encouragement of synagogue communities and clergy.

The Reason for This Book (Howard's Story)

When I was studying for my bar mitzvah in the late 1970s, it all seemed pretty straightforward. Students (boys only, at the time) were assigned a teacher (cantor or sexton), put in a trope (biblical cantillation) class with some other boys, given a pink- or green-covered booklet and a cassette tape, and then chipped away at learning some Torah reading and a Haftarah for a Saturday morning bar mitzvah. Girls celebrated bat mitzvah—if they did at all—on Friday nights by chanting a Haftarah from a very thin blue book. Over a period of months, students learned what they needed to. Most students got it using this "trope and tape" method. Those who struggled (or did not have voices that pleased the cantor) did less.

I didn't think much about b'nai mitzvah or the learning process until I started getting calls from religious schools in the late 1980s, when I was a special education teacher and social worker. Rabbis and religious school principals wondered what to do about students who weren't "getting it." I started working with synagogues and with these students and families, and I haven't looked back since. I have developed a reputation as the go-to person for b'nai mitzvah for children with disabilities and unique situations. I have come to appreciate that the b'nai mitzvah service and learning process are not one-size-fits-all. Both the service and the teaching—even for those marking the occasion in a synagogue—must be sensitive to the needs of each student's learning style, temperament, and circumstances.

How to Use This Book

We both knew that there were extraordinarily gifted people in the field of Jewish special education, as well as creative and committed clergy and families, who had already developed these kinds of ceremonies many, many times. There is simply no physical, cognitive, or psychological challenge that cannot be met, indeed, that has not already been met. The knowledge gained and strategies forged are there to be shared. Here they are, together in one place.

In this book, you will find chapters written by experts from all over the world, including the most expert of all—people with lived experience of disability who share the story of their b'nai mitzvah. This combined wisdom is yours to adapt to your needs. Given the infinite permutations of ability, and the unique personhood of each person with a disability and each family, we have purposely not categorized chapters by disability (autism, cerebral palsy, blindness, etc.) but by challenge: nonverbal, mobility, learning difference, vision, or hearing.

In each chapter, the author or authors share strategies, techniques, and reflections from their own vantage points. Throughout, we have sprinkled vignettes in sidebars as supplements, drawn from forty years of experience working with students, families, and clergy around b'nai mitzvah. These are written by us, except as noted otherwise. Except for the first-person reflection chapters, called "Voices," all the names of specific children or families have been changed to protect their privacy.

As a family member, clergyperson, or educator, you may choose to read this book from cover to cover, or you may let the table of contents or the index lead you to the parts most relevant for your situation. There are common strategies, no matter what the challenge, so we encourage you to explore. We hope that you will find something in this book that addresses your needs, offers you valuable guidance, and inspires you and your community to forge a path all your own, based on others' experience in responding to similar challenges.

While we hope there is valuable information for every reader in each chapter, some are more directed at parents, some at clergy, some at educators. In general, the first section is geared more toward families, and the second section leans more toward clergy and educators. The "Voices" chapters are first-person stories written by people with disabilities and will be of interest to all readers. Also, in the spirit of the principle of "Nothing about us without us," the slogan popularized by the disability rights movement, we recommend each chapter to the b'nai mitzvah child if they are able to understand its contents.

We cannot overstate the courage it takes for a child with disabilities and their family to confront the public milestone of b'nai mitzvah. After enduring many years of hearing an actual or implicit no, feeling outside the community or less than, and sometimes being overwhelmed with medical interventions, b'nai mitzvah children and their families should be saluted for the strength and bravery it takes to choose a b'nai mitzvah ceremony in community. We call on clergy, community members, educators, and families themselves to be gentle with the process. It is not easy to engage in trailblazing, and even harder to watch one's child do the bushwhacking before an audience. More than any other piece of guidance in this book, we implore you to begin with empathy and to start all considerations with "yes."

A Different Spirit is named for Caleb, the biblical character who is sent by Moses with eleven others to scout the Promised Land. Ten of the twelve return with alarmist news, spreading fear that the land is unconquerable. Only Caleb and Joshua report the land's beauty and that its challenges can be overcome (Numbers 13:30–14:24): Caleb "quieted the people before Moses," saying, "If pleased with us, Adonai will bring us into that... and give it to us." God responds, "But My servant Caleb, because he was imbued with a different spirit and remained loyal to Me—him I will bring into the land that he entered, and his offspring shall hold it as a possession." We all have things to learn from our children with "different spirits"; indeed, they may show us the way to a kinder, more interesting, and more inclusive world.

A Note about Terminology: Disability, Gender, and Hebrew Transliteration

We have adopted several conventions for this book that undoubtedly will shift as attitudes, research, and culture evolve. We want to explain our reasoning and fully acknowledge that with time the conventions we have chosen may become inadequate or inaccurate. We hope that this will be forgiven as a limit of prescience rather than intention.

We have done our best to use the most current terms that people with disabilities prefer at the time of this book's publication. Those terms changed even as we were editing this book, and will no doubt keep changing. We recognize the limits of the printed word and apologize for changes we have not foreseen.

As our notion of gender expands, so, too, will the language used to describe the *b'nai mitzvah.* The Hebrew language assigns every noun as masculine or feminine—hence *bar mitzvah* for boys, and *bat mitzvah* for girls. Some synagogues have adopted new nomenclature for this milestone to reflect identities that are not binary—*b-mitzvah, brit mitzvah, simchat mitzvah, bet mitzvah.* For the purposes of this book, when speaking about the experience in general, we have chosen *b'nai mitzvah* (translated as "children of the commandments"), which is plural and inclusive of all genders. When a writer is talking about themselves or about a specific child, they have chosen the term appropriate for that individual child.

The Hebrew alphabet contains twenty-two letters, all of which are written with different characters from English. As a result, transliteration of Hebrew words into English characters will result in spelling differences. It is acceptable to write, for example, *b'nai,* or *b'nei,* or *bnai,* or *bnei,* or even *benay.* For consistency, we have chosen one spelling for each Hebrew word in this book to use throughout. A glossary at the back of the book specifies the transliteration and definition of each Hebrew term.

*

Overview:
A Different Path

This book explores an array of ideas and options for creating b'nai mitzvah that honor children with disabilities. Before that, the Overview section starts with brass tacks: the essential tenets of Jewish law, American disability law, and cultural precepts that explain where we are with respect to inclusion of people with disabilities, and to where we can aspire.

* CHAPTER 1 *

Accepting All:

Creating a Culture of Inclusion and Belonging

Shelly Christensen

Shelly Christensen is senior director of faith inclusion and belonging at Disability Belongs, a nonprofit that works to change how society views and values people with disabilities. She strongly believes that Jews have a moral imperative to promote inclusion. Citing examples from Jewish foundational narratives, this introduction to the history and philosophy behind inclusion in the Jewish community contends that inclusion elevates the spirit of the Jewish community.

Twenty years ago, I was hired to direct the Minneapolis Jewish Community Inclusion Program for People with Disabilities. My charge was to guide all Minneapolis Jewish organizations toward adopting a culture of inclusion. I began with calls to clergy, executive directors, education directors, and lay leaders at synagogues, schools, and other agencies. After I explained the purpose of the inclusion program, one respondent said, "Shelly, it's so wonderful that you are doing this work. But we don't need your help—we don't have any of those people here."

How could it be that there were no people with disabilities in the Jewish community? According to the United States Centers for Disease Control and Prevention, more than 20 percent of the population has a disability. That would mean Jews with disabilities could number as high as 1.5 million. No Jews with disabilities, indeed.

A Moral Imperative: The Backstory

Two laws passed by Congress, the Individuals with Disabilities Education Act (IDEA) in 1975, and the Americans with Disabilities Act (ADA) in 1990, provided the legal mandate for including and supporting people with disabilities in education and community life. Faith communities, however, aren't covered under either law, except for some employment requirements of the ADA. The late Rabbi Lynne Landsberg, former senior adviser on disability issues for the Religious Action Center of Reform Judaism, called these laws "moral imperatives" for the Jewish community.

Under the ADA, a person with a disability is someone who has a physical or mental impairment that substantially limits their ability to perform one or more major life activities. This includes any number of life functions, such as eating, walking, breathing, thinking, feeling, learning, and communicating.

The ADA protects the civil rights of people with disabilities so that they can fully participate in society. When you see a curb cut, an automatic door opener, ramps, accessible parking spaces, sign language interpreters, and accessible restrooms, these are products of the ADA in public and private entities. Although religious organizations aren't covered by the ADA, the guidelines laid out in regulations can be used to implement the moral imperative Rabbi Landsberg spoke about.

The Individuals with Disabilities Education Act (IDEA) provides for a free, appropriate, public education in the least restrictive environment for all children. The IDEA significantly enhanced participation and inclusion of children with disabilities from birth to age twenty-one and provides all children and their parents with legal rights to public education.

After the passage of the IDEA and the ADA, Jewish parents whose children were receiving support services in public schools raised their expectations for inclusive Jewish education as well. Parents recognized the benefits of inclusion and began to advocate for their children to attend religious school with their peers without disabilities. "Parent power was one of the forces that drove us to include children with disabilities in Jewish education," said Dr. Sara Rubinow Simon, a pioneer in Jewish special education.

More than thirty-five years ago, Dr. Simon and Rabbi Dr. Marty Schloss invited leaders from Jewish educational agencies across North America to join the Jewish Special Education International Consortium. This group helped advance inclusive religious education and share ideas about successful special education practices; it was key to recognizing people with disabilities as full members of the community, entitled to access to education, worship, volunteering, and social participation, just like anyone else.

Historically, and certainly before the passage of the ADA and the IDEA, people with disabilities did not enjoy the same liberties to participate in Jewish life as those without disabilities. Sometimes synagogues and other Jewish institutions had physical obstacles that made buildings, parking, and playgrounds inaccessible to people using wheelchairs or walkers, or people living with asthma and other physical conditions. Inside Jewish buildings, there were different obstacles, including lack of access to physical spaces like the sanctuary, classrooms, and restrooms, and lack of access to resources such as sound systems, large-print and braille prayer books, and American Sign Language (ASL) interpreters. Even more egregious were attitudes about the ability of people with disabilities to pray in the manner of the congregation or to learn within the rigid methods of many Jewish schools. Not that long ago, many Jewish communities were so focused on academic success that children with disabilities were not even allowed to learn with their nondisabled peers. Many were denied access to Jewish education altogether.

While some Jewish day schools and supplementary schools began including students with disabilities in the late 1970s, this was very much the exception until fairly recently. Before that, it was unusual to hear about a synagogue or school that encouraged parents to enroll their children with disabilities. Some parents were told that the school simply could not educate their child, or they found that their children were unceremoniously removed from the student rolls after only a few classes. Some schools, responding to pressure from parents or perhaps a board member with a child or grandchild with a disability, offered students a seat in segregated "special-needs" classes. Marginal expectations were held for these segregated classes, and there was no distinction between ages, as if all children with disabilities would learn at the same level. Learning Jewish skills to prepare for *b'nai mitzvah* was not usually part of the curriculum. Without the education, students with disabilities lacked the resources to take part in this important life-cycle event.

Jewish Text and Tradition Are Inclusive

Throughout the Torah we encounter people whose lives exemplify the diversity of our Jewish communities. In Genesis 32:2 and 32, Jacob wrestles with a heavenly being and leaves the encounter with a physical disability. In Genesis 29:17, the Torah says that Leah had vision impairment, but nowhere does the Torah indicate that she was considered "damaged." Moses pleaded with God not to appoint him as the spokesperson of the Israelites because of a disability related to speech: "Please, O my Lord, I have never been a man of words, either in times past or now that You have spoken to Your servant; I am slow of speech and slow of tongue" (Exodus 4:10).

God then asks Moses, "Who gives humans speech? Who makes them dumb or deaf, seeing or blind? Is it not I, Adonai?" (Exodus 4:11). We must pause and consider that God doesn't see Moses as a person with a disability. God sees Moses's gifts, strengths, and abilities, and in the very next verse provides the very first documented accommodation in history—Aaron will speak for Moses publicly.

Inclusion and belonging are Jewish values. The Torah teaches that humans are created in the image of God (Genesis 1:27). The Torah also instructs us to welcome the stranger into our midst—thirty-six times. Just as Abraham and Sarah opened their tent flaps to welcome three strangers and offer their hospitality (Genesis 18), we can do the same by inviting people with disabilities to belong, not as passersby, but as valued community members. The Talmud reminds us that *kol Yisrael areivim zeh bazeh*, "All [the people] of Israel are responsible for one another" (*Shevu'ot* 39a:22).

Proverbs 22:6 commands us to "Train a child in the way they ought to go; they will not swerve from it even in old age." Investing in the education of all Jewish children, including those with disabilities, should never be an afterthought. Jewish education, taught in the way that the child learns, is a sacred responsibility and obligation.

A Unique Prayer Book

As she continued to build education programs for people with disabilities, Dr. Sara Simon noticed that synagogue prayer books were not appropriate for people with cognitive disabilities. In response, in memory of her late son Joshua, she and her family funded *Yehoshua Hazak* [Joshua Strong]: *The First Siddur* [prayer book] *for Children with Learning Differences*. The prayer book uses icons developed by the education company Mayer-Johnson to make the Hebrew text more accessible for children with disabilities. Other prayer books have since been published for use by people with disabilities. The Hebrew siddur *B'chol D'rachecha* (translated as *In All Your Ways)* credits *Yehoshua Hazak* as its inspiration. *The Koren Yachad Siddur*, which strives to reach readers of all skill levels to join in prayer, is another example.

—*H.B.*

Parents are understandably hurt and angry when their child with a disability is denied a Jewish education. For parents whose hopes and dreams for their children include Jewish learning, youth group participation, and b'nai mitzvah preparation and celebration, the grief may be overwhelming.

Let's look at the case of Yoav, a child born with spina bifida, who uses a wheelchair. The synagogue education director brought the matter of his bar mitzvah before the synagogue board, since it would have required making accommodations to the regular service. Some members of the synagogue board, not knowing much about Yoav, felt that lowering the desk on which the Torah scroll is opened to chair level would disrupt the congregation's tradition of reading the Torah from the *bimah*. No one asked Yoav or his parents for their thoughts. Yoav's parents were understandably devastated when told of the board's decision not to allow the bar mitzvah. Hurt, disappointed, and angry, his parents decided to take Yoav and his two younger siblings out of the religious school and left the synagogue altogether.

Yoav's parents did not give up their dream of their son celebrating his bar mitzvah, however. After a rigorous search process, they found an inclusive synagogue where Yoav could pursue his bar mitzvah journey. He joined his peers in a cohort where they learned prayers and blessings, and Yoav also had his own tutor, who prepared him by using his strengths and his learning style. Yoav was motivated and practiced nearly every day, experiencing success and pride in his accomplishments.

On the day of his bar mitzvah, the reading desk was moved from the bimah to the floor so Yoav could have full access from his wheelchair. Yoav proudly chanted his Torah portion and shared his *d'var Torah* (Torah teaching) with confidence. The joy he and his family experienced enveloped the whole congregation.

Belonging Is the Key to Inclusion

Bet Shalom Congregation in Minnetonka, Minnesota, has been our family's partner in fostering Jewish identities for our three sons, and now our grandchildren. Our sons flourished in the synagogue religious school. When one of our boys was diagnosed with autism, his teachers and the education director met with us to collaborate about ways to support him. The school and synagogue practiced inclusion for all its students. It never occurred to me that there was any other way. Our family simply felt a sense of belonging, and that we were cared for, valued, and respected.

I realized over time that people with disabilities and those who love them want more than inclusion. They want to feel this same sense of belonging. Belonging acknowledges that everyone has needs—and everyone also has talents, gifts, strengths, and a desire to contribute to the well-being of the community. Belonging erases distinctions about who is in and who is out. It promotes diversity and equity and tears down divisions between "them" and "us." A culture of belonging strengthens the community and all those who want to belong.

Attitudes continue to change and we make greater strides toward acceptance and inclusion. This is partly as a result of children with disabilities fully participating in preschool and religious school classes. Through regular, natural interactions, friendships are formed and attitudes change.

Programs in Israel

Most Israeli children—both religious and secular—have historically marked b'nai mitzvah in some way, although generally with less fanfare than in the United States. Families of both boys and girls often celebrate with parties (including those who do not have synagogue ceremonies). The sixth grade is considered the b'nai mitzvah year, and most schools, and some organizations, both secular and religious, have adopted programs that run over the course of the year. There are also group b'nai mitzvah ceremonies, such as those held for children on kibbutzim, for children of new immigrants, or children of soldiers killed in action.

For children with disabilities, however, b'nai mitzvah provides a sense of connection to previous generations and to the Jewish people throughout the world, and it provides one of the few normative rites of passage. A child with disabilities may not participate in others: graduating from high school, getting a driver's license, being inducted into the army after their eighteenth birthday. Consequently, participation in b'nai mitzvah allows them to experience a life cycle event that is normative in Israeli society.

—Gila Vogel, PhD
Founder, B'nai Mitzvah Program for Children with Special Needs, Masorti Movement, Israel

What Have We Learned from B'nai Mitzvah Journeys?

How we all love hearing the stories about the b'nai mitzvah of children with disabilities. They almost always all end the same way: "There wasn't a dry eye in the house!" These stories touch us powerfully because they help us recognize the possibilities when a child is appropriately supported. To stand before the Torah and the congregation, coming to Jewish adulthood in the tradition of our people, is more than cause for celebration. It is a moment where once uncertain hopes and dreams are fulfilled. It is a declaration made by a young person taking their place among the Jewish people, connected to the chain that began with Moses, and lovingly passed down from generation to generation.

These are the key values I have learned, from years in the field, about best practices for b'nai mitzvah for children with disabilities:

- B'nai mitzvah is as important to families of children with disabilities as it is to families of their nondisabled peers. Clergy and educators need to listen to parents' hopes and dreams for their child.
- Parents are partners in the process. Parents know best about their child's strengths, learning style, what works for them, and even their worries. These all contribute to making the experience of learning appropriate for the child.
- Don't assume that a child with a disability is unable to do what their nondisabled peers do. Set aside preconceived expectations to understand and observe how each child learns and progresses. No one can predict what they will be able to accomplish until they are given the opportunity.
- Listen to the b'nai mitzvah child. Get to know them. Suspend "This is how we do it" thinking and tailor training to the child's interests and way of learning.
- To the greatest extent possible, children with disabilities should be included with their nondisabled peers in b'nai mitzvah preparation group activities, providing support based on the child's needs. They are part of a community of their peers who may have been together throughout religious school. For a young teen, this promotes well-being and a sense of belonging.
- Have high, not low, expectations. As the child progresses, expectations can be adjusted. Set the bar at the right height for each person—never too high or too low.
- Presume competence. By adopting an open approach to discovering the way to teach a child according to their needs, they will succeed.

* Ensure that each child is matched with a tutor or teacher who is flexible and supportive, works well with diverse learning styles, and can communicate effectively and empathetically with the child and their family.

Let Torah be your guide. Torah teaches us that each human being is created in the image of the Holy One. Moses and so many biblical people have what today would be considered a disability. Having a disability is not an obstacle to fulfilling God's purpose. Let us make sure that every child has appropriate b'nai mitzvah training and support to fulfill this sacred obligation. The child's understanding of the text provides them with a deeper awareness of Torah's relevance to their lives and their relationship with the world.

CHAPTER 2

Created in God's Image:

The Message of Our Tradition

Rabbi Menachem Creditor

Rabbi Menachem Creditor, the Pearl and Ira Meyer Scholar-in-Residence at UJA-Federation of New York, lays out the meaning, history, and evolution of b'nai mitzvah. Drawing on traditional Jewish texts, he demonstrates that b'nai mitzvah for children with disabilities is an affirmation of the essential Jewish tenet that we are all created in God's image.

B'nai mitzvah ceremonies serve not only as rites of passage but also as opportunities for young people to connect with their heritage, deepen their understanding of Jewish teachings, and be recognized by their community as having arrived at a new moment. In the sacred weave of Jewish life, few moments hold as much significance. Young souls step forward to claim their place within the covenant, embracing the responsibilities and blessings bestowed upon them. This transformative ritual moment marks the transition from childhood to adolescence and from witnessing to participating.

The evolution of the b'nai mitzvah spans centuries, reflecting organic shifts in Jewish communal practice and the recognition of the importance of a coming-of-age ritual for young Jewish individuals. Ancient references in the Talmud speak of the physical changes that accompany puberty and of the notion of emerging adulthood. It was believed that at this age (traditionally twelve for girls, thirteen for boys), individuals become accountable for their own actions and are capable of fulfilling religious obligations. This understanding gradually gave rise to the practice of the b'nai mitzvah, which marked the formal recognition of a young person's entry into the adult Jewish community.

Origins

Originally, bar mitzvah was a relatively simple ceremony, often taking place in the synagogue, where a young man would be called to the Torah to recite a blessing or read from the sacred texts. Over time, the ritual evolved to include additional components, such as delivering a *d'var Torah* (Torah teaching) or speech to the congregation, demonstrating the b'nai mitzvah's understanding of Jewish teachings and values.

As ceremonies often do, this one serves as an external recognition of something larger—that a child has morphed into the next stage of life. A person does not "have" a b'nai mitzvah. They become one, and the ritual marks this moment. Ritual reflects something larger.

The formalization by Rabbi Mordecai Kaplan of the bat mitzvah in 1922 in America extended the power of this communal ritual to young women as well. The more recent addition of the *b-mitzvah,* a gender-neutral way to refer to the ritual, has expanded the experience to include those young people who would not identify as either bar (son) or bat (daughter) but rather in a nonbinary way. These changes reflect a crucial part of the b'nai mitzvah experience—affirmation. By celebrating this liminal moment in a young person's life, their community is saying, in effect, "We see you and we love you."

The rabbis of the Talmud worked hard to get to this point of "we love you." Several ancient texts made their work difficult. For example, biblical passages in the book of Leviticus harshly invalidated priests with any type of blemish (*mum*), deformity, or disability from service. Such priests were barred from raising their hands to offer the priestly blessing. As is often the case, these words in the Torah have been interpreted by sages—ancient and contemporary—to reflect evolving notions of physical appearance, of cultural expectations, and of holiness itself. The rabbis who codified the Mishnah and Gemara (collectively known as the Talmud) were obligated to preserve the Torah law concerning priests with blemishes but offered a creative workaround. They acknowledged that people's discomfort sprang from their lack of familiarity with and exposure to disabilities. They therefore allowed a priest to perform his job if the people in the community were "accustomed to him" (*Megillah* 24b).

From (a) the categorical exclusion in the Torah of a priest with a blemish from holy service, to (b) the Mishnah's narrower definition of *blemish* as a visible physical difference, to (c) the Gemara's later acknowledgment that familiarity with different kinds of people changes communal norms, a process of greater inclusion over time is evident (*Megillah* 24b). While these interpretative stages retain the problematic basic concept of a priest's exclusion (and, therefore, the exclusion of a ritual participant in a more modern Jewish context), the trajectory of evolving Jewish communal norm-setting is made clear: the goal of sacred community must be to work with text and shrink the barriers that keep individuals from claiming their place as equals in community and welcome before God.

All of this is, in fact, a fulfillment of the ancient wisdom of Rabbi Akiva, who said:

> Beloved is a person for they were created in the image [of God]. Especially beloved is a person for it was made known to them that they were created in the image [of God], as it is said: "For in the image of God was humankind made" (Genesis 9:6). Beloved are Israel in that they were called children to the All-Present. Especially beloved are they for it was made known to them that they are called children of the All-Present, as it is said: "You are children of your God Adonai" (Deuteronomy 14:1).
> —*Pirkei Avot 3:14*

In other words, the basic love due to every child stems from our recognition that they are created in God's image. But when we affirm every child as having been created in God's image, we show extraordinary love. The Jewish community's commitment to seeing every person, regardless of their physical or mental abilities, as included in the Covenant is nothing less than the extension of God's extraordinary love. We must ensure that all young people, including those with varying abilities, have the opportunity to participate fully in this milestone experience, enabling them to celebrate their unique identities and contributions within the rich tapestry of Jewish life. We must also remember that whatever a child does or does not do within the ceremonial framing of the moment, they are beautiful in God's eyes and should therefore be in our own.

✻ VOICES ✻

My Bar Mitzvah Led Me Home

Stephen Shore, PhD

Stephen Shore, professor of special education at Adelphi University, is a frequent speaker and writer about autism. He reminisces about his early childhood as a boy with autism, and the way that his own bar mitzvah offered an unexpected gift, decades after the fact.

בראשית ברא אלהים את השמים ואת הארץ:
In the beginning, God began to create heaven and earth.
(Genesis 1:1)

The first lines in the Torah, introducing Creation, are the beginning of my bar mitzvah reading from the Torah. I am an autistic person who, at age two and a half, was recommended for institutionalization. Yet I am now married, work as a professor of special education, travel internationally giving speeches on autism, and regularly pray at synagogues run by Chabad, a Chasidic sect that is open and welcoming to all Jews.

I teach about what I call "The Four A's of Autism": **Awareness** of autistic characteristics; **Accepting** these predilections as traits to be worked with, as opposed to against; **Appreciating** what autistic people contribute to society; and **Action** to fuse awareness, acceptance, and appreciation together. In intuitively employing these four A's, my parents helped me have a successful bar mitzvah, and today, a full Jewish life.

The Autism Bomb

After eighteen months of slightly faster than typical development, I was struck with regressive autism. As with about 30 percent of us on the autism spectrum, I lost functional communication, had meltdowns, and became a very challenging toddler. Because of the lack of understanding of autism at that time, it took a year for my bewildered parents to find qualified doctors to identify and address my condition.

Fortunately, my parents rejected the professionals' recommendations of institutionalization and instead confronted a gaping lack of support, knowledge, and expertise on how to reach and support an autistic child. Proceeding on intuition alone, my parents assembled what would today be considered an intensive home-based early intervention program, emphasizing music, movement, sensory integration, narration, and imitation. But my parents' attempts to reach me failed.

My parents then flipped their technique and started imitating me, and soon I became aware of them in my environment. They imitated my flapping sounds and other autistic behaviors and entered my world. As instructed in the biblical book of Proverbs (22:6): "Train a child in the way they ought to go; they will not swerve from it even in old age." We must teach the child in the way they learn.

Early Intervention, Grade School, and Jewish Education

The most memorable of my parents' homegrown early intervention activities involved music. Classical and some folk music played all day and night. We moved, sang, communicated, and did activities to music. We listened to Theodore Bikel singing the Yiddish folk song "Tumbalalayka" so often that we wore out the record.

At age four, with speech starting to return, I was reevaluated and upgraded from "psychotic, strong autistic tendencies, and atypical development" to merely "neurotic." My highly focused interest in wristwatches appeared at this time; one day my parents found me disassembling a watch. I would pop off the back, extract the motor, and remove some of the gears to spin them around. Then I'd reassemble the watch and it still worked—with no pieces left over. Soon my repertoire expanded to include alarm clocks, radios, and other battery-powered electric devices. Unbeknownst to my parents, they were practicing the imperative, "May you leap from strength to strength," as was commonly said by the late rebbe of the Chabad-Lubavitch movement.

At age six I entered regular kindergarten, a social and academic catastrophe for me. Today I am encouraged that ever-increasing numbers of school systems are required to document their anti-bullying programs by their state departments of education. Academically, I was about a grade behind in most of my subjects. I spent the bulk of my elementary school days reading library books about my interests at that time, such as music, electronics, earthquakes, weather, aviation, space exploration, and volcanoes. I'd spend my days at the back of the room consuming stacks of books, taking notes, and copying diagrams. At that time it never occurred to educators to teach me mathematics via my interest in astronomy. Since I was not a behavior problem, teachers left me to my own devices.

At the time, my family's Jewish life consisted of Shabbat, observance of holidays, and Sunday school at our family's Reform congregation. I found time at temple unpleasant because of scratchy formal clothes, a service in a crowded room that required alternating between standing and sitting, and stories that seemed the same each year. And, my bully classmates were in the synagogue as well. Eventually, my parents realized that Jewish education at our synagogue wasn't working out well, so we stopped going.

When I was in middle school, my parents connected with the more intimate Congregation Kehillat Jacob and its very kind and accepting leader—Rabbi Samuel Korff—who accepted our relatively nonobservant family with open arms. I felt much more comfortable there and spent many hours in the rabbi's library, searching for the oldest books I could find. As they were all in Hebrew, I could not read further than their publication dates.

Preparing for Bar Mitzvah

Given our relatively low level of observance, I was very surprised one day to learn that my brother, aged fourteen, and later I, would be celebrating our bar mitzvahs. My brother, two years older, was diagnosed with mild to moderate retardation and received many accommodations. Although he was and remains able to read only a few simple words in English, he was blessed with a good memory. With support, he got through the pre- and post-Torah reading prayers, and an abbreviated reading of his Torah and Haftarah [reading from the Prophets] portions.

My parents planned for my celebration on my thirteenth birthday. At that time, I could just barely recognize the word שלום/*shalom*. Sessions with Hebrew tutors failed, as I was unable to decode phonemes to Hebrew letters and words. One day, a cantor from our synagogue recorded all the prayers, the verses from the first three days of the Creation story, and the Haftarah on a cassette tape. This specific action is one of many examples where my parents transitioned from mere awareness of my autistic characteristics to acceptance. They realized that working with my echolalic tendencies would be a pathway to success.

I spent a half hour each day listening to and following along with the tape recording, memorizing increasing lengths of material. My auditory memory freed me from having to learn to read Hebrew. By my bar mitzvah I had all my reading down pat—right down to imitating the cantor's low gravelly voice! I enjoyed the slight echo from my place on the *bimah*. I remember being initially distracted by the person using the *yad* (Torah pointer) to follow my readings in the Torah, but I soon found it interesting to see where I was as I chanted my piece.

Encounters of the First Kind with Chabad

Like many in my circle of Jewish friends and acquaintances, I drifted away from observance as a college undergraduate, with an occasional rekindling with the Hillel student group.

In 2015, working as a professor at Adelphi University, I felt an urge to observe the High Holidays in a synagogue. Happy to discover that the closest one was barely a mile away, I bicycled to Chabad Mineola to find a standing-room-only service about to begin. As I entered from the back of the room, the rabbi immediately noticed me and cried out, "Come to the cheap seats in the front where there's plenty of room!" Rabbi Anchelle Perl went one step further and pointed to one of the benches at the side of the bimah. Soon, he called me up for an *aliyah* [call to the Torah]! Fortunately, I remembered enough from my bar mitzvah studies to get through the blessings—with assistance from others at the bimah.

Not bad, and *worthy of a return trip*, I thought. Indeed, when I returned soon after, the service was again warm and inclusive, and, to boot, Rabbi Perl invited me to dinner at his house afterward. Shabbat in synagogue followed by dinner and discussion became a great routine that came with Jewish education as a bonus.

I found the congregants friendly and typically stayed for about twenty minutes after services to socialize. Soon I was spending hours learning about Chabad, discovering traditional observance combined with a welcoming acceptance of all Jewish people, wherever they are in their journey of practice, knowledge, and understanding of Judaism. I found their philosophy similar to that of the Four A's of Autism. There was much emphasis on building awareness of Jewish heritage and practice, a warm acceptance of all Jewish people at all stages of observance, and an appreciation that valued people for who they are. Finally, I found that rabbis and others involved in Chabad embodied the fourth A—Action—with all their work and efforts in opening their homes and lives to all Jewish people.

Chabad Surfing, Near and Far—One Shul at a Time

Being a part of the Jewish community at Chabad Mineola became an important part of my life. However, my international travels to speak about autism regularly caused me to miss Shabbat and other holidays at home. Fortunately, I learned that Chabad is a massive international network, and from then on, I continued observing Shabbat at Chabad synagogues in other lands.

These days, once travel to a conference is confirmed, I always check for the closest Chabad house to the conference.

No matter where I travel, be it Shanghai, Moscow, New Delhi, Nice, or Kyiv, stepping over the threshold to a Chabad house is like returning home. When I memorized the sounds and words of the Shabbat service for my bar mitzvah so many years ago, I had no idea that this learning would give me a passport to discovering home in the Jewish community all over the world.

* PART 1 *

A Different B'nai Mitzvah

Before embarking on the learning process that ultimately leads to the b'nai mitzvah service and celebration, there are many important discussions and decisions that must take place. Part One introduces these considerations, including choices about service style, location, support team, teaching approach, inclusion of family members, and type of celebration.

✻ VOICES ✻

The Two Best Days of My Life

Jacob Artson

Jacob Artson, an autistic man who is minimally verbal, communicates via his keyboard. He lives in Los Angeles, where he advocates for inclusion and justice through his writing, speaking, and participation in programs. Jacob describes his own bar mitzvah and that of his twin sister.

A bar mitzvah for a person with autism is unique in ways you'd expect but also in ways you might not expect. I am a minimally verbal person with almost no functional speech. And it is also very difficult for me to sing words. But I deeply, deeply love Judaism and wanted to have a bar mitzvah near the same time as my twin sister's bat mitzvah.

The first decision we had to make was whether we would have our *b'nai mitzvah* together, like most other twins. I would have deferred to whatever Shira felt was right, but my mother insisted we do each one separately. At the time I did not understand her thinking, but now I am extremely grateful that we all listened to her. Separating our celebrations let us each shine—not only in our own right, but also to be able to enjoy our twin shining. I have always been extremely attached to Shira—she is like a part of my body. When we were growing up, she was my best friend, companion, social secretary, mentor, and cheerleader in her quiet way. I followed everything she did. So naturally she went first, on the Fourth of July, which fortunately landed on a Torah reading day that year. Mine followed on the Sunday of Labor Day weekend, which was a Rosh Chodesh (new month), when Torah is read. It was our Hebrew birthday.

Experiencing my family planning my sister's bat mitzvah was eye-opening for me. My father is a rabbi, and rabbis' kids are under a lot of pressure to be superstars. My sister has some learning differences, too, and learning Hebrew was incredibly difficult for her. She also did not like being the center of attention, so having a huge service in front of the entire congregation clearly was not happening. Because her bat mitzvah was customized for her, I was able to feel that my bar mitzvah was truly legitimate, and not just a poor version of the original.

Growing up, I had been to a few b'nai mitzvah of family friends, so I only had one vision of what b'nai mitzvah could be and obviously that was not going to be me. But hearing my parents discussing with my sister what her bat mitzvah might involve helped me understand that becoming bar mitzvah meant, for the first time, making a public statement to my community that I am a member, with full citizenship, even if I look and act very differently from most others.

Ultimately, my sister's bat mitzvah was the best day of my life. I was so incredibly proud that she learned her Torah reading, which she memorized, thanks to her good auditory memory. She read beautifully, and she looked so poised and confident. The party was a blast too. We had dancing and silly games, and our whole family came together. I sat through most of it and only took one short break to get re-regulated when I got overwhelmed with pride for her. I also loved being in the family pictures and seeing her being loved by everyone as much as I love her. Perhaps the best part, though, was seeing my parents beaming at her with joy and love.

The process of preparing for my bar mitzvah was pretty stressful. My dad found a rabbinical student who had experience working with kids with autism, but I was still scared and overwhelmed by the whole idea. I couldn't imagine having to sing the Torah blessings in front of people even though I had sung them to myself hundreds, if not thousands, of times since I was a toddler. Once we started, my mom realized what was happening and we switched gears. My mom had the brilliant idea that I study with my dad and write a siddur (prayer book) commentary, so that there would be a fallback plan in case I got overwhelmed and couldn't do my Torah blessings. I loved the opportunity to learn more about the morning prayers and make them my own. I also loved writing my bar mitzvah speech and bringing my own perspective to the *parashah* (Torah portion).

For me, the bar mitzvah was the process more than the day itself. I was too overwhelmed with emotion to focus, so we went with Plan B and everyone there read part of my siddur commentary. At the end of the service, everyone came up on the *bimah* for Adon Olam (the service-concluding prayer), while I sat in the audience. I will forever have an image in my mind of everyone smiling at me and supporting me. So, looking back, my bar mitzvah was one of the best experiences I have ever had. It just wasn't a single day.

✱ CHAPTER 3 ✱

Beyond Physical Access:

Creating an Inclusive Synagogue Community

Rebecca Wanatick

Rebecca Wanatick is the director of Disability Inclusion & Belonging at the Jewish Federation of Greater MetroWest NJ and oversees its ABLE program (Access, Belonging & Life Enrichment for People with Disabilities and Their Families). She offers concrete guidelines for how synagogues can create truly inclusive communities, both in their physical structure and their attitude.

Becoming a *b'nai mitzvah* is quite an accomplishment! Reaching this goal begins years before the actual *simchah*, and being part of a community is often how we begin our Jewish engagement. For people with physical disabilities, finding the right community shouldn't be a challenge, but we know that sometimes it still can be.

We want our synagogues and all their congregants and prospective congregants to walk or roll into those spaces and feel at home, not like they are strangers in a strange land, trying to navigate difficult terrain. This is how we build community from the beginning.

Synagogues can be places of belonging in two ways: the physical architecture of the building; and the language, attitudes, and practices shared within the community. While each area is critical to creating a community of belonging, this chapter is dedicated to the ways in which we consider the community as a reciprocal relationship, one in which each member has the opportunity to gain from, and contribute to, their community or congregation.

Building a sense of community in our congregations requires us to think about the ways in which our congregants and their families engage with our physical space, and how they feel about this experience. B'nai mitzvah is often a time when our children have the opportunity to give back to their community, especially as they lead their congregation in prayer. We want all families to experience this sense of community and belonging long before their child reaches b'nai mitzvah age. How families experience our physical spaces from early on in their synagogue engagement will influence how they approach their child's simchah. Physical access—and how we engage with it—is a key component in how we create community.

Rabbi Avi Weiss: Early Access and Inclusion Champion

For decades, rabbis like Avi Weiss of the Hebrew Institute of Riverdale in New York have been concerned with ensuring that everyone feels welcome in their synagogues. Rabbi Weiss insisted that his synagogue give up "precious real estate" in both the men's and women's sections of his Orthodox synagogue so that wheelchair users could easily wheel up to the bimah. In addition, Rabbi Weiss has been modeling ways to interact with and include people with mobility challenges. "My policy is that, when I see somebody in a wheelchair, I walk up to them to say hello. People with disabilities often feel they are not fully part of the community. As a rabbi, it is my responsibility to step up and model being inclusive. For example, this could be dancing with them at a wedding—even if they are seated. There are always ways to be inclusive. We have to stop thinking in boxes—that there is only one particular way. That some people are inferior, that they are second level." Rabbi Weiss believes that "everybody has a [figurative] wheelchair. Everybody has limits." And he feels that the way we treat the most vulnerable is a test for all who come to his synagogue.

—H.B.

We can learn from those in the public sector who do this sort of work every day. Creating physical spaces using the concept of Universal Design (UD) is our ultimate goal. According to the Center for Excellence in Universal Design, UD "is the design and composition of an environment so that it can be accessed, understood and used to the greatest extent possible by all people regardless of their age, size, ability or disability." Keeping UD in mind not only benefits those with physical disabilities, but also young parents with strollers, someone with a temporary injury requiring crutches or wheelchair use, and certainly our aging congregants. When we think about the physical access to our spiritual spaces, we are meeting the needs of many in our congregations. The reality is that if we are each lucky enough to grow old in our congregations, we will all benefit from many of these UD features. Creating inclusive congregations is good for all members of the community, not just those with disabilities.

While congregational spaces using UD practices are the ideal, we recognize that our synagogues are not legally bound by these guidelines or those of the Americans with Disabilities Act, and making some of these modifications may be considered cost prohibitive. Yet we are bound by our Jewish teaching that says, *Kol Yisrael areivim zeh bazeh*, "All [the people] of Israel are responsible for one another" (*Shevu'ot* 39a:22). This mutual responsibility leads us to care for and support one another to the best of our abilities. In actuality, creating physically inclusive spaces is often feasible, and does not need to be cost-prohibitive. There are many low-cost or no-cost accommodations by which we can creatively adapt the environment and materials to best meet the needs of each individual.

Inclusive congregations have a sense of mutual responsibility and work to ensure that their members' needs are being met. The first step lies with synagogue professionals and lay leaders, who then extend the learning and practices to the greater congregational community. Below are some key features that are reflective of inclusive congregations.

How Synagogue Professionals and Lay Leadership Teams Can Prepare

It takes education and awareness to successfully build inclusive community. The following are offered as best practices, and it is important to revisit these on an annual basis to ensure that the congregation is best meeting the needs of its community:

- Complete a community inclusion audit to assess access needs. You can find a sample audit online from the Jewish Federation of Greater MetroWest NJ.
- Conduct inclusion training for staff and board members on an annual basis.
- Use an inclusive events checklist with all constituencies of the congregation when planning events. You can find an example online from the Jewish Federation of Greater Washington.
- Provide usher training annually, which includes informing the lay leadership about disability etiquette, how to welcome congregants with accessibility needs, accessible materials, assisting with a lift or orienting to a ramp, and pointing out accessible seating areas.
- Include security and safety training to assist someone with physical access needs in case of an emergency.
- Offer professional development for educators annually, with an inclusion focus.
- Provide best practices training for marketing professionals on how to make websites more accessible to people with visual disabilities and marketing materials that depict a diverse Jewish community inclusive of people with disabilities.
- Establish an inclusion committee and ensure that the committee is actively engaged in promoting inclusion in every aspect of synagogue life.
- Include people with disabilities on the leadership team or staff.

Honest Conversation

There is an important concept that refers to people with disabilities as "Needs Knowers." In short, who knows best about what a person with a disability needs? That person! While inclusion committees are important and should always include people with disabilities, they may not consider the very specific needs of an individual.

Planning a *b'nai mitzvah* for a person with any disability requires honest communication between families and clergy about every aspect of the service. Families will be experts in thinking of every detail of the service and in what ways specific choreography, rituals, or customs may be challenging and stressful. It's important to discuss the support needs required. Initial conversations may address the best day and setting for the b'nai mitzvah service. For example, for synagogues that strictly follow *halachah* (Jewish law), permitting the use of microphones or PowerPoint presentations on Shabbat will likely be problematic, so a non-Shabbat option could be proposed.

Subsequent meetings may address such topics as length of the service and possible sensory breaks in the middle of the service for the b'nai mitzvah, or access to the bimah and carrying the Torah for a wheelchair user.

The family of Jason, a young man with cerebral palsy who uses a motorized scooter, helped the clergy understand that having Jason come up to the bimah at the start of the Torah procession for his bar mitzvah, instead of joining the actual procession, would save both energy and time.

When Seth, another young man with cerebral palsy, had his bar mitzvah, he and his parents asked the rabbis *not* to place their hands on his head when offering the Priestly Blessing, as it would destabilize him, possibly leading to a fall. Seth's mother, Laura, notes, "Instead of touching his head and blessing him, the rabbis knew that Seth likes to be tightly wrapped—so they wrapped him tightly in their *tallit* (prayer shawl) and lifted him up and carried him—like a Torah!"

By simply sharing these concerns in a straightforward way, the rabbis could make simple modifications to their synagogue customs. Families who don't attend synagogue regularly may be less familiar with those customs, so it is particularly important that they attend services several times in advance and get a sense of the service flow.

—H.B.

Signaling

Marketing and communications should reflect the value placed on physical access in the actual space. When individuals and families are seeking out a community, they will often explore a website and marketing materials before even setting foot in the physical space. If families can't envision themselves in your community, even at first glance online, they won't walk or roll through the door.

Here are some questions to consider:

- Do the images on the webpage and marketing information include people with disabilities? Representation matters. We want to be able to see ourselves in the communities in which we participate. This needs to be done with sensitivity and permission so as not to be perceived as tokenism.
- Is there an inclusion statement on the website and in the marketing materials? One example may be, "Building an inclusive community is a priority for us. Contact us and we will make every effort to meet your needs."
- Individuals with visual disabilities need to be able to access all written materials. Are the website and social media pages accessible to someone using a screen reader? Is the weekly/monthly newsletter accessible using a screen reader or available in large print?

* Is there a contact person listed on the website and marketing materials for individuals to reach out to for greater support or to answer inclusion questions?
* Is there information on the website about accommodations in place in the congregation? For example, be sure to point out accessible parking and entrances, inclusive classrooms, assistive listening devices, and large print materials.
* Are announcements from the *bimah* also printed for those who need a visual format, and available in large-print if needed?

Engagement

The congregation's public face should reflect its value of inclusion. The goal is for people outside the synagogue to recognize it as one that is welcoming to everyone, even if people know very little about the synagogue itself.

Outside the Community

Consider the ways in which a congregation can demonstrate an inclusive mindset and the ways in which it practices community outreach:

* A member of the inclusion committee should be available at public events.
* Share photos and flyers of past events that include the diverse community of which you are a part.
* Membership and school materials and applications should include information about meeting accessibility needs.
* Materials should be made available to engage a diverse set of participants (large-print, fidgets, plain text or visual materials, QR codes to easily access web content).
* Be ready to speak about how individuals with disabilities meaningfully participate in the congregation.
* Offer building tours as part of an open house, to allow community members to explore the spaces and understand the accessibility features available.

If the People Are Accessible

My synagogue has many physical barriers that we are currently trying to address (lack of access to the *bimah*, restrooms, religious school, and other areas). But what has kept me here for more than thirty years is the fact that the people are accessible and welcoming. Unlike my experience at other synagogues, where I often felt invisible, the people at my synagogue are friendly and will actually talk to me (not just to my service dog!), and they will seek out my opinions and ask me what I need.

Synagogue clergy and educators should reach out to young people with disabilities and their parents, and survey their accommodation needs in becoming b'nai mitzvah. Recognize that every person with a disability is unique and may need different accommodations—or none at all.

I had my b'nai mitzvah service as an adult. As a wheelchair user, I was lifted up the step to the bimah, and the Torah was brought to me and placed on a lower table with sufficient knee clearance for me to access. We need to ask young people with disabilities and their parents about what they need, and involve them in the decision-making process.

For young people with disabilities and their parents, remember that you deserve to have a meaningful b'nai mitzvah service. Do not be afraid to speak up and ask for what you need. There are many community organizations and resources that can help synagogues and their staffs to identify creative ways to accommodate people with physical, sensory, intellectual, mental health, autism, and many other types of disabilities. And, remember that people with disabilities should not just be tolerated, accommodated, and included—we should belong at our synagogues.

—Wendy Elliott-Vandivier

Within the Community

When new members are welcomed to the community, we have the opportunity to discuss an individual's physical needs and the ways in which they want to be engaged in the community. Keep in mind that longtime members of the community may have changing needs too. Consider surveying the congregation to determine any changing congregant access needs. A new family will complete a membership application, which may now include access needs, but many long-standing member families should be surveyed as well. For example, one congregation recently shared that they only had two accessible parking spots, but their aging congregation needed more.

Many of our facilities are older and were designed during a time when UD and access were not at the forefront of design practices. There are many instances where the outside, program, and spiritual spaces are not fully accessible. Being able to enter the building is not enough; there are many ways in which we can make accommodations within the building that are no cost or low cost.

Here are some additional ways to plan for physical access needs as you move forward.

Outside the Building

- Provide assistance for all events when the door does not open easily.
- Ensure that accommodations for drop-off allow for those in need, including senior adults, to facilitate access to the building before parking the vehicle.
- Provide clear signage for those with and without visual disabilities.
- Make sure that walkways to and from the parking area are clearly marked, well-lit, and free of obstruction.
- Ensure that the parking lot includes appropriately spaced, reserved spots clearly marked with the International Symbol of Access close to accessible entrances.
- Clearly mark the main entrance or the side entrance and make sure it is accessible for a wheelchair or another assistive device. Place a second mezuzah low so it is accessible to a wheelchair user or someone short in stature.

Motorized Scooters and Shabbat

There are currently several scooters on the market that are halachically approved for use on Shabbat. Using a standard motorized scooter on Shabbat would be considered a violation of traditional Shabbat laws. GramaChip Technologies utilizes a Jewish legal loophole, known as a *g'rama*, which permits indirect activation in scooters and other electronic devices on Shabbat. Amigo Scooters also provides a halachically approved mobility vehicle for use during Shabbat. They are certified by the Zomet Institute in Israel and use a special timing circuit that fulfills the "no-work" requirement for Shabbat observance.

—H.B.

Non-Worship Areas inside the Building

* Ensure that doorways and halls are free from obstructions and swing open without impediment.
* Make sure there are no area rugs in the building that might cause those with difficulty walking to trip or might make wheelchair access difficult.
* Use non-fragrance soaps in restroom areas.
* Provide signage that is clear for those with and without visual disabilities.
* Make sure that classroom and public meeting areas provide seating designed so all individuals can have access to a desk or table when necessary.
* Ensure that restrooms (at least one per floor) have accessible toilets, sinks, mirrors, towel dispensers, and doorways.
* Ensure that elevators, lifts, or ramps provide accessibility to the entire facility.

Spiritual Areas

* Reserve seating for individuals with physical disabilities, and make sure the seating area allows extra space for wheelchairs or other mobility devices.
* Welcome and encourage individuals with hearing loss to sit up front.
* Ensure access to *tallitot* (prayer shawls) and *kippot* (head coverings).
* Move the podium and microphone to floor level to be accessible when the bimah is not accessible.
* Ensure access to large-print prayer books.
* Ensure access to assistive listening devices. Provide a sign language interpreter when a congregant requires this accommodation.
* Provide adequate reading light/visibility on the speaker's face to facilitate speechreading/lipreading or sign language.
* Ensure that all signage is clear for those with and without visual disabilities.
* Ensure that the Torah ark is accessible.
* Provide a visual schedule for those who may need one. Gateways: Access to Jewish Education provides one on their website.

When I speak about inclusive synagogues, I often quote *Pirkei Avot* 2:16, "It is not your duty to finish the work, but neither are you at liberty to neglect it." We have certainly come a long way toward building a fully inclusive Jewish community, but we still have a long way to go. I look forward to the time when we no longer need to use the phrase *inclusive community*, because our Jewish communities are places of belonging for all.

✱ CHAPTER 4 ✱

It Takes a Community:

Building Support for the B'nai Mitzvah Journey

Gabrielle Kaplan-Mayer

Gabrielle Kaplan-Mayer, an author, educator, and disability advocate, is director of virtual content for Ritualwell, an online resource of inclusive Jewish rituals, and editor of Jewish Disability Inclusion News. She details ways that parents can assemble a planning and support team including professionals, family members, and friends to assist in the b'nai mitzvah process.

The Circle Around Your Child

We all know the adage: "It takes a village to raise a child." For parents raising children with disabilities, your village likely includes not only friends and family but also the numerous professionals who help to support your child and aid in their educational and therapeutic growth: teachers; doctors; occupational, physical, and speech therapists; and behavior support professionals, who may spend hours each day in your family's home. Often, the relationships between these professionals and your child are hugely significant: they may understand your child's unique strengths and challenges in different ways from how your own family and friends do.

Very often, when a parent discovers that their child has a disability and/or receives a medical diagnosis, they seek out parents in similar circumstances, whether through in-person support groups, online forums, personal connections made in school, or social or therapeutic programs. If you are fortunate to have these kinds of relationships as part of your village, those friends can be a major source of support as you prepare for and celebrate your child's becoming *b'nai mitzvah.*

When you think about the community that has surrounded you and your family through your child's life so far, what image or metaphor comes to mind? I often use the word circle when it comes to those who surround my son George, age twenty-three, with their love and protection.

For me, a *circle* of friends—family members, George's teachers, therapists, and fellow parents who share similar experiences—feels powerful. George has multiple disabilities—he is nonverbal, has severe autism, and also has an intellectual disability—and we are now working on his transition to adult life. He also had a bar mitzvah service and party. My circle was invaluable during the planning of that milestone; I continue to turn to them when I am struggling and need someone to listen. I can ask my circle to send good vibes to George when we have a big school funding meeting coming up. Some people in our circle will play ongoing roles in George's life. All the people in our circle love and care deeply about George—and that brings me great comfort.

Think of a metaphor that describes the people who are cheering on your kiddo. Maybe you have a team? A crew? A pack? A posse? Give it a name. So often, people with disabilities and their loved ones feel isolated because we live in a society that marginalizes us. It takes power, effort, and intention not only to claim your tribe, but to celebrate the *community* that celebrates your child.

Now consider how you can use this valuable group of people who support you and your family throughout this rite of passage, the b'nai mitzvah process.

It's also never too late to reach out or expand your village of support. Connecting with one other parent who relates to your experience or finding one community leader to support your b'nai mitzvah can make all the difference!

I've made some of the closest friends of my adult life by connecting with parents who are also raising children with disabilities. Some folks I have been fortunate to meet at in-person programs, but some I found in online support groups, and those relationships are meaningful and very real.

There are Jewish community groups that offer social or support programs, both online and in person, to connect with other Jewish parents raising children with disabilities. Some options to explore include Jewish Family Service, Jewish Disability Inclusion News, PJ Library, and Friendship Circle.

Steps to Creating a B'nai Mitzvah Team

Think back to other major life-cycle events that you've been part of or helped to plan, such as your wedding or your child's circumcision or naming ceremony. You knew to tap friends and family to help. The same is true for planning a *b'nai mitzvah*, except you'll be expanding your circle of helpers.

Maybe you were fortunate enough to have had a close relationship with your rabbi or wedding officiant, had that special friend who helped you to pick out what you wore, or found an event planner who made you feel like all your event details were being handled with care.

For your child's b'nai mitzvah team, you'll bring an intentionality to gathering the people who can support you and your child throughout the process.

Of course, your child may have ideas about whom they would like to be on their team and whom to invite to their b'nai mitzvah. They may want to include favorite teachers or therapists. They may have friends from school you know and those you don't know—feel free to reach out to their teacher if you need help contacting parents. If your child is part of any social or recreational extracurricular activities, they may want to include friends from those settings into their special day. Work with your child to imagine both who could support them in the process of becoming b'nai mitzvah—and whom they would most like to have at their side as they celebrate!

Consider the following categories of people to add to your team.

Your Religious Community: Clergy, Tutors, and Educators

Even if you are a member of a congregation and the rabbi, cantor, or educator knows your child well, they may not be familiar with planning a b'nai mitzvah for a child with disabilities. In my experience, however, more and more Jewish professionals want to understand disability inclusion and support members of their community who have disabilities. So you'll want to start a discussion about your child's strengths, challenges, sensory needs, and any other factors that may affect the b'nai mitzvah process. The synagogue professionals you'll be working with may not have experience or knowledge of your child's needs, but hopefully they have a willingness and a desire to learn. That openness is what you need on your team!

Sometimes, especially in larger congregations, there may be formal systems and requirements around b'nai mitzvah in place. Depending on your child's kind of disability, these requirements may or may not be appropriate for them. Chat with the clergy or educator you'll be working with about how to make modifications as needed. Give them a sense of your child—what they are excited about when it comes to their b'nai mitzvah, what they love about being Jewish, and what kinds of accommodations they may need to prepare for their service.

If for any reason you experience resistance or defensiveness, those professionals either don't have the understanding of what your child needs or just aren't sure how to handle those needs. Have a second conversation in which you emphasize how important a b'nai mitzvah is to your family and for your child to feel included. You can suggest that they reach out to Matan (mataninc.org) or connect with other clergy who have worked with students with disabilities. Sometimes people need time to process changes to the systems that they have come to rely on. You may find that there is one person on the professional staff who especially "gets" your child and has a special connection with them. That individual may take the lead on the b'nai mitzvah preparation process and help their colleagues to understand more clearly how to support your child.

If your family is not affiliated with a congregation but wants to hire a private tutor or rabbi to prepare your child for b'nai mitzvah and to lead their service, there are a number of resources to turn to. Many major metropolitan areas have rabbis or tutors who work independently in this capacity, and the major rabbinical schools can put you in touch with students who do tutoring and lead life-cycle events. Also know that one need not be a rabbi or cantor to officiate at this life-cycle event. The essential thing to do before enlisting a rabbi or educator to join your child's team is to have a similar conversation as described above.

Ideally, you will find someone who has experience working with children and adolescents with disabilities. And, sometimes, a professional without experience—but who comes to you with a strong desire to learn about your child's needs—could make for an excellent team member. Whoever you work with, ongoing communication is an essential part of any good team.

A Rabbi Shows the Way

For Becca Hornstein, cofounder of Gesher Disability Resources, key bar mitzvah prep for her son, Joel, involved show-and-touch sessions with their rabbi. Joel has autism and is deaf, and the rabbi met with him and Becca weekly at the synagogue. "Every Thursday after school the rabbi met with Joel and me. I would sign [sign-language interpret] for Joel, and the rabbi would take him around the building,introduce him to various things around the synagogue and in the sanctuary. This is an important aspect of communicating a Jewish essence to a child with disabilities. It's not necessarily what you say. It's what you touch. It's what you hear. It's what you smell. It's what you see. It's the multisensory aspect of religion, and that should be considered for all children, not just children with disabilities, but for all children. You teach them through all of their senses."

—H.B..

Key Professionals in Your Child's Life

As you consider people from your "chosen family" whom you want to bring into your child's b'nai mitzvah planning team, consider those therapists, teachers, and other important professionals who can play an essential role in preparing your child and helping them to feel at ease on the day of the celebration.

Some team members you may want to call forward and the roles they could play:

Speech therapist: If your child receives speech therapy, their speech-language pathologist can bring a wealth of knowledge and skills that will assist the clergy, tutor, or educator who is preparing your child to become b'nai mitzvah. You can engage the pathologist for a session or two that focuses specifically on b'nai mitzvah preparation, and they may be able to integrate some of what your child is working on in ongoing sessions. For example, a speech therapist could support a young person who uses a communication device or other assistive technology by working with them to program icons related to the service onto their device. For a child who struggles with voice and articulation, you could ask your rabbi for a transliteration of the entire passage of their Torah or prayer reading, which a speech therapist could then offer techniques to support.

Occupational therapist: Book a session with your child's OT to come see the space where the b'nai mitzvah service will take place. They may notice things about the light and acoustics that would not have occurred to you, and they can offer creative ideas about accommodations that can help to support your child.

Physical therapist: Similarly, a physical therapist could play a crucial role for children with physical disabilities in helping to determine necessary accommodations. A PT can help a child navigate the sanctuary space and the *bimah* or help determine whether walking with the Torah is possible and whether any accommodations for that might be needed. A PT may also have suggestions for the best path for the child to take from their seat to the bimah, for example, if they need to save time and energy.

Behavior therapist or support person: For children who need behavioral support, the person who knows how to help them in school or other secular settings can share their wisdom during the b'nai mitzvah process. They can help to set up a reward or other positive behavior support plan in conjunction with the tutoring process and look ahead with you to the day of the service. For example, your child might benefit from having a room or dedicated space to decompress if they need a break, or some kind of reward in order to participate.

If your child receives services at home or at school that provide a one-on-one paraprofessional to support their behavior, you may want to include that person on your b'nai mitzvah team. It was important for me to have a support person in place for my son's service because I knew that he often needs to take breaks. My husband and I wanted to stay in the sanctuary for the entire service, and having someone he felt safe with to take him on breaks was very effective.

Nanny/babysitter: If your child has a close relationship with someone who has provided childcare in your home, that person might also be helpful by being on hand to lend support during the service and celebration.

Teacher: If your child had a pivotal teacher in their lives, inviting them could be very meaningful and comforting to your child. For example, we created a social story to help my son prepare for his big day and loaded it onto his iPad. When his teacher was working on reading with him, they would sometimes look at his bar mitzvah social story together. Looking at the story with his teacher reinforced what we were talking about with him at home and no doubt added to his sense of readiness.

Another example: Max is a young man with cerebral palsy who adored one of his teachers, Susan. Max chose to invite her to his bar mitzvah. He was so excited to know she was coming, and he waved at her from the bimah. Susan beamed with pride as if Max were her own son. As soon as the ceremony ended, Max got off the bimah and made a beeline straight for Susan.

Music therapist: A music therapist or music teacher may have useful suggestions on how to help your child learn prayers or the Torah reading. Some b'nai mitzvah will take to the trope system of musical notation in the same way they might have learned to read music for piano or guitar. Others may use their extraordinary auditory memory to learn a Torah reading. The music teacher may also have suggestions on how to best project from the bimah and how to maintain proper pacing and delivery.

Consider honoring and thanking these wonderful professionals during your child's ceremony. In synagogues that offer group *aliyot* (calls to the Torah), consider inviting "all teachers and professionals who helped them reach this milestone" to come up for an aliyah! You could simply name them and offer gratitude in a printed program, speak about them in remarks or at a toast if they will be joining your party, or even have a special blessing for teachers, helpers, and "chosen family" within your ceremony. Your b'nai mitzvah child could also offer the thanks themselves.

The Tefillin Therapist in Munich

Rabbi Yisroel and Chana Diskin, longtime Chabad emissaries in Munich, Germany, worried that their son Zalman, who has autism and is hearing-impaired, might never celebrate his bar mitzvah. "It dawned on me that he won't be able to say a blessing or count in a minyan (quorum of ten Jewish adults)," Chana recounts. "I was very upset; it insulted me!" Chana knew that Zalman had some religious awareness; for example, he clearly understood Shabbat rituals and customs.

The Diskins thought creatively and brought Zalman's non-Jewish, Singaporean autism specialist, Lynn, on board. Lynn had helped Zalman through difficult situations in the past. Perhaps she could also teach him to put on tefillin (phylacteries)—an essential part of his family's tradition for a bar mitzvah.

The Diskins were nervous—Zalman was unpredictable and impulsive, and often exhibited difficult behavior. He refused to get on the school bus at the start of the school year, hit others, and once flushed an expensive cochlear processor down the toilet.

Lynn had helped solve Zalman's refusal to get on his bus by creating a step-by-step picture book. She asked Rabbi Diskin to create a video on how to wrap tefillin, which she used to create another step-by-step book. Lynn illustrated two boxes—one representing the head and one representing the arm—and showed that each has a home: the tefillin bag and not the floor. Lynn then practiced with Zalman using a plastic tefillin prototype, since Zalman was likely to throw it.

On the Sunday morning of his bar mitzvah, as the time for the recitation of the Sh'ma prayer neared, Zalman was escorted into the service, wearing his tefillin. "He kept them on through two lines of the prayer!" says his proud mother. "Everyone was visibly moved. Then, he got frustrated and left the service."The Diskins will never forget that the unsung hero of Zalman's bar mitzvah was a non-Jewish autism expert who figured out the way to reach—and teach—their son.

—H.B.

Extended Family and Friends Who Are Chosen Family

It is important to look honestly at your family and close friend relationships as you plan for your child's b'nai mitzvah.

Don't hesitate to reach out to others to help you carry out the details of the day. A chosen family is made up of people who have intentionally chosen to love and support each other through life's good times and challenges. As with the family members to whom you feel close and connected, reach out to your friends who are like family. They can be there, too, to listen and support you, to play an honorary role in your child's big day, even to help you with the ever-present last-minute schlepping that always comes with hosting a *simchah*!

Begin by thinking about which family members have been with you along the way since your child's diagnosis, and who have been advocates, champions, and listeners. These are important people who will most likely continue to play a role in your child's life as they transition to adulthood. You'll want them to be present for your child's b'nai mitzvah ceremony and perhaps to play an honorary role. This gesture can recognize the role of grandparents, godparents, cousins, aunts, and uncles—those people whose presence is important not only in the present but in imagining your child's future full of community and connection that extends beyond parents and siblings. You may also want to engage these family members as a supportive presence throughout the process.

You might have cousins with whom you're not often in touch and who haven't played a supportive role in your child's life. If you feel the call to reconnect with them, go for it. But it doesn't have to be at your child's b'nai mitzvah. Many of us imagine that our child's b'nai mitzvah service and party will also be a family reunion of sorts, bringing together grandparents, aunts and uncles, and cousins of different generations. Depending on the kind of service and celebration that is best for your child, it may not be wise to invite every extended family member to your child's b'nai mitzvah. You can explain this to those extended family members, and arrange another time to get together.

There are many ways that your close family members can take an active role in the service. For example, if your child will read one aliyah, there may be others in the family who would be honored to chant other Torah readings at the service. Having grandparents participate in a "passing down the Torah" ritual can be a beautiful tradition. That tradition involves the officiant inviting various generations to the Ark and explaining how the b'nai mitzvah is part of a tradition dating back to Moses. According to our tradition, Moses received the Torah on Mount Sinai and passed it down to his successor, Joshua, who in turn passed it down to the elders of Israel, and ultimately to the great-grandparents, grandparents, and parents of the b'nai mitzvah. It's a symbolic way of honoring the idea that the b'nai mitzvah is receiving Torah from those who came before.

My father, Steve, has been a dedicated grandfather to my son George throughout his life. Initially, I had hoped that we could teach George how to hold the Torah with supports in place so that he could march through the sanctuary at his bar mitzvah. During the tutoring process, we discovered that George's fine motor skills, challenges with body awareness, and generalized sense of anxiety did not allow him to do so. Instead, we invited Pop-Pop Steve to carry the Torah through the sanctuary in George's honor. This was a wonderful way for my dad to participate in a deeply significant ritual moment in the service.

You may have artists or creative family members or friends who would be excited to help you with any task, from designing invitations, to creating centerpieces, to playing music as part of your service. At our service my brother Jon played Matisyahu's "One Day," a favorite song of George's, on guitar. Finding those special ritual moments and honors was very meaningful for my husband and me and helped George to see and experience all of the people who love him dearly as part of his bar mitzvah service.

There was another way that we engaged a wider circle of community around George's bar mitzvah. We envisioned George's bar mitzvah as an opportunity to build education and awareness, and emailed the friends and family that we planned to invite to our simchah a few months ahead of the service and asked them to read a book about disability awareness in George's honor.

You Are Not Alone

Ultimately, we all want the process of becoming b'nai mitzvah to increase community for you and your child. That will last well beyond the day itself.

A friend of mine shared with me how his son Josh, who is autistic, has continued to find community at his synagogue, post–bar mitzvah. "Since his bar mitzvah, Josh has become a very active member of the synagogue, attending services every Saturday morning, being called for an aliyah, and just enjoying learning more and more of the service."

May every child find the unique ways that they can offer their gifts and become part of a community.

Help from Near and Far

At a school about an hour from Boise, Idaho, a Modern Orthodox boy from New Jersey was prepared for his bar mitzvah. The team included the bar mitzvah teacher in Connecticut, a supportive team in Boise, and Zoom. This was a relief to Nate's parents, who had worried about his bar mitzvah for years.

Nate's therapist and treatment team at Cherry Gulch, a therapeutic boarding school for boys (which was not Jewish) in Emmett, Idaho, and Rabbi Mendel Lifshitz at Chabad Lubavitch of Idaho in Boise were key members of the bar mitzvah team. School therapists ensured that Nate met with the teacher on Zoom each week at thdesignated time. Throughout the bar mitzvah learning process, members of the treatment team drove Nate nearly two hours round trip to meet with the Chabad rabbi. Once, the rabbi opened a real Torah scroll and the three practiced together—with Nate and the rabbi at the Chabad House, and the teacher on Zoom.

On the bar mitzvah day, when Nate finished chanting Torah, the community did something they have never done before: they applauded. Nate came down from the bimah and told his parents, "This is the best I've felt in my whole life!"

Despite the distance from his family and from a large Jewish community while Nate was in Idaho, his bar mitzvah learning experience and his in-person New Jersey bar mitzvah were smooth and affirming.

—H.B.

✻ CHAPTER 5 ✻

Start with a Dream:

Ideas for Services, Celebrations, Guest Lists, and More

Gabrielle Kaplan-Mayer

Gabrielle Kaplan-Mayer, an author, educator, and disability advocate, is director of virtual content for Ritualwell, and editor of Jewish Disability Inclusion News. After many years in the field and raising her own son, she knows her way around party planning for a child with a disability. This chapter focuses on inspiration for families.

My son George is nonverbal, has severe autism, and an intellectual disability, and was also an active participant in preparing for his bar mitzvah in ways that we had specially designed for him. His *aliyah* (call to the Torah) was recorded onto his iPad, and he practiced pressing the button to play it; he finger-painted a colorful collage of the parting of the Sea—his Torah portion—that hung in the sanctuary during his service; and he practiced singing the Sh'ma prayer in his loudest voice (George can produce some sounds vocally when he sings though he can't speak—his loudest singing was a whisper). George's service was an hour long and took place on his actual thirteenth birthday, a Monday morning (which happened to be Martin Luther King Jr. Day), so that we could avoid a large Shabbat crowd at our synagogue. We approached his party as an extension of his service.

For us, that extension meant hosting a simple brunch in the synagogue social hall following his service, so that George didn't need to navigate a transition to another space (this choice was also appreciated by many of our elderly relatives).

George had attended the *b'nai mitzvah* parties of his older cousins and some family friends—and that usually meant wearing noise-canceling headphones and sitting outside the main room where the DJ was playing music that was still too loud for him to tolerate. We knew that any kind of celebration following his service would need to be sensitive to his significant sensory and attention needs.

We had a simple setup for the celebration—no glaring lights or loud DJs, just some of George's favorite rock/pop music playing through a speaker at a modest level. We invited his wonderful music therapist to lead a program for the kids after they ate, which was enjoyed both by his peers with developmental disabilities and his neurotypical friends and cousins. The music therapist gathered everyone into a circle, shared instruments like tambourines and egg shakers, and sang children's songs as everyone helped to make a band. Many adults who didn't have kids with them made their way over to enjoy the fun! We also hired a professional Mickey Mouse character—George's favorite cartoon because of his lifelong obsession with the movie *Fantasia*—to make the rounds and add to the festivities.

It's natural to want to wish the b'nai mitzvah kid a hearty "mazel tov!" and to shower them with hugs and good wishes after their service—but lots of social contact at once is overwhelming for George. Instead, we set up a table with pretty paper and pens where people could write messages and notes of congratulations for George. We let our guests know that we would be sure to read George all of their loving words after the bar mitzvah excitement had wound down—when he could really take them in.

Although we were carefully planning the party to support George's needs, we also knew that being part of any festivities following the service might be too overwhelming for him. We hired a favorite babysitter, who knew George well, to hang out with him during the party if he preferred not to attend the whole event. This turned out to be very helpful, because George *did* need time with the sitter, away from the party, to sit quietly and play on his iPad before he was ready to join the fun again. We, in turn, could focus our attention on the guests.

George's service and his celebration were truly beautiful rituals, marking his turning thirteen with love, affection, and community. Know that families can plan a celebration that is just right for each child. It can be beautiful, memorable, and completely unique.

No One-Size-Fits-All

Disabled is an umbrella term for individuals with learning, physical, intellectual, developmental, hearing or vision, or mental health disabilities, or a combination thereof. A party for a thirteen-year-old who has dyslexia or another kind of learning disability wouldn't necessarily warrant any kind of special planning—while preparing for their b'nai mitzvah service would require it. But for another thirteen-year-old who has social anxiety or social skills deficits, planning an appropriate celebration means taking their unique challenges into consideration.

Below is advice gathered on my own journey and from the words, experiences, and perspectives of many parents who have created meaningful celebrations to honor their children becoming b'nai mitzvah.

Not all of the ideas and suggestions presented here will resonate with your child's specific needs—but hopefully these ideas will inspire you to create a celebration that is reflective and supportive of them.

Avoid the Cookie Cutter Party

When parents are planning their children's b'nai mitzvah parties—whether they consciously realize it or not—they face a lot of pressure to keep up with their peers. The lavish, over-the-top party is common, and there may be tension between the opportunity for a meaningful ritual and the social pressure to throw a party in keeping with the community's expectations. An "alternative" party is still outside the norm and can feel hard to consider.

When a traditional party isn't the best option for your child, it is actually an opportunity to step back and plan a meaningful, personal celebration, independent of others' expectations. Creating a unique celebration not only supports your child and your family, but offers a memorable experience for your guests and will contribute to our communal creativity about options for the future. Remember, there are thousands of thirteen-year-olds who don't have disabilities, who also really hate DJ parties and dancing, and who would probably love to celebrate their big day with an outside-the-box party. There are plenty of adults who can't stand yelling across the table because the DJ's music is just that loud. Many parents who create alternative types of parties—whether their child has a disability or not—report on how much their friends and family loved their different and personal way of celebrating.

Start by Dreaming

To create a unique and supportive b'nai mitzvah celebration for your child, begin with an open heart and mind. Take a deep breath . . . grab a pen and paper (or Google doc), and see what arises as you answer these questions:

- What kinds of activities does your child love to do? An activity doesn't have to be a formal hobby per se, but could include any kind of activity that engages them and makes them happy, whether that's building with Legos, listening to music, cooking, etc.
- What are some kinds of outings that are fun and relaxing for your child? Favorite local places where your child feels comfortable? This location could be a nature center you visit frequently, a bowling alley your child loves, or a favorite restaurant.
- What kind of food does your child like best? Many children and teens with sensory issues prefer or avoid certain types of foods.
- Who are the people who are most important to your child—and your family? This could include extended family and friends and also therapists, teachers, and classmates—people who have supported and nurtured your child.
- What time of day is your child's energy level strongest? Are they a morning or an evening person? When you've attended parties or formal occasions, how long does your child's energy and attention generally last?
- What type of sensory issues affect your child? Are they sensitive to noise, crowds, or lights? Do they seek out or avoid certain kinds of sensory stimulation? Have you encountered environments that are challenging for your child from a sensory perspective?

Clothing Accommodations

While there are often clear synagogue norms, many b'nai mitzvah are uncomfortable in a suit or dress, which will affect comfort or performance. Ties may feel too tight around the neck, tags may bother or chafe, and some girls feel awkward or exposed wearing a dress. Max, who has autism, arrived at synagogue in a sports coat and slacks, and later changed into shorts and a T-shirt. In Israel, formal clothing wouldn't even be considered; most people, no matter their ability, wear sandals, sneakers, and a pair of "nice" pants.

—H.B.

Where and When

As you move from dreaming into planning, remember that you have many options about when the party should be held.

Consider whether a nontraditional location could be an option. Perhaps you never thought of your child's favorite Chinese restaurant as a party venue—but if that is a comfortable place for your child, it's worth finding out if they have a room for events. If the zoo is a favorite place, investigate whether they have a party space. And, of course, throughout the planning, be sure to bring the b'nai mitzvah child into the conversation too.

Consider, too, your child's energy levels. If they wane in the afternoon, a long luncheon following a morning service might not be as appropriate as an evening party, after they've had a chance to go home and rest for a while.

When Donna Cohen was planning her daughter's bat mitzvah, they chose a Sunday Rosh Chodesh (new month) date for the ceremony and party rather than a Shabbat morning. By holding the event on Sunday, the synagogue would have fewer people in attendance, and they could have a more intimate luncheon.

Perhaps just one big event in a day—the b'nai mitzvah service—is best for your child. You could hold a simple *kiddush* (social time after synagogue service) reception afterward, and plan a party to be held the next day or later in the week. A *havdalah* service (Saturday evening, ending Shabbat) could be an option as well.

For some families, the celebration could be an outing that the child would really enjoy, such as a favorite museum, zoo, or aquarium; a sensory-friendly sporting event; or a ballet or musical. It could also be a festive meal held in your home, backyard, or a park in your community.

Along with immediate family, you might invite cousins, grandparents, and/or some classmates to make the experience even more celebratory. The celebration need not take place the weekend of the service—for some children who become overwhelmed in social situations, it may be preferable to gather a week, or even a month following the b'nai mitzvah service.

Budget

For any family planning a b'nai mitzvah party, it's essential to begin with a clear sense of your budget and to make choices that reflect the reality of your budget. There is far more economic diversity in the Jewish community than we generally acknowledge, and parents raising children with disabilities are all too familiar with the economic hardship related to disability that other families do not face. Children with disabilities often have medical, therapeutic, pharmaceutical, respite, and caregiver expenses that can affect a family's ability to save money. Within our Jewish communities, there are still programs in which children with disabilities pay higher tuition or extra program fees to participate. Real inclusion will only exist when we have a communal conversation about this disparity and find creative ways to share the expenses for children who need extra support to participate in community. There should not be a family tax on having a disability—especially when families may already be struggling financially. Know that there are many ways to create a meaningful, special party for your child without spending a fortune. It's ok to just host one party! Many families feel pressure to host a whole weekend of events for their out-of-town guests, including a Friday night Shabbat dinner and also a Sunday brunch. These additional events can become too much for many children with cognitive, sensory, and attention challenges—and can add stress to parents who are working with a modest budget. Remember that your event does not need to conform to others' expectations of a b'nai mitzvah weekend.

It's also important to consider additional expenses that may be needed for the b'nai mitzvah celebration of a child with disabilities:

* **Add support people to the guest list:** Are you considering inviting all of your child's classmates to the celebration? Some of them may need a support person, incurring the cost of additional meals. As we did for our son George, many parents hire a childcare worker or paraprofessional to be on hand during the celebration so that you, as the parents, can stay focused on your role as party hosts. Include the fee for that person (along with their tip) as a line in your budget.
* **Don't forget alterations.** For children with physical disabilities or sensory challenges, and for those with short stature, it may be difficult to find a suit or party dress off the rack and you may need to have your child's clothing custom made

The Guest List

You may be feeling pressure as you consider whom to invite to your child's party. Sometimes grandparents have expectations about inviting all of the extended family . . . even when that means second and third cousins whom your child may not know. Perhaps you've been invited to many celebrations by members of your synagogue community, and now you feel you must reciprocate at your family's simchah.

I would like to wave a magic wand right now and let you know that the right way to make a guest list is to consider what is best for your child. Maybe your child LOVES big parties—if so, and if you can afford it, make a big guest list! If a smaller party is going to work with their needs, then go that route. And if it's more important for their happiness and comfort level that beloved therapists and teachers come, invite them, even if it means other people get left off the list.

If your celebration will be a smaller event, perhaps on another day, or won't be a formal party at all, it's fine to invite the extended community only to the service. A small kiddush reception following the service is a lovely way to celebrate with everyone present that day.

Children with social anxiety and/or social skills deficits can be challenged by the prospect of coming up with a list of friends. As parents, it can be upsetting to acknowledge that our children don't have many friends. But this is the reality for some children, and not necessarily a cause for despair. There is a range of human need for friendship, and we all fall somewhere on that spectrum. Social skills, like any developmental skills, continue to grow in time, so a thirteen-year-old who struggles with friendship may discover their best friend at sixteen or eighteen or thirty-five.

If your child doesn't have many friends to invite to the party, that is simply where they are. Plan your event accordingly—and perhaps instead of a DJ-focused party with lots of games for kids, find a fun party game or activity that kids and adults can engage in together.

Thinking through your guest list may take some time and some negotiation. Keep your focus on your child and on your family's well-being. If you hear from someone whose feelings are hurt because they didn't receive a party invitation, let them know that this event was designed to support your child's needs. Anyone who is on your team will understand.

Your Child's Role in Party Planning

Just as most families' party planning involves considerable negotiation between parents and child, when planning a celebration for a child with a disability, it's equally important to give your child a voice in sharing their desires—even as you will need to set boundaries around what is possible for your family. For example, when planning their daughter Elianna's bat mitzvah, parents Susannah and Bernie knew that a Disney theme was important to her. For Elianna's needs, it was necessary to modify the party in certain ways, such as limiting the guest list, but it was easy to make Elianna's wish for a Disney-themed party come true.

Too many choices can be uncomfortable for young people with cognitive disabilities. Party planning is no exception. An open-ended question like "Where would you like to have your party?" could be abstract for a child who is a concrete thinker. Instead, for some children, two choices might work best. Instead of asking "Where would you like to have your party?" you could say, "For your bat mitzvah celebration, we could have a pizza party at the synagogue OR we could go to the bowling alley and have a party there with some friends and your cousins." For some children who think visually, you could use photos to present choices of location, food, and activities.

If your child has a particular request for a party theme, activity, location, or guest list, consider what accommodations might be needed to make their hopes for the party come to be.

Raffi, a young person on the autism spectrum, wanted a party with a DJ playing music and leading party games like Coke and Pepsi, which he'd played at other parties. His parents knew that many of Raffi's classmates who have intellectual disabilities might not be familiar with the games and might need help following the DJ's directions. Raffi's parents hired two teenage girls who had been helpers in a program that Raffi attended to assist the DJ with running the games. Raffi and his friends had a blast at the party.

For help in achieving your child's wishes for a particular activity, reach out to your child's teachers and therapists for their ideas. Professionals with expertise in working with children and teens with disabilities may have insights that will be extremely helpful to your planning. Fellow parents who are b'nai mitzvah veterans can be a helpful resource too. Don't hesitate to join social media groups about b'nai mitzvah planning—your child may have a disability, but good ideas are universal. You don't have to figure this out on your own.

Party Planning and Inclusive Design

Keep the idea of universal design in mind as you plan your child's party—accommodations to make the party accessible for your child may also benefit lots of your guests. For example, you may want to designate a quiet room where your child can go to decompress from the main events of the party, listen to music, or play with a calming toy. If you're holding the party in your synagogue's social hall, the quiet room could simply be a lobby area or a classroom. When guests know that a quiet room is available, it may be used by others who also need a break—children, teens, or adults.

Susannah knew that her daughter Elianna benefits from fidget toys. So rather than just bringing some of Elianna's fidgets to the party, she placed bowls of fidgets throughout the party so that other kids and adults could use them too.

Another parent needed to protect her son's dietary needs. This child is allergic to peanuts and tree nuts, and is also on a gluten- and dairy-free diet. The caterer made sure that all of the food was nut-free, and set up a clearly marked buffet table of only gluten- and dairy-free food across the social hall from the food containing gluten and dairy. Many guests commented on how much they appreciated that clear separation of food.

Physical accessibility is also important to consider. A family whose child uses a wheelchair or has mobility challenges knows it is crucial to find a physically accessible event space—including bathrooms. When you choose an accessible venue because of your child's needs, you're benefiting all of your guests—especially elderly relatives who use walkers or canes.

Preparing Your Child for the Party

Social stories with words and pictures that depict a social experience are a simple learning tool. If social stories benefit your child, create one about the experience of the b'nai mitzvah service and also what will happen at the party. Describe the event's location, who will be there, what food will be served, and what activities are planned for the party. More information about social stories and examples is easy to find online.

A visual schedule is also beneficial for some children. Include the timeline of events that will take place at the party with as much detail as your child needs. For example:

- Snacks and drinks
- DJ plays games with my friends and me
- Lunch is served
- Dancing the hora
- Cake is served
- Time to say goodbye

Go over the schedule in advance with your child. Read it to them again the day of the event. Have a copy printed and easily accessible. Visual schedules can be posted with Velcro, so that a child can "check off" the activity as it occurs.

There may be elements to the party that will be new experiences for your child. It was important to the Goldstein family to include dancing the hora at Elianna's celebration—but Elianna needed practice learning the dance. Practicing the hora became another way the family helped Elianna get ready for her big day.

If being lifted in a chair will be part of your party, children with sensory needs or poor balance may require practice. They would also benefit from a chair with arms. Being lifted in a chair and bounced in rhythm to the music is certainly a novel experience—but not a welcome one for everyone. If your child has seen older relatives or friends being lifted in a chair and they want that experience, they should certainly have the opportunity, but a little practice can ensure that it's the fun, festive experience it's meant to be and not one that produces anxiety. This is certainly something to practice with a physical therapist in advance. One family showed their child videos of people being lifted in chairs during the hora, and that was enough for their son to decide that being lifted in a chair was not for him.

Preparing your child for the party location is also important. For children who experience anxiety in novel situations, a comfortable, familiar venue can significantly alleviate stress. If your party is being held in a restaurant, a park, or another place that is new to your child, be sure to visit it several times before the event itself.

Communicating with Extended Community

Even when you have a supportive circle of friends, it's natural to feel some anxiety about how your extended community will react to a celebration that will be different in some ways from typical simchas that they've attended.

One way to decrease your stress and gather support, is to send an enclosure in your invitation, or post details on the website or in a separate email, explaining what to expect at the service and party. If you have more religiously observant guests, they might appreciate knowing if the service will be modified. Make sure they know if the dress is casual or more formal. If the party's length will be shorter than the average b'nai mitzvah celebration, guests may appreciate knowing that. Explain that the party will celebrate your child's strengths, just like the service.

For some of your guests, your child's b'nai mitzvah may be the first time that they have experienced the beauty of this ritual for a child with a disability. Whether you prepare them for what to expect or not, they will likely enter the experience with love, compassion, and a positive attitude toward your child and your family.

What Do You Need?

When planning your child's celebration, it may feel counterintuitive to consider what you need to make the event a success, and how you can reduce your own stress. Take time and consider this question, however, because your child's b'nai mitzvah ceremony is a coming-of-age moment for you as a parent too. It may also be the first time in a long time that you've been able to bring together friends, extended family, and community members for a celebration. You deserve to be present, interact with your guests, and savor the moment.

In addition to hiring a support person for your child, you may want to include an event coordinator in your budget. It can be challenging to watch out for your child, greet your guests, and manage the caterer and other vendors. A trusted event coordinator can take some of that responsibility off your shoulders.

If hiring an event coordinator is not possible within your budget, reach out to a family member or a few good friends and ask them to help with party management. Someone could be in charge of making sure that vendors arrive and know where to set up; someone else could make sure guests know where to leave cards and gifts; someone else could mingle among the kids and make sure that everyone has the support they need. It can be hard to ask for help—but there are undoubtedly people who want to help make this day special for you and your family. They will be happy to take on a task so that you can be fully present and able to celebrate.

Vendors

How does your son or daughter react to being photographed? You may want to capture this milestone moment in family portraits, but you'll want to consider how and when that should be done.

It's common at a Saturday night dinner dance to pull together the grandparents, cousins, and extended family to get some portraits. Many photographers have certain standard party shots that feature the b'nai mitzvah kid. If taking pictures is stressful for your child, plan to take those family portraits at an alternate time when everyone can be relaxed. You'll definitely want to get recommendations for relaxed photographers who can go with the flow—and not put undue pressure on your child. Even a chill photographer may not have experience working with a child with disabilities. Let the photographer know about your child's needs before you hire them.

Other professionals who work in the party/event industry often have standard operating procedures for events, but these may or may not work for your specific party.

When you're hiring any vendor, talk openly with them about the kinds of accommodations that you're planning. For example, food trucks have become popular at lots of parties—but some food trucks mean guests have to wait in long lines. This may not work for kids with attention challenges or cognitive or physical disabilities. If you're using a DJ, look for solutions beforehand, such as keeping the music at an acceptable level, providing headphones, staying away from using strobe lights (which can be seizure-inducing for some with seizure disorders), and creating a space on the dance floor accessible for those using wheelchairs. Perhaps the food truck vendor can make some things ahead of time and place them on a table set up next to the truck.

Any quality vendor should be happy to accommodate necessary modifications; they want your business. Communicate your vision in advance, and don't sign a contract until you're clear that the vendor understands your vision and can adjust to your needs. If a vendor isn't amenable, they are not the professional with whom you want to work.

Party Ideas

Example: A Nature Party

Neither Emmett (who uses "they/them" pronouns) nor their parents like loud parties or crowds, so they ruled out a large DJ/dance party. Emmett and their parents lived an hour from a nature center that they really loved and remembered that it was available for private events. The nature center featured walking trails, a boat to take party guests out on a lagoon, and an indoor/outdoor room for food. Emmett had a *kiddush* luncheon buffet at the synagogue immediately following the ceremony, but the family chose to hold the nature party the next day, when everyone would feel more rested.

Why It Was Perfect: The atmosphere of the nature center was very calming for Emmett and for guests, as it turned out. People could walk the trails, take a boat ride, or sit on a lovely outdoor patio where cold drinks were served throughout the afternoon. All of the guests came together to enjoy a picnic lunch and an ice cream sundae bar, one element that Emmett especially wanted to include in the party.

Example: A Party Within a Party

Leon and Ali are brother and sister, fifteen months apart, who became b'nai mitzvah together. They have the same genetic disorder that affects their cognitive function and motor coordination, and both are nonverbal and use communication devices. Leon and Ali both love music and enjoy social gatherings. Their mother wanted to create a party immediately following the service that would be just right for them—and at the same time, wanted to host a cocktail hour for adult friends in the social hall. Leon, Ali, and their friends had their own room with kid-friendly food, live music by a local Klezmer musician, their favorite caregivers, and two movement therapists whom their mom knew very well. Leon and Ali's smart mom also filled the social hall with comfy bean bag–style chairs, so that sensory-friendly seating was available and the kids weren't expected to sit at tables.

Why It Was Perfect: Leon and Ali were able to enjoy their own party, and the adults could celebrate in the way that was right for them.

Example: A Theater/Improv Party

Eli is a self-advocate with autism. He knew that he wanted a celebration that would include the people closest to him and that would revolve around a favorite activity. As he and his parents dreamed up possibilities, they realized how much Eli enjoyed theater at his Jewish overnight camp. His mom got in touch with the camp drama teacher. She lived several hours away but was really excited to lead Torah-based theater improv games for Eli's party after a *kiddush* luncheon.

Why It Was Perfect: The intimate number of friends and family (less than thirty) was the ideal number of people for Eli to relate to and feel comfortable with. The theater improv activity was fun for the intergenerational group, and Eli loved having a favorite teacher lead the activity.

Example: A Purim Party

Nathan, a young person with an intellectual disability, mood disorder, and autism, was born on Purim. He loves the holiday and had a bar mitzvah service on a Shabbat afternoon just a few days before Purim. Nathan and his family dressed for the service in costume, and so did the rabbi. Nathan enjoyed Purim carnivals, so his parents asked their synagogue educator to use carnival games in storage for Nathan's bar mitzvah party. In the synagogue social hall immediately following Nathan's service, Nathan's family set up games like ring toss and pin the crown on Queen Esther—fun and basic enough for Nathan and his classmates.

Why It Was Perfect: The carnival atmosphere was fun and focused for Nathan and his classmates, as well as Nathan's young cousins, and many adults, who got into the spirit and took turns playing.

Example: The Trip of a Lifetime

Benji, who is nonverbal and has autism, and Max, his neurotypical twin brother, became b'nai mitzvah in a small family service in Israel. Their family chose to take a dream trip instead of throwing a party. The b'nai mitzvah was held in Jerusalem at the Western Wall, just after their thirteenth birthday.

Why It Was Perfect: Benji and Max's parents knew that it would be challenging to create a party that would be right for both boys. They were each excited about going to Israel and prepared for their bar mitzvah in ways that were meaningful for their different abilities. Their family trip to Israel provided an opportunity to be together in a Jewishly meaningful place and to extend their celebration of this shared milestone event.

As you can gather from these fun, creative celebrations, a b'nai mitzvah party can take infinite forms. What matters is that people who love your child and your family come together to celebrate your child's life and the remarkable milestone.

—G.K.-M.

CHAPTER 6

Envisioning the Experience:

A Checklist for Getting Started

Rebecca Redner and Arlene Remz

Rebecca Redner, an educational specialist at Gateways: Access to Jewish Education in Boston, and Arlene Remz, Gateways' founding executive director, are passionate advocates for the right of every child to participate in Jewish education. In this chapter, Rebecca and Arlene provide a checklist that clergy and educators can use with families to address the nuts and bolts of envisioning b'nai mitzvah for a child with a disability.

Activating Creative Thinking

One of the first steps in creating a positive *b'nai mitzvah* experience is to think creatively about how to build a service around each child's strengths and challenges. At Gateways, our b'nai mitzvah intake form was originally meant to help parents communicate their child's needs, as well as their own preferences, to their child's teachers and clergy.

We found that the act of filling in this form also expands parents' conception of what b'nai mitzvah can look like by presenting options many didn't realize were possible.

Creating Initial Goals

Once you have had the opportunity to imagine what your child's b'nai mitzvah might look like, it is time to bring together the entire b'nai mitzvah team. The core members of the team include the parents, the clergy, and the educator who will be overseeing the child's instruction. Additional team members may include the child themself, religious or secular school educators who have a deep understanding of the child, behavioral specialists, speech and language pathologists, and occupational therapists. The parents' vision for their child is the starting point of the team meeting. The parents share the b'nai mitzvah they envisioned as they completed the intake form. The clergy and educators can then help them refine that vision and determine concrete steps to bring that vision to life.

These meetings don't always start with all the team members on the same page about what the child is capable of or what the service will look like. However, everybody can usually agree on certain guiding principles. We have found that articulating these principles at the beginning of the first meeting helps the team focus on the child's feelings and experiences, and feel empowered.

B'nai Mitzvah Guiding Principles

Principle #1: It is essential that the learning process, and the b'nai mitzvah itself, be positive experiences. The main goal must never be about how much a child is able to do or how well they can perform. The top priority is for the child to come away from this process feeling good about being Jewish and eager to continue their participation in Jewish life. Sometimes this may involve adjusting our expectations so that the child doesn't feel stressed.

Principle #2: A b'nai mitzvah is about more than just a single day; it encompasses the overarching educational process that takes place in preparation for that day. Preparing to become b'nai mitzvah is an opportunity for children to learn skills that contribute to their continued participation in Jewish life as adults. This might mean cutting back on skills that the child may only use once in favor of skills that the child might use every week. For example, instead of learning to chant a Haftarah portion—a reading from the books of the Prophets—the child might learn how to recite additional prayers from the Shabbat morning liturgy.

Principle #3: The child should actively participate in both learning and in the b'nai mitzvah service in a way that is meaningful and accessible for them. Every child is capable of engaging in meaningful actions during the b'nai mitzvah ceremony.

The b'nai mitzvah visioning form can be a powerful tool for helping the team to communicate expectations and envision a path to success. Additionally, it helps the team to place the child's unique needs at the center of planning, so the b'nai mitzvah is molded around what will work best for the student, rather than trying to force the student into the mold of a typical b'nai mitzvah experience. By enabling the team to focus on how to make the b'nai mitzvah experience accessible, meaningful, and positive, an effective intake form guides them on their first steps to success.

B'nai Mitzvah Visioning Form

When could the ceremony take place?

* Saturday morning
* Saturday evening
* Rosh Chodesh (new Jewish month) that falls on a Sunday, a Monday holiday, or during a school vacation week

  A Monday or Thursday [days when the Torah is traditionally read in synagogue] morning during school vacation week
* A Monday or Thursday evening during school vacation week
* Festive holidays such as Sukkot, Purim, Hanukkah, or Shavuot
* During the time when the child regularly attends religious school or b'nai mitzvah tutoring
* Other: ____

Considerations:

* When is the child at their best? Are they an early bird or a night owl?
* Does the child take medications that wear off as the day goes on?
* Will the child need to use electronic devices that not all synagogues allow on Shabbat?
* Is the child familiar with the routine of going to synagogue on a certain day or at a certain time?
* What is the Torah portion for that date? Is it a portion that will have meaning for the child?
* How many congregants attend the synagogue's Saturday morning service? Will the child feel comfortable with that number of people?

How long would the ideal service be?

* 15 minutes
* 30 minutes
* 45 minutes
* 1 hour
* 2 hours
* Other: ____________

Courtesy of Gateways: Access to Jewish Education.

- How long can the child usually focus on a task at home? At school?
- What will the child do during parts of the service when they are not leading or participating? Can they rest or reset during this time?
- Are there points in the service where the child could take breaks, either off the *bimah* (podium) or out of the room?
- Is the clergy willing to cut out parts of the service to make it shorter? Will the congregation be open to parts of the service being cut?
- Are other children with disabilities being invited to the service?
- Will it be difficult for them to sit through a long event?

Where could the ceremony take place?

- Large sanctuary
- Small chapel
- Rabbi's study
- School
- Home
- Summer camp
- JCC
- Other: ______________________

Considerations:

- In what setting is the child most comfortable?
- Is the child familiar with the space?
- Is the space large and overwhelming?
- Is the space cluttered and full of distractions?
- Is the space sensory-friendly (no harsh fluorescent lighting, no perfumes, not too much ambient noise, no echoes)?
- How many people might attend the ceremony without overwhelming the child?

Courtesy of Gateways: Access to Jewish Education.

How might the child participate?

- Reciting prayers (verbally, in sign language, or with AAC—Augmentative and Alternative Communication)
- Chanting Torah (verbally, in sign language, or with AAC)
- Delivering a *d'var Torah* (speech about the weekly Torah portion)
- Doing a mitzvah project
- Greeting congregants
- Sitting on the bimah
- Calling page numbers
- Wearing a tallit (prayer shawl)
- Making music
- Dancing
- Carrying the Torah
- Dressing and undressing the Torah
- Opening and closing the ark

Considerations:

- What are the child's strengths?
- What would the child enjoy?
- How does the child communicate at school and at home?
- How does the child usually participate in religious observances? Do they recite prayers? Do they perform actions such as uncovering the challah on Shabbat?
- What kind of sensory stimulation does the child enjoy most? Touch? Sound? Movement?
- What kind of sensory stimulation is the child sensitive to? Are they overwhelmed by noise? Does visual clutter overwhelm them?
- Does the child feel comfortable being in front of a crowd?
- Does the child get easily fatigued?

Courtesy of Gateways: Access to Jewish Education.

What might the child learn, do, and be exposed to during the b'nai mitzvah preparation process?

* Learn the words of the prayers
* Learn the meaning of the prayers
* Learn to decode Hebrew
* Learn about holidays
* Learn about the meaning of becoming b'nai mitzvah
* Learn about the basics of Judaism
* Do a mitzvah project
* Attend services in synagogue regularly
* Learn to chant a Torah portion
* Learn the story of their Torah portion
* Compose a d'var Torah speech
* Create an alternative d'var Torah such as an art project or a digital presentation
* Form a relationship with the clergy
* Form relationships with other Jewish children of the same age

Considerations:

* What will help the child be comfortable on the day of their b'nai mitzvah?
* What does the child enjoy learning?
* What do you want the child to get out of this entire experience? What feelings and skills would you like them to come away with?
* What will help the child to "own" their Judaism?
* How does your family celebrate holidays at home? How would you like your child to participate in holiday observances?
* What will contribute to the child becoming an active adult participant in Jewish life?

Courtesy of Gateways: Access to Jewish Education.

CHAPTER 7

Sibs in the Spotlight:

Remembering the Needs of Siblings

Jessica Leving Siegel

Jessica Leving Siegel, founder and president of the Center for Siblings of People with Disabilities and author of Billy's Sister: Life When Your Sibling Has a Disability, *reminds readers that celebrating b'nai mitzvah is a family affair that includes the siblings. She shares the research and her personal experience of sibling dynamics in "mixed ability" families, and offers ideas about how to create a welcoming, uplifting b'nai mitzvah experience that includes the whole family.*

While parents no doubt experience a roller coaster of emotions in the months leading up to the momentous occasion of seeing their child with a disability up on the *bimah*, don't forget: if there are other kids in the family, these siblings are on an emotional roller coaster during this time too. And it's probably not the same one as their parents.

Though many siblings are excited for their brother or sister's big day and eager to play a role, neurotypical brothers and sisters experience a whole host of challenges and joys during this time that aren't always top of mind for the adults involved. A brother or sister may be nervous for their sibling, jealous of all the attention directed toward the *b'nai mitzvah* in the family, or even feeling guilty that they aren't doing enough to help their sibling be successful or to help their parents to manage the stress of it all.

Whatever it is that siblings are feeling—don't assume they'll tell you about it. In fact, one of the most frequently noted characteristics of "sibs" (the commonly accepted term for non-disabled siblings in a family where one or more children has a disability) is that they often keep their emotions close to the vest, *especially* if they sense that parents or others are already overwhelmed trying to address the needs of a child with a disability.

The Emotional Life of Siblings

"Parents are already spending a lot of time, money, and emotional energy on tending to the child with the disability, and the 'well' sibling doesn't want to burden the parents further—so they just keep it inside," says psychology professor and sibling research specialist Dr. Avidan Milevsky, one of the preeminent researchers on sibling issues. Dr. Milevsky's research has shown that siblings of children with disabilities have a statistically significant higher likelihood of developing internalized behaviors and disorders (such as anxiety, depression, and eating disorders) later in life if not provided with adequate support when they're younger. This is likely due to sibs' propensity to shove feelings down and turn inward, especially during stressful situations (such as a b'nai mitzvah).

Celebrating a b'nai mitzvah in the family is a wonderful and exciting time. And it can be a wonderful and exciting time for sibs, too—perhaps even a pivotal, affirming time—*if* parents, clergy, and others take a few extra steps to consider their needs.

There are all kinds of ways to create a welcoming, uplifting b'nai mitzvah experience that is truly inclusive of every child in the family—including sibs. Not only can including sibs in the b'nai mitzvah set them up for better mental wellness now and in the future—it will also help you maximize the possibilities for a beautiful, memorable day and a stronger sibling relationship that the whole family will benefit from for years to come.

My Brother, Billy

My younger brother, Billy, was diagnosed with autism and epilepsy when I was eight years old. Since childhood, Billy has been my best friend, my partner-in-crime, my confidant. . .and, at times, a huge pain in the butt.

In these ways and many others, we're just like any other siblings. But there's no denying that his disability also makes our relationship different—or that it indelibly shaped the course of my own social-emotional development.

I don't consider myself scarred for life by being a sib. In fact, because so many caring adults in my life helped validate my feelings throughout my childhood, and because I was able to access the resources I needed as I grew older, I credit my sibling experience with helping me develop into the leader that (I would like to think) I am today. And, my relationship with my brother is stronger now than ever.

I do, however, believe that I am among the lucky ones.

As an adult I've taken an interest in exploring sibling issues, and I started a nonprofit devoted to addressing some of the challenges siblings face at all ages (the Center for Siblings of People with Disabilities, www.siblingcenter.org). Through my work, I've had the opportunity to speak with quite a few of my peers—and while I'm not a psychologist or a researcher (I leave the statistical stuff to Dr. Milevsky), I've developed what I believe to be a pretty strong understanding of what we'll call the "typical neurotypical sib."

I'm also Jewish and had a bat mitzvah—and watched my own brother's bar mitzvah with lots of complicated emotions (How would he do when it came to chanting the prayers? What if he did something embarrassing? Why were so many more people crying during his ceremony than during mine?).

I'm also a former journalist—and journalists are big fans of asking experts a lot of questions and then acting like they know everything. So, I asked experts a lot of questions, and now I'm excited to tell you everything I learned.

Note: *I use* Mom and Dad *for simplicity's sake throughout this chapter, but the insights and advice are intended for all family structures and communities.*

Supporting Siblings 101

It's critical to ensure that even sibs who are excited to participate in their sibs' b'nai mitzvah know the difference between taking on extra responsibility as a choice and feeling pressure to assume a "parentified" role in their siblings' ceremony preparations—whether that pressure comes from others (parents, extended family, or community members) or from themselves.

Parents of "parentified" kids have not *purposefully* abdicated their roles—sibs often take on that role out of love for their sibling and a genuine desire to see their sibling live their best life. It's a beautiful desire, but it needs to be nurtured with care.

"The sibling relationship is usually the longest-lasting relationship in a family, and brothers and sisters will likely be involved in the life of the child who has special needs longer than anyone—including the child's parents," according to Don Meyer, founder of the Sibling Support Project and creator of Sibshops. Taking time now to tend to sibling needs will pay infinite dividends for everyone long into the future.

Sibling Needs Vary

No two sibs are exactly alike. There are, however, many emotions that are common among siblings of those with disabilities. When it comes to b'nai mitzvah time, here are several that we might expect:

Fear/Anxiety

- "What if he can't learn it in time? Or messes up and feels embarrassed? What if I feel embarrassed?"
- "What if people can't understand what she's saying? Or she has tics in the middle of her *parashah* (Torah portion)? Or falls coming down the stairs from the bimah?"
- "What if . . ." The possibilities are literally endless.

Jealousy

- "How come my sibling is getting more attention than me?"
- "Not nearly as many people cried at my b'nai mitzvah. I worked really hard too, y'know . . ."
- "Wow, Mom and Dad are really going all out for this party and invited the whole town. Bet they won't care this much when it's my turn."

Guilt

- "Am I a bad person for being jealous of her? I shouldn't feel so angry at her, but I can't stop feeling it."

* "Mom and Dad seem so stressed about his bar mitzvah. I feel terrible that my lameness in math means they have to find me a tutor when they're already so overwhelmed. What's wrong with me?"
* "I should help Susie study more to learn her Torah portion. It's my job as her sister."

Left Out/Invisible

* "XYZ would have been neat to do during the ceremony. . .Too bad no one even asked my opinion."
* "Wow, seems like every person in the synagogue knows Susie's name now. Wonder if they know who I am."

Joy/Pride

* "Wow, that was really cool seeing him accomplish that."
* "I can't wait until she sees the video; she's going to love it."
* "This was so much fun!"

All the above feelings are common, normal, and valid. None of them are a judgment on what parents or community members have or haven't done to support siblings up until this point.

They *are*, however, excellent opportunities to start a conversation with the sib to help them explore the situation further and to build healthy coping skills. More on that later in this chapter.

Including Sibs in the B'nai Mitzvah Ceremony

Leverage the special relationship sibs have with their brother or sister with a disability. Whether it's something as major as chanting the Torah portion for a sibling who can't speak, or as small as helping with a blessing, many sibs both desire and appreciate the opportunity to have a formal part in the ceremony or simply to be recognized in some way. (At my brother's bar mitzvah, for instance, the rabbi included a special section in his speech where he talked about our relationship. I remember how meaningful it was for me to feel seen, too, in that moment.)

Brothers and sisters may have their own creative ideas—like holding up flash cards or giving special hints if their sibling forgets a word while on the bimah. In more open prayer communities, there may even be opportunities to include special blessings to acknowledge the sib or add a song or skit that the siblings in the family perform together.

If there's a youth service or a youth group that the nondisabled child is involved in, that may be a natural fit for banding together with peers to offer group support, whether during the preparation or the ceremony itself. You may even find, as one Silver Spring, Maryland, mom did, that leveraging sib connections makes inroads for inclusion that shift the entire synagogue's culture.

"Because my older son, Tani, and his peers were in charge of running the youth service when Uriel started preparing for his bar mitzvah, it seemed only natural to the other kids that, of course, they would help him," says Dina, whose son Uriel has Down syndrome. "Uriel became sort of a fixture in the service even after [his bar mitzvah]. Tani and his friends set the example that this is how you include. And they still do that to this day, even after Tani graduated."

Want more ideas? Reach out to your rabbi, extended family, friends, and other networks. Maybe make a post in a local parent or family support group for your child's specific diagnosis. Try browsing Ritualwell (www.ritualwell.org) to see if anything there could be adapted for your family situation.

There are tons of wonderful ways to recognize and honor the special relationship of siblings. If your sib genuinely wants this honor and recognition, it's a smash hit of win-wins: a beautiful, inspiring moment in the ceremony for everyone, and some very well-deserved attention and credit for the sib.

Ideas to Get the Wheels Turning

- Ask siblings if they'd like to give a speech during the ceremony.
- Find a special blessing that sibs can recite.
- Ask the rabbi or cantor to give a special call-out to the siblings in a way that feels meaningful.
- Light a candle to honor siblings during a candle-lighting ceremony.
- Give siblings a special sign to hold, or perhaps a name tag or ribbon identifying them as the brother or sister of the b'nai mitzvah.

- Ask sibling to steady the hand of the b'nai mitzvah or push a wheelchair.
- Invite siblings to have a friend sit with them during the ceremony—and/or let them invite a few friends to keep them company at the party.
- If sibs are part of a youth group, consult the youth group leader to see if there's a way to involve the group—perhaps during a group *aliyah* (call to the Torah) or a special presentation during the ceremony or party.
- Write thank-you notes to everyone in the community who helped the b'nai mitzvah child get to where they are today—and be sure to include one for each sibling.
- As appropriate, remind the b'nai mitzvah child to acknowledge their sibling(s) during their speeches. Sometimes getting recognition directly from the affected sibling is the most meaningful of all.

When Siblings Don't Wish to Participate

Or maybe they want to be involved, but just a little. Give them space to change their mind—in either direction—up until the last minute.

Either way is okay.

There are a lot of difficult emotions that the b'nai mitzvah experience can bring up for a sib. It's not a judgment on how much they love their sibling, their parents, or even how much they value Judaism. Remind them, and remind yourself, that all emotions are valid. Even if they're unpleasant or not what the adult wants to hear.

Whether you're a parent, a clergy member, or another community member, if a sib says, "I really have a lot on my plate right now with school and sports, and I just don't think I can help tutor Susie for her parashah," the best thing you can do for that sibling is thank them for being honest with you, and with themselves, about what they can commit to. Remind them that it's not their job to tutor their sibling, and reassure them that you as the adult will make sure Susie has the support she needs.

You can also check back in a few weeks and see if maybe there's another, less time-intensive way they'd like to be involved. If yes, great! If no, also great. No matter what, make sure you let them know that you respect their choice.

Special Considerations for a Double B'nai Mitzvah

Parents of twins or siblings considering having a b'nai mitzvah for one child who is affected by a disability and another who is not should proceed with care. It can certainly be a wonderful, moving experience. But please, take the time to check in with *both* siblings to make sure no one is feeling shortchanged—and look into options for each child to have separate times to shine. For instance, maybe one child can lead services Friday night, while the other leads Shabbat morning services.

"We opted to have the events a year apart in order to give our neurotypical child a chance to shine on her own," said Lori, mom of twins. "We had the realization that they needed completely different settings and services. Our son with needs often dominates the family in many ways, and this was an opportunity to tell our daughter that she also comes first sometimes."

Helping Siblings Feel Supported

Remember: the goal is to help kids learn to manage their complex emotions, not to eliminate them. Sibs in families affected by disability most often get into trouble when they don't express their emotions—or, worse, when they feel so guilty about having what they deem to be a "negative" feeling that they shove it down and try to pretend they didn't have it in the first place. A little extra effort at learning to name and manage emotions now can continue to benefit everyone in the family for, literally, the rest of their lives.

This can also be a great opportunity for sibs to see that, in fact, their brother or sister with a disability can indeed accomplish more than they thought. Seeing their sibling learn to do something without their help may also reassure them that it's okay for them to step back when they need to—that it's actually a positive thing to let other people help sometimes.

Consider also connecting sibs with peers who get it. See if you can connect your sib with the nondisabled child from a family with a similar makeup to talk about their sibling's b'nai mitzvah experience. If you can't find anyone, find a Sibshop near you and encourage the sib to get involved. (Sibshop provides siblings of children with disabilities with resources and peer support.)

Encourage embracing conflicting emotions. It is both normal and possible to feel joy and embarrassment, pride and fear, etc. (The Disney movie *Inside Out* is also a great resource for teaching this concept!)

Siblings Who Are Really Struggling

While many siblings just need a little extra care and compassion to help them navigate the complex emotions outlined above, some may need a bit more. If you find that the sib in your life is really struggling—whether with anxiety, depression, or other mental health or behavioral issues—please don't delay in getting them access to an age-appropriate therapist who can provide early intervention.

Suggested Responses to Complex Emotions

In my family, we love scripts and social stories, so. . .I have a gift for you! Let's take another look at the big list of emotions and hypothetical sib quotes discussed earlier, now with some suggested responses plugged in.

Concern	Suggested Response
Fear/Anxiety: What if he messes up?	It sounds like you're feeling worried about what will happen if your brother doesn't meet expectations. Which part worries you in particular? Let them respond, then. . . Hmm, yeah, you're right. That could happen and it would be a bummer. But in our family/in this community, it's the effort that matters. We believe in providing everyone with all the resources we can to help them perform to the best of their ability—that's the part we'll celebrate, no matter what.

Concern	Suggested Response
Fear/Anxiety: What if she does something that embarrasses me in front of the whole synagogue?	I can understand feeling worried about your sister doing something embarrassing. It's okay to feel embarrassed by family members sometimes. Have you felt embarrassed by her at shul before? Tell me about it. It might feel good to let it out.
Fear/Anxiety: What if. . . ?	It seems like you're feeling uncertain and worried about a lot of things right now. Let's work on learning how to get used to that feeling, since we can't control the outcome. It gets easier to sit with these feelings the more we practice doing it!
Jealousy: How come my sibling is getting more attention than me?	I can see why you might feel that way. You have every right to feel upset. Is there a way we could include you in the ceremony or party so that you'd be able to feel more a part of things?
Jealousy: I don't want to participate. I'm just jealous. There's nothing you can do to fix it. It just stinks	I hear that. There will probably be times when she gets more attention or praise than you, and I can see why that feels unfair. The best I can do is remind you that I see how hard you work on everything, and I know it's not always easy for you either. I'm proud of you.
Anger: He always gets everything he wants just because he has a disability.	I can see why it would feel that way and I understand why you're mad. Sometimes when I'm mad, I [journal/take deep breaths/go for a walk]. Could we try that together?

Concern	Suggested Response
Guilt: I wonder if I'm a bad person for being jealous of my sister.	It's normal in all families to feel jealous and angry sometimes. She may have a disability, but she's still your sister and you're allowed to be mad at her, as long as you express your feelings in a healthy way. I'm never going to judge you for having a feeling. In fact, if you tell me how you're feeling early on, I might even be able to help you find some ways to navigate the situation.

Creating a positive experience that is welcoming and inclusive of siblings can be a mitzvah unto itself that lays the foundation for a healthy sibling relationship for years to come.

Yeah, maybe I scared you in the first few pages. But now that you've made it this far, what I hope you'll actually come away feeling from this chapter is inspired. Or, at the very least, a little better prepared and motivated to meet sibling needs head-on and open the door for some fruitful conversation.

Truly, some extra consideration for sibling needs in the months leading up to b'nai mitzvah can change the course of that sibling's life. It can help them to develop healthier communication and coping mechanisms and a stronger sense of self—not to mention stronger community connections and a new understanding of Jewish values in action.

Ultimately, the child with a disability benefits too, from having a healthy, well-adjusted sibling who loves them for who they are and is able to do so while holding fast to his/her own identity and boundaries.

How's *that* for a mitzvah?

CHAPTER 8

A Happening:

Invoking the Arts to Express the Soul

Elaine Hall

Elaine Hall is an acting coach to child stars, with and without disabilities, founder of the Miracle Project, and author of such books as Seven Keys to Unlock Autism: Making Miracles in the Classroom. *Here, she recounts the journey to the bar mitzvah of her son with autism, and offers arts-based practices to give voice to each child's wisdom.*

"My bar mitzvah is going to be a happening," my twelve-year-old, nonspeaking, autistic son, Neal, types with his speech therapist, Darlene, during one of their communication therapy sessions.

"It is when I make a commitment to the Torah," he continues.

"Is that right?" asks Darlene, whose expertise does not particularly include Jewish studies.

"Exactly right," I say.

For years my cousin Gloria had sent me articles about kids with disabilities becoming a *b'nai mitzvah*. She emailed me about the importance of building a spiritual community for Neal, often suggesting that I take Neal to synagogue and to religious school. I thanked her for her caring and encouragement, but I knew in my heart that I would not follow through. Between being a single mom, trying to stay financially afloat, dealing with medical insurance, attending Individualized Education Program (IEP) meetings, taking Neal to speech therapy, occupational therapy, *therapy* therapy. . . adding religious training was far from my most immediate concern. Neal and I did pray together each night, every morning, and before most meals. I reminded him often about his own relationship to God. We celebrated Shabbat together at home; and when I could find childcare, I attended weekly services at my neighborhood synagogue, on my own.

What I didn't tell my cousin about were my disastrous attempts at joining synagogue life as a family. The last time we had even tried, Neal was barely four years old, and the sounds and sights of people totally overwhelmed him. Neal turned into a screeching, whirling mess; I turned into an embarrassed and profusely apologetic mom trying to carry a flailing Neal out of the sanctuary. Neal shook his head "No, no, no!" I felt people's confusion and helplessness, not knowing what to say or do. Worse were the few gawking, pitying, and judgmental stares invariably turned in our direction. As kindhearted and well-meaning as the rabbi, cantor, and congregation were—and they *were*—they just didn't know *how* to include us. And neither did I. Then.

The Marriage of Profession and Spirit

You can imagine my surprise eight years later when a Los Angeles–based nonprofit hired me to create a b'nai mitzvah program for individuals on the autistic spectrum. Previously, I had worked in Hollywood as an on-set acting coach/consultant for Walt Disney Studios, Universal Pictures, CBS, Sony, Nickelodeon, and other networks. I also taught movement, musical theater, and creative dramatics in local private schools and Jewish day schools. I loved working with kids and was even described by the *New York Times* as the "child whisperer." Many of the young actors I taught called me "Coach E," but what I really wanted was to be called "Mama" by my own child.

Because I was not able to give birth biologically, I adopted Neal, a toddler from Russia. He was not able to speak and was later diagnosed with apraxia and autism. (Apraxia is a neurological condition that makes it difficult or impossible to make certain movements, including producing speech.) When traditional therapies did not work for him, I turned to what I knew best and drew upon my experiences in the arts to connect with him. Rather than trying to pull my son out of his autistic world, I chose to enter his. When he spun in circles, I spun with him, and we played "Ring around the Rosie." When he flapped his hands, I flapped mine, too, and we became birds "flying" through the room. Some professionals told me that I was enabling his autism, but I knew that when I entered Neal's world with creativity and joy, we connected. And what does any mother want but to connect with her child? Fortunately, I found other autism experts on the East Coast, such as the esteemed Dr. Stanley Greenspan and Dr. Barry Prizant, who offered me the clinical insights I needed to support what I was doing and encouraged me to use my background in the arts to reach my son.

As I used expressive arts to connect with Neal, he slowly began to emerge and engage, developing vital communication and self-regulation skills that decreased his anxiety and enabled him to participate in the world around him. I began to train others to help me better reach my son, ultimately developing an evidence-based methodology called Inclusion from WithIn®, which uses creativity to bring out the best in individuals with and without disabilities.

Building an Arts-Based B'nai Mitzvah Program

In 2007, when I developed an arts-based b'nai mitzvah program, I was thrilled to combine my love of children with autism and creativity with my love of God and Judaism. I had created a theater and film program for kids with autism and other disabilities called the Miracle Project. I felt certain that the qualities at the core of the program I had created—love, acceptance, creativity, and joy—could be applied to religious education. And they could.

I gathered colleagues from the Miracle Project's original team, including the cantor and another religious educator, and trained new Jewish educators and volunteers in my methodologies. We built a unique, arts-based b'nai mitzvah program to reach children and teens whose parents may never have dreamed of participating in this celebration. Miraculously, the year that I began the b'nai mitzvah program was the year that Neal would turn thirteen, the year that he should become a bar mitzvah. There are no accidents.

I reached out to the autism community to find Jewish families like mine who might be interested in having their child participate in the b'nai mitzvah program. Many were hesitant; so many had been hurt by negative experiences in synagogues. As a result, many of the families had little to no affiliation with a synagogue, so I felt it was important to start from our beginnings, our history, and what bound us to Judaism and tied us together.

At first, some of the parents were concerned that their autistic child could barely read English, let alone Hebrew, and would not be able to lead a congregation as they had seen other teens do for their b'nai mitzvah. I assured them that we would find ways for their child to be successful and to shine.

In God's Image

I also reminded these parents that the cornerstone of our Jewish tradition is that we are all made *b'tzelem Elohim*, in the "image of God" (Genesis: 1:27). The Torah does not read that some of us—but rather that *all* of us—are created in God's image. So, it naturally follows that if we are all made in God's image, our neurodivergent children, who perceive the world differently, are indeed inherently whole. They are not "less than" because of their disability, nor "more than"; they simply *are*, as every human being, made of the same earth, with God's breath blown into them (Genesis 2:7). The Hebrew word for this breath is *neshamah*—"soul."

So often the spiritual nature of a child with a disability is downplayed or even ignored by professionals. I had come to believe that a spiritual life was essential for all children. In our afternoon b'nai mitzvah classes, the same young people who, earlier that day at school, had kicked, bitten, or melted down into a tantrum were able to come together and quietly share their deepest feelings. They communicated with each other about love, friendship, and taking care of the Earth. They talked about their personal relationship to God. Some used assistive technology to speak their words; others had no words at all. Some spoke out in ways that they had never spoken before. They seemed to have had an intuitive grasp of concepts steeped in spirituality, such as generosity and gratitude. When we asked them to define *neshamah*, one nonspeaking, autistic boy, who used an Augmentative and Alternative Communication (AAC) device, typed the word *Radiance*.

Our Practice

We met each child where they were, making relationship paramount. Connection was more important than mastering any skill or learning trope (biblical cantillation). It was important to me that we break down the meanings of the weekly prayers, making them meaningful for each student. Our participants learned the Modeh Ani (prayer said upon awakening) and told us what they were grateful for each day. One child responded, "I am grateful for my mother for taking me to my therapies." Another child said, "I am grateful for my grandparents for watching me so my parents could both work."

I brought in b'nai mitzvah buddies—neurotypical peers who were celebrating their own b'nai mitzvahs that year, or who had recently celebrated theirs—to connect with each child. We included relevant, meaningful, and age-appropriate art projects, movement activities, breathing, singing, playing instruments, role-playing, and acting out the weekly Torah portion. Using a Hebrew letter yoga chart together we shaped our bodies into Hebrew letters by standing side by side to form Hebrew words. We created a tzedakah (charity) box to collect coins for people in need, and we discussed ways to be of service and give charity. We presumed competence and understanding, and, accordingly, taught all aspects of our Jewish values and traditions, making the curriculum experiential, meaningful, and joyful.

We used the actual sanctuary to practice opening the ark, and holding, carrying, and kissing the Torah. We made the entire experience accessible, meaningful, individualized, and personal. We presented the *parashah* (Torah portion) of the week and openly discussed ways to use the lessons in the Torah to help us with our personal difficulties. We used creative dramatics to act the stories, and brought in costumes to make the scenes come alive.

Children and teens who once had little to no connection with their Judaism learned when to stand, when to sit, how to be in synagogue, how to carry a Torah, and what to do when you receive an *aliyah* (call to the Torah), and they were able to generalize this into other environments. Parents who had once felt isolated and alone quickly became part of this dynamic community. To quote Psalms 126:5: "They who sow in tears shall reap with songs of joy."

Neal's Bar Mitzvah

As classes progressed, Neal typed with his speech therapist that his bar mitzvah would be a happening and that it would be when he made a commitment to the Torah. As I wrote in my memoir, *Now I See the Moon: A Mother, a Son, and the Miracle of Autism,* when Neal typed, "God helps me find patience with my autism," I knew that he had an innate understanding of the importance of this celebration.

For several years I had recited the *Sh'ma* prayer with Neal every night before he went to bed. The word *sh'ma* can be translated as "hear" or "listen." How perfect that the one word Neal was to utter at his bar mitzvah celebration was "LISTEN," the word he put forth to me, a word he knew so well. We taught him to say it. We showed him how to place his finger on his lips and whisper "Sh," then press his lips together to make the "ma" sound. Just like "Mama," we said.

For his bar mitzvah ceremony, Neal wore a colorful prayer shawl that he'd painted himself. During the ceremony, he literally danced his own prayers, moving with grace and joy across the *bimah.* He took my hands, and as we did when he was four years old, we spun together in swooping circles. For the Torah blessing, we input the blessings into Neal's talking device. He pushed the appropriate buttons before and after the Torah reading and, using a *yad* (Torah pointer), he pointed to the passage in the Torah.

Suddenly, looking out at the seventy-five guests watching him, Neal became overwhelmed and ran out into the lobby. I ran after him, hoping he could continue, as I knew how much this meant to him. We were joined by two of his friends, one, another b'nai mitzvah student with autism, the other, neurotypical.

"Neal, you are doing great," they told him. "You're doing great."

We were all silent together.

They offered Neal some snacks. He used the bathroom, gathered himself together, and returned to the synagogue to complete the ceremony.

Neal chose to sit with his friends as Jeff, his stepfather-to-be, read the speech that Neal had typed with his therapist.

> *"To be Jewish is to take the Torah as the word of God and live your life as God has said. The people of God live by the Torah. They are to be rewarded. The greatest gift is my mother. She rescued me from a different life. I know that everything I have started that day. God put us together so I could*

have Mom. The greatest gift is my mom. I am a leader of my thoughts and decisions. It is the right and responsibility of a boy to learn what God wants and expects of us, then to listen and set an example. I get to be smart and teach people about differences. To pick a humble act, I have to say it is how I show patience to my life each day. I have to be humble to God when I am challenged with autism. My humility comes in my love and humor. Thank you to Rabbi Avi for being real and being a great teacher. Thank you to my mom and Jeff. Perfect love is what they give. Thank you to all the people who support us."

Neal's face was lit by his glowing smile. As a klezmer clarinetist played, the congregation danced through the aisles. That day, Neal and I were transformed. Neal's face radiated a new sense of purpose, of accomplishment, of responsibility. I experienced a sense of belonging, of peace, and of joy that is every Jewish parent's divine right. The congregation was elevated. I recall a ninety-eight-year-old woman saying to me, "That was the most spiritual experience I have ever had."

Bridging and Belonging

Our challenge today is to rethink the word *inclusion*. Do we ever say, "I am included at Temple Emanuel?" No, we say, "I belong to. . ." Today, Neal and I go to Nashuva, a prominent community of prayer located on the west side of Los Angeles. Every Rosh Hashanah, Rabbi Naomi Levy calls Neal to the Torah to open the ark. When I first thanked the organizer for giving Neal this honor, she responded with, "Of course! He is a valued member of our community." At Nashuva, we are not "included"—we belong.

The arts can be a bridge to belonging. Psalm 96 encourages us to "sing unto God." I have witnessed young adults who have minimal speech lead a congregation in song. In Exodus 31:1–6, we read about God requesting the artist Bezalel to build the Mishkan (the portable Tabernacle), because Betzalel was an artist who "possessed a divine spirit." I have seen young people with disabilities create sculptures, paint exquisite works of art, or design professional-quality animation. The arts create a bridge into the soul of those who experience the world differently. If we nurture that soul and allow their spirit to shine, we will witness miracles.

Follow Their Lead

What interests your b'nai mitzvah student? Where do they light up? Let go of any preconceived notions of what a b'nai mitzvah celebration should be or look like. Our tradition invites us to "Train a child in the way they ought to go; they will not swerve from it even in old age" (Proverbs 22:6). I like to interpret this as teaching a child in the way that they learn best.

There is a story by Rebbe Nachman of Breslov about a prince who decides he is no longer a human but a turkey. He sheds his clothing, sits under the dining table picking at crumbs and bones, and refuses to do any of his usual activities. The king, deeply distraught, hires the finest doctors in the land to cure his son, but to no avail. Finally, a wise man, requesting no money, asks to meet the prince. Instead of trying to cure the turkey prince and pull him out of his world, the wise man joins the prince in his. The wise takes off his own clothes and gets on the floor with the prince, claiming to be a turkey too. Over time, the two develop a trusting relationship and become friends. The wise man starts to suggest to the prince that turkeys can also wear clothes and eat at a table. Step-by-step, the prince chooses to enter the typical world. The wise man does not set out to change the prince, but rather to understand him. Through connection, transformation occurs.

Create a trusting relationship with the b'nai mitzvah student. Join their world first before you ask or expect them to be part of yours. Be patient, calm, and curious about what interests them. Think creatively, outside the box. Nurture the relationship above all else. Follow their interests, whether they love music, movement, art, Disney stories, drumming, or gardening. Find your way into what is meaningful for the child, and, through shared positive emotional experiences and being in this liminal space together, create an environment to begin to teach Torah.

Let each child shine in whatever way allows their neshamah to light up.

Include the Child

Include the child's perspective on their b'nai mitzvah. How would they like to express themselves? Who do they want to invite to the ceremony? Do they wish to have a party? Or would they prefer something quiet in the rabbi's office or even in their own home?

Include the Family

When I first meet with parents, I invite them to begin their child's b'nai mitzvah year as their own spiritual journey, reflecting on their own childhood memories. The smells of their grandmother's challah, lighting candles with their mother, sitting in temple with their father playing with the *tzitzit* (ritual fringes) on his tallit (prayer shawl). I invite them to start incorporating meaningful rituals into their own lives. Slowly their own, sometimes buried, Jewish identity resurfaces and the celebration becomes a profoundly moving family affair.

Techniques for Using the Arts

Whether you are a parent, teacher, or clergy member, presume competence. Using the arts should not be limited to just cutting and pasting Hebrew letters on a dreidel, reading Bible stories, or teaching children how to dance the hora. We can use every aspect of creativity—music, movement, storytelling, singing, visual art, video—to allow self-expression in whatever form to create engagement and spiritual meaning—traditional, individual, and communal.

To transition from the outside world into the b'nai mitzvah tutoring class, I often start a b'nai mitzvah session with an art project based on their parashah. For example, if we are discussing Deuteronomy 6:4–9, "*Sh'ma Yisrael, Adonai Eloheinu, Adonai echad* (Hear, O Israel! The Lord is our God, the Lord is one), we might create a mezuzah, a small box to attach to the doors of Jewish homes that contains parchment with the words of the Sh'ma. We have used glass test tubes or clay for the container, decorating it, purchasing an authentic scroll, and later placing it on our door in the company of our family members.

We may use movement to embody the Hebrew letter shin, which is the first letter of the word sh'ma. I have used the book *Aleph-Bet Yoga: Embodying the Hebrew Letters for Physical and Spiritual Well-Being* by Steven A. Rapp, as a resource.

I may teach the Sh'ma to the students through American Sign Language, or drum the rhythm of the prayer. We discuss what the prayer means to them. We may also add in meditation, to consider what God may be saying directly to them.

For each b'nai mitzvah student, we learn their Jewish name and how it is spelled. We use yoga to embody each letter and then explore through Jewish stories or Torah what their Hebrew name means. We can dramatize their story and act out what their role was in our history.

Traditionally, b'nai mitzvah takes place near the child's thirteenth birthday on the Hebrew calendar. In that case the portion of the week is predetermined. For the actual b'nai mitzvah ceremony, we similarly explore creative ways to teach and celebrate, led by each child and customized for their interests and skills. A b'nai mitzvah date could also be chosen based on a Torah portion that aligns with their interests: for those who love to dance, they can include their friends or family through Exodus 15:20-21, evoking Miriam and the women dancing and singing as they cross the Sea of Reeds. A student who loves science more than the expressive arts may choose as their portion Leviticus: 25:1, which focuses on our responsibility to the land. They can align the scientific explanation of caring for the Earth with the Torah's mandate of a seven-year cycle in which the land is left to rest. Animal lovers may enjoy having Genesis 6:9–11:32, the story of Noah and the Ark, as their parashah. If they enjoy drawing, perhaps they can illustrate a book, create animation, or write a poem. Our tradition is full of amazing stories. A budding young filmmaker can write a script, directing friends and family members to become characters.

Be open, be willing, be innovative. When we begin to open our minds to alternative and creative ways to teach and celebrate, the possibilities are endless. I have spoken with cantors who, burned-out after numerous years of teaching neurotypical b'nai mitzvah students, feel enlivened when they begin approaching the same material when teaching children, teens, and young adults with disabilities. Many then start to incorporate more creativity with their neurotypical and nondisabled students as well. Trust yourself, trust your student, trust our tradition to allow new ways of expressing and awakening Judaism.

Call on the community for support—a dance teacher, an art teacher, a guitarist. With help from community members, I have seen amazing things: a bat mitzvah student who spoke only a few words, but who loved to move her body, danced her Torah portion; a young thespian enlisted his friends to dramatize his portion; another child drummed his part. A shy young man created a PowerPoint presentation, recording his voice in advance, and led the congregation through an exquisite, multiplatform presentation without having to be on the bimah or speak a word. I saw two teenagers who had not previously been involved in their Jewish community write songs that were included in their celebration:

I am grateful God gave me life.
I am grateful for my Mom and Dad. I am grateful for my friends.
I am grateful God answers my prayers.
Baruch Atah Adonai Eloheinu, Melech Ha'olam. Melech Ha'olam
I am grateful God answers my prayers.

Practice Makes Progress

Break down every activity, every song, every dance move into small attainable tasks so that the child can master the tunes and movements. Help them to feel confident in their own ability.

As often as you can, practice everything that the child will be expected to do in the exact environment where they will be doing it. Ask your synagogue to let you into the sanctuary months before the event, and then invite others to witness your child being on the bimah, or in your backyard, or in the office where the celebration will be occurring. Desensitize your child to being watched. Just as we did in the Miracle Project, film some of these practice sessions and ask someone to edit it together so you know that when the actual event happens, if the child (or parent) is too anxious to be in public, you can show the video. We schedule our b'nai mitzvah celebrations on Mondays and Thursdays when the Torah is read, or on Hanukkah, rather than on Shabbat, to allow video to be played and to film the event.

Opportunities to Celebrate Together

I urge you not to wait for the b'nai mitzvah date to begin celebrating. Let every moment, every choice, every activity be a celebration. Remind yourself and your student or child how extraordinary they are just by being who they are—a beautiful child created in the image of God, *b'tzelem Elohim*. When it comes time for the actual date, it will only be an extension of a newly formed habit that is as essential to our tradition as any prayer.

For the Family

A month before the date of the b'nai mitzvah celebration, we gather the child and their family to create their own silk tallit and *kippot* (head coverings), using silk fabric paint. The results are beautiful, and the bonding with family is amazing. Document the meaningful moments of the year through photos or video.

For the Congregation

Bring in neurotypical peers as b'nai mitzvah buddies to work together with the b'nai mitzvah. We call this "reverse inclusion." Allow for everyone to learn and grow together. Do not think of this relationship as a "mitzvah project," but as a way to foster a sacred relationship. Some of our buddies have become advocates for disability rights in their schools; others have raised funds for education or raised awareness through blogs. Keep the actual relationship and time with their neurodiverse peer sacred and unique, not a "project."

As much as you can, include the congregation in the entire b'nai mitzvah experience, even in nontraditional ways. One of my most memorable experiences was attending the bar mitzvah of a Miracle Project student held in a large, Modern Orthodox synagogue in Los Angeles. Throughout most of the service, the young man sat with his family in the congregation. When he was called to the Torah, it took him a great deal of time using his walker to reach the bimah. In those five to seven minutes that it took for him to walk up to the bimah, the congregation was silent. We all walked with him in sacred silence, and experienced a meditative moment as he reached the bimah and opened the Ark. To this day I have never witnessed a congregation that silent, that respectful, that inclusive. Truly a holy moment.

With experiences such as these, I wonder why all synagogues don't always include those with disabilities in participating in and leading services. Why wait for a once-in-a-lifetime b'nai mitzvah celebration or even once-a-year Jewish Disability Awareness, Acceptance, and Inclusion Month in February? I look to a time where it is as natural to include individuals of all abilities in synagogue life as it is now natural for women in Reform and Conservative synagogues to read from the Torah. This day will come. Start with the b'nai mitzvah.

Closing and Opening

I offer one of my favorite tales that we performed in our first Miracle Project production in 2005. It is called "The Boy and the Flute." (*Note: a variation of this story appears in Chapter 14.*)

> *Meir was a good boy. He always listened to his parents and helped out around the house, but no matter how hard he tried, he couldn't learn to speak. Instead of going to school, Meir tended his father's cows. Every morning he led them to a meadow, where he would take out his flute and play them the most beautiful tunes. When he put his flute away, the cows knew it was time to go home. Meir was thirteen when his father took him to the Ba'al Shem Tov [a Jewish mystic from the early 1700s believed to be the founder of Chasidic Judaism] on Yom Kippur. "Maybe the presence of such a great man would do Meir some good," his father thought. For a while, it even seemed to work. Meir was excited to be in the same synagogue as the Ba'al Shem Tov, but he was also very sad that he didn't know how to pray. As the long service came to an end, Meir had an idea. Reaching into his pocket, he pulled out his flute and began to play. This is how even I can pray, he thought proudly. No one agreed, though; in fact, the entire congregation was outraged. How dare this boy disturb their prayers? They jumped up from their seats to throw Meir and his father out of the synagogue. Even the Ba'al Shem Tov rushed toward them; however, the Ba'al Shem Tov looked at Meir and hugged him. "Thank you," he said. "All Yom Kippur I wondered whether our prayers would be answered. We said all the words, but we lacked the passion. Then I heard your flute, so simple and sincere, and I knew our prayers would be answered." The Ba'al Shem Tov turned to the congregation. "I see you've risen to thank this boy. After all, his flute opened the Gates of Heaven to our prayers."*

I invite you, dear reader, to open your heart, open your mind, and open your soul to those who experience the world differently. Let yourself and your congregation hear the authentic prayers of one who plays the flute.

✶ CHAPTER 9 ✶

By a Lake or in a Tree:

Celebrating in a Camp Setting

David Neufeld, PhD

David Neufeld is dean of learning support at Jewish Community High School of the Bay in San Francisco. He explains the hows and whys of holding b'nai mitzvah at summer camp.

It is Shabbat morning on a sunny day during a *Shabbaton* (a weekend program that involves communal worship, study, meals, and socializing) at a camp in Northern California, and the bar mitzvah boy is in a tree.

His mother and brother, who are celebrating their *b'nai mitzvah* in a family ceremony, are below. Everyone is beaming. The rabbi leads the service while the people sitting in the amphitheater—steadily shifting every few minutes to escape the sunlight streaming underneath the redwood canopy—look on with joy on their faces, singing and celebrating the occasion. Nobody cares that one of the day's honorees is currently perched ten feet above everybody's head instead of being at the Torah. That's just what he likes to do, and they're happy he's doing it. The brother on the ground quietly recites the blessing over the Torah, the rabbi gently offering him words when he stumbles. A few minutes later, the bar mitzvah boy's mother, who was not allowed to have a bat mitzvah in her traditional religious community in New York when she came of age, tearfully speaks about how meaningful it is to have a bat mitzvah today, at age 58, alongside her sons. She is older, queer, and hard of hearing. Her boys (both adopted) have profound developmental challenges, and the family has never felt welcome at any synagogue. A b'nai mitzvah in her community was simply out of the question. But not here. Not at camp. Here, where there are no preconceived notions or judgments about who can have a b'nai mitzvah and what that should look like, anything is possible.

For many families with children with disabilities, a traditional b'nai mitzvah ceremony at a synagogue, with its predetermined structures, rituals, and behavior expectations, is impossible. Despite the progress that we have seen in the inclusivity and flexibility of many contemporary synagogues, being called to the Torah in the midst of a synagogue congregation remains out of reach for many children with disabilities. For some families, a traditional setting would be overwhelming to their child's sensory system. For others, the behaviors and vocalizations of their children would be too much for the congregants: Their children have been shushed too many times, and they want nothing to do with a synagogue. And some families, despite the goodwill shown to them by the community and its desire to accept and embrace them, have simply never felt at home. For those families, a camp setting can be an excellent alternative.

A Little History

Much of my experience with camp b'nai mitzvah for children with disabilities was gained while serving as the Director of Inclusion at Jewish LearningWorks (formerly known as the Bureau of Jewish Education) in San Francisco. From 2002 to 2017, we ran an annual Special Needs Family Camp weekend for families with children and young adults with disabilities. It was started by a woman named Flora Kupferman in response to a growing need for families with children with moderate to severe disabilities to have a Jewish community to call their own, and where they could feel comfortable, surrounded by other Jewish families who intimately understood the joys and challenges of having a child with a disability. For many of these families, Special Needs Family Camp was the only place where they could be themselves and connect to their Judaism without fear of not fitting in.

Services at Special Needs Family Camp had three main features: a custom siddur (prayer book) with readings and prayers that spoke to the experiences of families with children with disabilities; music; and an ironclad "no-shush" policy. The kids could be themselves—making whatever noises and movements they needed to make in order to feel comfortable—and this in turn made their parents feel comfortable. Camp became a second home to many families who returned year after year.

One year during the camp weekend, a twelve--year-old camper diagnosed with what was then called high-functioning autism told his mother, "This is my community. These are the people I feel most comfortable with, and I want to become bar mitzvah with them." This, from a child who almost never spoke in terms of feelings and belonging! His mother immediately began crying, and so did the camp director. So, the camper worked over the summer with the educator who had been the song leader, and the following year the first bar mitzvah in the history of Special Needs Family Camp was held. The camper read the blessings over the Torah, chanted a section of the weekly parashah (Torah portion), and a new tradition was born.

Over the years the specifics and ways people did their b'nai mitzvah at camp changed, but one thing that never changed was the feeling that permeated each one. No matter what the b'nai mitzvah child did or didn't do, every person in attendance bought in, honoring the child and celebrating the achievement earnestly, joyfully, and without inhibition. At every b'nai mitzvah, the love, support, and excitement of both the family and community were palpable. Faces hurt from smiling, tears flowed, and everyone knew they had witnessed something incredible.

Jewish Disability Family Camps

While Jewish LearningWorks Special Needs Family Camp closed in 2017, there are several other camps and camping movements that offer disability family camping opportunities for families with a child with disabilities. These include National Ramah Tikvah Networks' Camp Ohr Lanu at Ramah California (Ojai, CA), Camp Yofi at Ramah Darom (Clayton, GA), and the Tikvah Family Shabbaton at Camp Ramah New England (Palmer, MA). B'nai mitzvah could be celebrated in the context of any of these programs.

—H.B.

In my experience, there are two main benefits to a camp b'nai mitzvah: flexibility/freedom of expression and radical inclusion/acceptance.

Flexibility and Freedom of Expression

At camp, loose structure makes flexibility easier. The possible use of outdoor space, lack of formal expectations about what a b'nai mitzvah ceremony should look like, and the ability to make it as simple or complex as one might wish (my advice: err on the side of simple) are enormous benefits of having a camp ceremony. Sometimes camp b'nai mitzvah look like b'nai mitzvah anywhere else. In general, though, camp b'nai mitzvah tend to be less formal in terms of length, attire, and overall tone than in a traditional synagogue. Over the years I have seen many kinds of b'nai mitzvah ceremonies at camp, and all were magical. Here are a few examples:

- A more traditional type of bar mitzvah where the teen of the hour (who had good language and comprehension but very limited social skills) studied every week with a tutor for a year, then held his ceremony in the camp *beit midrash* (a place of study). He led the prayers, read from the Torah, and gave a *d'var torah*. In short, he did exactly what one might see in a traditional synagogue service, but with his beloved camp community.
- A bat mitzvah that took place during a camp song session. Rather than lead any prayers, the bat mitzvah girl (who had global developmental delays and limited language abilities) sat in the audience with everyone else and, only occasionally getting up, loudly and joyfully sang every song she knew along with the songleader. During one traditional song ("Bim Bam," which consists only of the phrases *bim bam* and *Shabbat shalom* repeated many times over), the congregation reacted each time she sang "Shabbat Shalom," energetically shouting it back to her.
- A nonspeaking boy on the autism spectrum wore a tallit (prayer shawl) and slowly carried the Torah around in a circle while singing the Sh'ma prayer, which his mother had taught him for the occasion. In general, this was a child who struggled with self-regulation and focus, often becoming distracted and losing control physically. In addition, he typically would not tolerate wearing extra things over his clothing. On this occasion, though, he was transformed. He was firmly in control of his body, kept the tallit on for the entire ceremony, and slowly and deliberately completed his walk with the Torah.

Radical Inclusion and Acceptance

At camp, people who don't fit in anywhere else can find a loving community that accepts them and appreciates them for who they are. In speaking to former directors, families, and clergy who have officiated at camp b'nai mitzvah, the main themes I heard consistently were total acceptance, respect for the unique circumstances of each family, a feeling of safety, and the joy and excitement for all that unfolds. Families spoke of feeling that their camp ceremony, no matter how simple, was truly a rite of passage and a milestone for their child and for them, and something that many of them had never thought possible. It is difficult to overestimate the impact of this kind of radical inclusion and acceptance from the Jewish community, especially if families feel it has been denied them because of their children's challenges.

This kind of inclusion has a profound effect on the campers as well. Remember the bar mitzvah boy who studied for a year and led the entire service from inside the beit midrash at camp? Fifteen years later, in the midst of the coronavirus pandemic, he called his bar mitzvah tutor (who had also been camp director at the time) just to check in. They hadn't spoken for years. He told her that he was thinking about people who had meant something in his life and wanted to reconnect with her. He spoke of how important his bar mitzvah was to him, and how grateful he was that she had made it possible. The inclusion and acceptance she had offered him in the form of his camp bar mitzvah had stuck with him, even through conflict, and had created a lasting impact that surprised even her.

The Mayor of Ramah New England

Tiki's supportive Israeli-born parents are sensitive to her intellectual and developmental needs and did not pressure her to mark her bat mitzvah. But Tiki saw her Camp Ramah friends celebrate their b'nai mitzvah at camp and wanted to do the same.

Tiki is like the mayor of Ramah New England. She remembers names and details about campers and staff past and present—and she keeps in touch with them on Facebook and via text messaging. Camp is where Tiki truly feels a sense of belonging.

Tiki was tutored throughout the year by Ariella Rosen, a longtime counselor and division head (and now rabbi), who has a brother with disabilities. Together they worked on a meaningful Torah portion and *d'var Torah* (Torah teaching). Rabbi Rami Schwartzer, the officiant, believes that campers who celebrate b'nai mitzvah at camp get to show their "true, real selves."

Leora, Tiki's sister, reports, "We were so moved by the service, her dedication to preparation, and the warmness of the Ramah community. Tiki's bat mitzvah was very meaningful for all of us. Tiki absolutely surpassed my Israeli parents' expectations. They were so immensely proud of her. We all spoke about it for many years. The impact of the bat mitzvah on Tiki's Jewish connection lasts until today. After our father died, Tiki often reflected that she is happy he was able to share in this special event."

"I think her bat mitzvah showcased her fearlessness," according to Tiki's sister. This confidence has carried over to other parts of her life.

—H.B.

Preparing for Camp B'nai Mitzvah with Your Child With Disabilities

One advantage of doing b'nai mitzvah at camp is that you are not beholden to anyone else's vision. Whatever requirements a synagogue might encourage or even require—time of day, use of Hebrew, reading from the Torah, or giving a d'var Torah—will likely not apply at JCC or Reform and Conservative movement camps. In Orthodox camps, traditional Jewish law will apply; at the same time, many options are available, including doing less, and in a relaxed setting. Families can choose whatever feels right to them and to their child.

When preparing for a b'nai mitzvah at camp, it's important to consider several factors:

- The setting: outdoors or indoors? One of the great advantages of camp is the possibility of using outdoor space, which may not exist in other religious and community settings. For many, having a b'nai mitzvah under the redwood trees, on the shore of the lake, or at the outdoor amphitheater may be the main reason to choose a camp setting. For families with children who tend to vocalize and be loud, open space to maneuver may be the best option. For children who wander or run, the walls of an indoor space with physical boundaries like doors and walls (and no bugs!) may be the better choice. Time of year and weather patterns will, of course, affect this as well. If you will be celebrating your child's b'nai mitzvah at camp during the rainy, snowy, or, in California, the fire/smoky- air season, the decision will be made for you.
- How formal/informal do you and your child want the ceremony to be? Over the years at Special Needs Family Camp, we had some ceremonies that looked like a traditional synagogue service, and some that were decidedly informal. We had b'nai mitzvah that involved a full year of Torah study and practice, and some that were planned and executed with little to no preparation. At camp, anything goes, and that is an enormous gift.

- Will clergy (either from camp or a home congregation) be involved? If a family already has a good relationship with a member of the clergy, I strongly recommend speaking to them about the ceremony. They can help provide options for observance, identify parts of the service that a child can participate in (with their own voice or their communication device), and provide a way into thinking about the day. If the family has no preexisting positive clergy relationship, there is no need to do this. Another option is to ask the camp director if the camp has clergy on staff—many camps do—who would be open to discussing your family's needs.

How Do You Design the Service, and What Kind of Jewish Learning Will You Need?

The easiest way to design a service will be to work directly with a clergy member or a Jewish educator who can guide you and help you choose the pieces that work best for you and your family.

That said, if for any reason—religious, personal, financial, the needs of your child—you'd like to design a service yourself, you can absolutely do that. The first step is knowing what the various parts of the b'nai mitzvah ceremony are. If you wish to learn the details, there are several excellent summaries online in many different formats that you can refer to, including video. Check out the Bimbam and My Jewish Learning websites, or check out the book *To Pray as A Jew: A Guide to the Prayer Book and the Synagogue Service* (by Rabbi Hayim Donin) for a chart explaining the structure of each service. You can also find online descriptions of a Shabbat service from specific denominations of Judaism (the main ones you will come across are Orthodox, Conservative, and Reform, and there are others like Renewal and Reconstructionist as well).

You can pick whatever parts are most interesting and most feasible for your child to do. Remember, though, there is no specific requirement for what someone must do to become b'nai mitzvah. If what will be most meaningful for your child is gathering with friends at camp on a weekday afternoon, taking a nature walk. or engaging in a guided meditation and expressing what nature means to them and their Judaism, that is absolutely fine—and the child may not need to learn anything new to do it.

If you do wish to pursue some formal or informal Jewish learning for the big day, there are two main ways to go about it. You can do it yourself or find a tutor. Useful suggestions throughout this book also apply to planning and preparing for camp b'nai mitzvah. If you choose to teach your child, start with some basic prayers or songs, participate in community prayer service, and consider having the student teach attendees Torah through art or music. Clergy—both those in your local community and those online—are also valuable resources.

Remember, your family gets to set the tone for the celebration. The most important focus is what will make it meaningful and engaging for you and your child. When you have b'nai mitzvah at camp, it's not about a performance or a big party. It's about becoming a Jewish adult in a beautiful setting in the ways that are most appropriate for your particular family and your particular child.

Jake's DIY Bar Mitzvah at Camp

Jake is funny, clever, and good-natured. He also has attentional and learning issues and attends a school for children with learning disabilities. His parents knew that a traditional bar mitzvah, like the one his older brother celebrated, was not right for him. They learned that a camp in Kent, Connecticut would be a perfect location for Jake's Shabbat afternoon bar mitzvah.

Jake met each guest in the parking lot and transported them to the campgrounds in a golf cart. This put him in a great, relaxed mood. Jake and his guests swam, played tug-of-war, used the zipline, and enjoyed many activities on the grounds throughout the day on Saturday. Much like a destination wedding, friends from all walks of life and family got to know each other through games and just hanging out. As the service time approached, everyone was relaxed.

The service started off outside. When rain clouds moved in quickly, everyone seamlessly moved indoors. Jake introduced prayers and co-led the forty-five-minute service, chanting beautifully from the Torah. Jake's hard work paid off in confidence and in pride.

—H.B.

Practical Tips for Families

Keep in mind the following as you go through the planning process—whether that process takes a year, a season, or a month:

* **Talk to the camp director**. If you know the camp where you'd like to hold the b'nai mitzvah, let the camp director know as early as possible. The director is your first point of contact and will have the best information about what your options are and what has worked well in the past. They can also connect you with camp clergy if you would like to have a more detailed discussion about the spiritual and religious content of the ceremony. The director will likely be your biggest cheerleader, your child's biggest champion (apart from you, of course), and the person who will be with you every step of the way from "Maybe we should do this" to "Mazel tov!"
* **Communication is key.** This will come as no surprise to any parent of a child with disabilities (and, really, to any parent at all), but clear, honest, and transparent communication can make the difference between an experience that is positive, rewarding, and meaningful for you and your child and one that is forgettable, uninspiring, or, in the worst case, traumatic. There must be open communication between the family and those in charge so that everyone will be on the same page about expectations, the child's capabilities, and how those two things intersect.

  Things you will want to discuss might include:

  * What are the child's interests? What are the activities that will get the gleam in their eye, give them a positive Jewish experience, and help them connect with their Jewish identity, whatever that might mean?
  * Will the service be in Hebrew, in English, or a combination?
  * Will the child read Torah, will family members, or will the clergy and other camp attendees? If the child is nonverbal, are there some nonverbal ways for them to participate or lead the service? If the child uses a communication device and is interested, would it be possible to record a Torah portion (or a blessing) in advance and have the child push the button to "read" it? Is there another way to access the child's personal Torah—their perspective or way of engaging with the world, the community, and Judaism? The clearer you all are on the answers to these questions, the more successful the ceremony will be.

- **Be flexible.** No matter how much you prepare, unplanned things are going to happen (for example, a bar mitzvah boy in a tree). Expect the unexpected, and have a plan to continue no matter what. Ask yourself, "What will we do if . . . ?"
- **Enjoy it!** The point of a b'nai mitzvah (and especially a b'nai mitzvah at camp) is to celebrate your child and all the lovable, maddening, and wonderful things about them. It's to celebrate you and the fact that your child has publicly committed themselves to Judaism. And to celebrate Judaism and Jewish life. No matter what happens before, during, and after this day, your child will have stood up (in body or spirit) in front of a loving and supportive community—who understands them and embraces them, who accepts them and your family for all that you are, and who will cheer them on no matter what—and said "I am here, I belong, and I matter to the Jewish people."

And that is certainly a thing worth kvelling (feeling proud) about—even from the top of a tree.

✻ CHAPTER 10 ✻

B'nai Mitzvah or Not:

When It Should Be off the Table

Rabbi Allison L. Berry and Matan A. Koch

Rabbi Allison Berry, formerly co-senior rabbi at Temple Shalom of Newton, Massachusetts, serves as director of the Betty Ann Greenbaum Miller Center for Jewish Healing at Jewish Family and Children's Service in Waltham, Massachusetts. Matan Koch, an attorney, is the former senior policy advisor at RespectAbility and a disability employment specialist. Here, Matan and Allison engage in an unfiltered dialogue with the editors of this book on a topic that few dare to address: Are there ever reasons not to pursue b'nai mitzvah?

B'nai Mitzvah or Not

Different Spirit *(DS): Thank you both for joining us. Given your respective backgrounds, we'd like to know your thoughts: Are there ever circumstances where, because of cognitive disability or temperamental opposition, a child should NOT have a b'nai mitzvah? What if you're not clear as to what the child understands? What thought process should parents go through in developing b'nai mitzvah for their child?*

Matan: Let's leave disability out of the discussion for a moment. Rabbi Berry: How would you have answered that question in your former role as a pulpit rabbi?

Allison: It's the question I asked every single family when we sat down for our first meeting together. I first asked parents to reflect on their own coming-of-age experience. I asked, "And what would you have done differently?" We went from there to a conversation about why they wanted their child to become bar or bat mitzvah. What I almost always universally heard was that people wanted their kids to feel connected to their Judaism, and, in a sense, connected to family, as in generations past and present, and to a chain of tradition that we are handing to one another. They wanted their child to experience affirmation that they had gained a particular set of skills to be an active Reform Jew—to have that literacy. We also heard that people wanted a reason to celebrate, which I thought was wonderful.

It's the child's own decision to decide what becoming b'nai mitzvah means to them. But it's about something so much bigger that I'm not sure the child understands until they're much older. And I'm okay with that. As long as the child feels they were a part of a decision-making process.

Matan: From my perspective, the single biggest thing is that the child is demonstrating some affirmative acceptance of Jewish responsibility, whatever that means for them, even if they will continue to understand it in different ways as they grow. My late father [Rabbi Norman David Koch] always referred to "accepting the responsibility" of becoming a bar or bat mitzvah; that was his phrase for it. I feel like that acceptance is key. Acceptance can look different for different children. A child with significant intellectual and communications challenges, who nonetheless has a spiritual connection to the Sh'ma prayer, may demonstrate it by saying the prayer. My twin nephews with disabilities shared their knowledge of the Torah portion with the congregation through a dialogue with the rabbi. The key is that, regardless of the words, and at whatever level they are able, they're really saying, "I'm ready to play my role. I'm ready to do my part. And this is me showing what that is."

My concern involves those rare cases when acceptance is just fundamentally impossible, not different. I believe that it's important to celebrate. But, for a child who has demonstrated little or no awareness of the world around them, for example, when there is no acceptance of what's happening, perhaps this moment is celebrating something else: a community's love and support for an individual. Maybe then the nomenclature is different.

Allison: I don't change the nomenclature because I think there is tremendous power in those words for families, to fulfill that yearning or hope a parent has, regardless of their child's challenges. Some of us even start planning this coming-of-age moment as soon as our children are born; my dad came home with a onesie the week my first son was born that read "bar mitzvah 2022."

Can B'nai Mitzvah Be Something Else?

***DS:** What about reframing b'nai mitzvah as presenting the child to the community, rather than a demonstration of ability?*

Matan: We do that in *brit milah* (circumcision ceremony), we do that at baby namings. At b'nai mitzvah, we present that child as an individual who is willing to step up and take their place in the community. The formative moment isn't when they chant Torah, it's when they're called to the Torah. It's when they have that first *aliyah* (call to the Torah), which is really the way of saying, "I'm literally standing up as an adult in this community to do an adult thing." This statement manifests in different ways.

Allison: My understanding of why we're doing this [the b'nai mitzvah ceremony] continues to transition. I used to think of it as a demonstration of how much the kids learned about Hebrew or Judaism or prayer. My understanding in recent years is that b'nai mitzvah is all about relationships. That kid needs to know they have an important voice to add to the fabric of our Jewish story. I talk about how each of us is a letter in the Torah. And today, as you stand up to become b'nai mitzvah, you're adding your letter to that history and to our text. And that letter is really important. We wouldn't be complete without you.

In our congregation, as we continued to redefine our priorities, we eased off prioritizing *Haftarah* (reading from the Prophets). Some of it is that the kids just don't get there. I told half to three-quarters of families, "We're just not going to do it. I would rather your kid feel great about reading Torah and feel great about leading prayer for the community and teaching us something, because these are transferable Jewish skills that will allow them to be in relationship with other Jews for the rest of their life. To me, that's success."

I don't want a kid to walk away thinking it was all gobbledygook that didn't mean anything, but rather that it was about the relationships created during this process that made them feel of value and that their voice matters. Some Jewish spaces are not welcoming to kids from interfaith relationships. I want all of my students to feel proud of their Jewish identity and their unique story.

Isn't a B'nai Mitzvah Based on Age Anyway?

Orthodox-practicing Jews mark a Jewish boy becoming bar mitzvah at age thirteen and a day while a girl becomes bat mitzvah at twelve and a day. Outside of Orthodoxy, the generally accepted practice is to mark b'nai mitzvah for all children at age thirteen. This may have evolved as a practical matter so that most b'nai mitzah in a given grade were celebrated over the course of one year and not two.

DS: *If the child is at least one day over thirteen, don't they become b'nai mitzvah no matter what form it takes? Why and how does understanding matter, and who is to assess that? For Elaine Hall, (see chapter 8), her son's bar mitzvah consisted of him saying one word: Sh'ma, the name of our central prayer.*

Matan: Yes, the person becomes bar mitzvah when they're thirteen anyway. But that's sophistry. We have the ceremony because we think it's important to demonstrate that you've accepted this change in your life.

Elaine's son, Neal, is a great example. Neal said Sh'ma [besides being the central prayer of Jewish faith, sh'ma means "listen"] at his bar mitzvah because that's what he understood. Neal is a perfect example of where I do believe adaptive b'nai mitzvah should go. The opposite, however, is an elaborate show where the kid doesn't even know what is going on, and the event is happening just for the benefit of the parents.

The most extreme example I can remember from my government work [Matan was appointed by President Barack Obama to serve as Member-Chair of the Governance Committee at the National Council on Disability] is someone who quite literally just had a brain stem and was being kept alive on machines; there was no physical brain left in his head to be having thoughts. I think we have to remember what we are—and what we are not—celebrating, and the celebration is about the individual's engagement with the community. The extreme versions are the versions where no engagement is possible.

Here's the reason I like to keep that model in mind: Let's assume we know that, for that particular kid, Adon Olam (the service-concluding prayer) is extraordinarily meaningful. A meaningful demonstration of their connection to the Jewish people might be having them up on the *bimah* and visibly reacting as the congregation sings Adon Olam.

But this hypothetical child uses an assistive communication device, so one could envision that someone might program the entire service into the assistive communication device and have the child press the button so that the entire service streams out of the speaker of the device. This could be good or bad.

My concern is with the understanding of the child. A child who directs that the entire service be programmed in the device is simply using an accommodation to communicate. A child who does not know what was programmed into the device is a prop. I don't want the child to become a prop. I want the ceremony to be based around what it means for the child to engage with the Jewish community.

I use the augmented communication device example because of the *opportunity* it presents to negate agency, not because it generally *does* take away agency. I'm not suggesting there's anything wrong with the notion that someone's entire service had to be programmed into a box, as long as the programming reflects very clearly what that person wants, as well as that person's understanding of what is going on.

Allison: I ask that every child teach something to the congregation about how Judaism speaks to them. Sometimes this manifests as a traditional *d'var Torah* (Torah teaching). Or sometimes the teaching moment happens in different ways, through art or music or even as a PowerPoint. My hope is to set expectations from the beginning that a successful b'nai mitzvah is defined by who the child and family are, and what Jewish life and practices are important to them. In the Reform Movement, we have incredible flexibility with these services.

Where we frequently run into problems is unfortunately when, for all sorts of reasons, it's hard for parents to partner with us. The most challenging bar mitzvah ever was when the parents' expectations weren't realistic. They wanted their child to learn a tremendous amount, and yet he was already struggling to learn the smaller section he had been assigned. We suggested multiple alternative paths that we felt would be equally as meaningful. The parents just couldn't get there. They wanted their child to look like everyone else. It was so hard. I had empathy for the parents, and I also wanted to meet the child where he was and support him.

But at a certain point, a kid's parents are a kid's parents. And it's important to respect that. We're not always able to do what we feel will work best for that child and with the child's agency. Those situations are when I beat my chest, and I say that this whole system has failed, that people have such staid ideas of what a b'nai mitzvah is, or that we live in a world where there is so much stigma that this poor family, these poor parents, are not even able to sit in a room with me and share their fears and their concerns and offer a full picture of what's going on with their child. And that's so painful. I wish that we could see every child for the incredible human being they are, and have every possible support system available, without budgetary limit, to meet every child where they are.

A Bar Kehila

Rafi is a rabbi's son, and he grew up attending his father's synagogue. When Rafi turned thirteen, his parents chose to mark the milestone with a *bar kehilah* (literally "son of the community") to honor Rafi's beloved reciprocal relationship with their community.

Rafi has multiple severe intellectual and developmental disabilities. He lacks the ability to understand the meaning of a bar mitzvah ceremony. But Rafi's profound place in the congregation, where he is "welcomed, accepted, and loved," was a blessing to recognize. Each Shabbat morning, the community had a rotation of volunteers stay with Rafi in the rabbi's office during services so his mother could attend the Torah service. They appreciated his enthusiasm for the music. And they enjoyed his regular presence on, and back-and-forth across, the *bimah*.

Rafi's disabilities are degenerative, and his parents, Susan and Avi, had grieved the loss of skills he had once worked hard to master. The *bar kehilah* was a way to "have a joyful milestone with him."

In creating a bar kehilah, Susan and Avi thought about what would be natural for Rafi. They kept it simple—each parent had an *aliyah* (call to the Torah), and each blessed him ritually. Special friends and family members brought festive food and music, and they kept it small to maintain the focus on Rafi. The congregation presented Rafi with a recording by the cantor and the synagogue board of his favorite songs, and a plaque reading, "His love of music, song, and prayer touched our hearts and enriches our lives." Years later, community members still consider Rafi's bar kehilah a spiritual highlight.

Susan acknowledges that Rafi's privileged position as part of the rabbi's family enabled them to create such a ritual for Rafi. Susan recommends that families choose what they want to recognize about their child—in Rafi's case, his communal relationship—in designing a nontraditional way to mark reaching age thirteen. Knowing some families with a child with a disability feel isolated, she encourages reaching out to a local rabbi or Jewish disability organization for help imagining the possibilities.

Rafi's father gave him this blessing at his bar kehilah:

May your smiles of delight never fade.
May you always be thrilled by the ocean.
May you always have reason to smile.

— *I.T.*

Matan: I come from a family of rabbis. As a Jewish professional myself, I sharply and vehemently disagree with those performative b'nai mitzvah that mean nothing to the child except that they had to check a bunch of boxes that their parents felt they needed to. That's a failure of the American Jewish system. That's a failure of us to help people understand their heritage, where they fit into it, and how to find their own place. And frankly, that's why we have such poor Jewish engagement among adults. Instead of spending time to find a way to help kids feel like they've connected, we put them through a laborious two-year rehearsal process to do a performance that they don't understand and that doesn't have meaning for them.

That said, go to the example that I use of programming the ceremony into an assistive communication device: A kid with understanding, who uses the device to communicate, still, at the base level, knows what's going on. Unless their Jewish training team really hasn't done their job, I could sit that thirteen-year-old down and ask, "What's Torah? Why are we reading it?" and they can give me the rote answers. They may not have a deep connection to it, but five years later, they might be able to reflect back on the experience and find new meaning in the choice to do it and the skills that they obtained to get there. Several years after their bar mitzvah, they may, as I saw many kids do in my time at a monthlong leadership program at the former URJ Kutz Camp, take the skills they learned to read Torah and finally read Torah at a time and a place that matters to them.

If, on the other hand, we design a ceremony that is simply beyond someone's level and ability to even follow what's going on, and stuff is being done for them, there is no chance of that epiphany ever coming. That's a tragic outcome, because you could have taken that time, that sacred moment when all these people are coming together, to create a new experience that was meaningful for them, at their level, and that they could reflect back on for years to come.

We Wanted the Exact Same Things

When Becca Hornstein moved to Arizona in 1983 with her son Joel, who has autism, she tried to find a synagogue for their family. All the congregations in her town explained that they didn't have any special education program because "there were no people with disabilities in their synagogues." Eventually, Becca found a welcoming home at Temple Chai in Phoenix. When she told the rabbi that she wanted Joel to have a bar mitzvah, Rabbi William Berk respectfully and sincerely asked Becca why she wanted Joel to have a Jewish education and a bar mitzvah. "My answer was that Joel, regardless of his limitations, his challenges, his struggles, was still a child of God, someone formed in the image of God—because God encompasses all of these special, unique qualities—and that Joel had value and dignity. Whatever Joel was able to achieve at the time of his bar mitzvah, we were going to celebrate that. If we were asking too much, then we were simply going to have a moment when he reached thirteen where everybody in Joel's life could say, 'Wonderful, mazel tov!' That joyful moment was what we wanted."

Becca reflects that "Parents of a typical child may want their children to have *b'nai mitzvah* to carry on or to connect their child to the traditions of their family and their community. Other parents may want to mark the growth transitions of their child." Parents of a child with special needs, she insists, want the exact same things for the exact same reasons. "I think that was my rallying cry, that Joel being different, having autism, having limited communication, didn't mean that what we wanted for him was any different. We still wanted him to carry on the traditions, to be bound to the culture and the religion and the community, perhaps even more than the parents of a typical child marking that growth. Joel deserved his place in our Jewish community."

—I.T. and H.B.

Honoring the Wants

DS: *Should the "wants" of "typical" children be similarly honored?*

Allison*:* One of my favorite b'nai mitzvah that I ever officiated was this young man who came into my office and said, "I don't want to do this because I don't believe in God. I hate this text stuff. These stories in the Torah are stupid and I don't see the point." I had a long chat with his parents after this conversation, who, in this incredible way, said, "You know, if in the end he really still feels this way, we won't do it. But will you spend some time with him? Will you do some learning with him one-on-one, and then let's see where he's at?"

So, he and I spent a good amount of time together. In one of our meetings, I remember asking him, "Why don't we write about that Torah portion you don't believe in? Why don't we write about what's wrong with it and what makes you angry about it? Because if I'm being honest, it makes me angry, too." Somewhat to my surprise he agreed to work with me.

Once the piece was written, I said to him, "So what do we want to do with this? It's an expression of who you are. And I think that this is a valid Jewish opinion." He argued with me, "But it's saying I don't believe in this." And I shared, "Sure. Jews debate what they believe and don't believe all the time. We wrestle—and that actually is the point."

In the end, he decided, "If I didn't have to do anything else, I would feel really proud for people to hear what I think and what I have to say about this." So, we moved forward and planned a very unique Jewish "coming of age" experience. We asked him to give the d'var Torah on a Friday night. Was it a bar mitzvah? We didn't call it that because we were all in agreement that we shouldn't call it that. But his mom and I talk on occasion still, and she'll say to me that that particular evening is something he remembers and continues to feel proud of. And, most importantly, he has not rejected Judaism.

Matan: Yours is sort of a gold standard example; you went exactly as far as the kid was willing to go and pushed him no further. But what the ultimate ceremony reflected, the one that you did not call a bar mitzvah, did not require him to say anything that he was not ready to say. That is exactly what I mean by respecting the agency of where the kid was at.

Now it becomes more complicated when disability, especially cognitive disability, removes choice. Sometimes it's about capacity. But that doesn't make it any less important. So, let's imagine for a moment that there is a kid with low communication ability, can't even use an augmented communication device. It's just challenging to figure out what they know. But we know that every week at services during Debbie Friedman's version of Mi Chamochah, they react differently than they do to every other fun and exciting stimulus in the world. We can observe a clear difference in reaction to that particular moment in the service, to their baseline, and to general fun and exciting things. It's clear that Mi Chamochah means something to them. We may never know what it means for them. They may lack the means to express to us what it means to them. But clearly and objectively, we can establish that it means something to them. This could be thoughtfully made into a meaningful b'nai mitzvah ceremony.

The reason that I get so worried about the b'nai mitzvah experiences is that families and educators may skip the work of saying, "Who is this person? What is meaningful to them? How do I reach them where they are?" We lose so much when we fail to respect the humanity and individuality of the children in question.

But What About Letting Understanding Come?

DS: *What about the idea of* na'aseh v'nishma *(we will do and we will hear, which is the Israelites' response to Moses's reading of the Book of the Covenant in Exodus), meaning we'll do the ritual first, and then listen and think about it. Isn't there something to be said for going through the experience and the ritual, and then discovering the meaning in it afterward, because we're all limited in our capacity to understand what something can be?*

Matan: It's really important that na'aseh v'nishma be balanced against the notion of *keva* (fixed prayers), *kavanah* (intention), and the understanding that when they said na'aseh v'nishma, they assumed the person in question could get some kind of understanding from an action. The ancient rabbis have whole discussions about people who are not subject to that if they don't believe the kavanah could ever be there.

I do this for a living. There's nobody left in the world for whom we really can't figure out what is meaningful to them, if sufficient time, effort, and energy is put in, with all of the technologies, communications devices, strategies, and experts that exist. There is a way to figure out what is meaningful to that child. If you haven't been doing the work yet, do it now. That should be the first step, before we talk about what happens on the bimah. Because otherwise opportunities get missed.

It can take time: my nephews are twin boys with disabilities. They were adopted at age seven. They had their b'nai mitzvah at age fifteen. It took a long time to get every service in place and understand what their needs were. By the time it got to getting their Jewish needs in place, it just took longer than age thirteen would allow. Figuring out what is meaningful to the child is always the focus. If the choice is to rush at the thirteenth birthday or postpone because you haven't figured out everything about who that kid is, then postpone.

Allison: What I always keep in front of me is that it is my job to say your kid is amazing. And I say it because they are, because of the unique person that they are. And I can't wait to figure out what makes them special and get to know them and bring that to the surface. And that's what we celebrate. I hope, some of the time, by sitting with a family and just giving them space, that we can get there.

Matan: I think it's a very powerful value statement and a very powerful notion.

DS: *We thank you both.*

⁂ VOICES ⁂

Wrestling with Theology, Pedagogy, Disability, and My Parents

Yishai Barth

Meir Yishai Barth, who goes by Yishai, is a PhD student at Cambridge University. He also has multiple disabilities, including cerebral palsy and visual impairments. Yishai is a lifelong disability activist.

"You expect me to get up in front of a couple hundred people, virtually everyone we know, and lie? I thought the whole point of what you've been trying to get through my head ever since I can remember is that lying is something we're not supposed to do. That it goes against Jewish values. It would be paradoxical for me to ritually affirm commitment to Jewish values by lying, don't you think?"

That was my first response to the idea of bar mitzvah one Shabbat morning when I was eleven and a half.

Both my parents responded with deep sighs, and my mother asked, "What lie is it exactly that you think you would be telling?" I couldn't believe my ears. I had told them, at least ten times in the previous year, that I was an atheist, that I didn't believe in God. That I had decided the entire idea was just a way for adults to have a socially acceptable form of an imaginary friend. That if there were a God, life would not be so absurd and innate disabilities would not exist.

My intimacy with interlocking disabilities and gifts—psychological, physical, and sensory—made this absurdity my go-to support for atheism. With increasing frequency, it seemed that the whole way people interacted with me vacillated between my strengths and weaknesses. Weaknesses like my struggles with motor skills, walking, hand-eye coordination, and my inability to read or write, and strengths like my ability to absorb auditory information, to strategize, to deploy language and communicate. I was treated as broken, subpar, and had to be protected or pitied. Or, I was seen as gifted, bright, admired. That contradiction made me feel like the world didn't make sense; the idea of God seemed stupid, and religion even more so, making my father's response really infuriating.

"We're not Catholics. There's nothing in this life-cycle event that affirms belief in God. . . There isn't even a word for religion in Hebrew." Despite my frustration, I took my father at his word because I had always known him as expert rabbi, and a liturgist, a specialist in Jewish ritual. However, it didn't solve my problem: doing this thing was equivalent to saying to the world, or at least my world, that I wanted to be a part of this thing called Judaism, that it mattered to me.

At the time, Judaism became my scapegoat for my anger toward everything that I was struggling with in my life. These included my frustration with my parents' seeming inability to understand anything about what I was experiencing, the internal emotional struggle I was waging as I grew more conscious of injustice in the world—and the immense obstacles that would inevitably face those who attempt to combat injustice, as well as my increasing feelings of alienation and isolation from peers that I experienced in our new neighborhood of Gloucester, Massachusetts.

In hindsight, I acutely recognize that it was far easier to scapegoat Judaism as an external factor for my social struggles than to confront my slowly dawning suspicion that those struggles were the result of a fundamental difference between my nature and those of my peers.

To support my scapegoating of Judaism, I conveniently ignored the fact that the only meaningful social success I had experienced since our move to Massachusetts had been during my two summers at Camp Ramah New England. There, I was able to build on common connections of Jewish heritage. At that time, those relationships felt ephemeral because the previous summer seemed forever ago and the next, forever ahead. These early friends seemed like unstable and strange things I was terrified of counting on, lest they proved to be disappointments. Finally, they didn't really matter much in my day-to-day life, because my closest camp friends lived more than an hour away. Therefore, I rarely if ever saw them during the year.

My parents' first approach in persuading me to undertake a bar mitzvah seemed ridiculous, leaving me with the impression that they had no idea how I felt about anything at all. They started talking to me about how much fun it would be to bring everyone together to celebrate my achievement. How there would be a huge party for me, the biggest I'd ever experienced, and everybody would pay attention to me and would get to see how amazing I was at public speaking.

But those arguments didn't make sense. If there was one thing I had had enough of, it was people's attention. People never stopped paying attention to me. I had never in my life walked into a room and not been noticed, whether by people who had known me my entire life or by strangers. And with regard to their other argument: no one who ever saw me be myself ever failed to tell me how smart or talented I seemed for my age.

Finally, my parents turned to lines of argument that eventually did work. The first was about becoming an adult within our tradition, about standing up and being counted as a man. On one level, my dad's argument resonated with me the way I'd seen it matter to quite a few of my peers whose bat and bar mitzvahs I'd started attending. And I suppose at some level I recognized that I had the same desire to be validated by the status of adulthood as did many pre- and early adolescents. But if that had been the only factor, the argument wouldn't have prevailed, because the ritual offered nothing but a pretaste of adult-esque validation. And outside the confines of Jewish ritual, people (of course) didn't really treat each other any differently than from before.

Nevertheless, even what I recognized as a quasi-validation of adulthood was still immensely alluring, because I had lived my whole life smothered in a tangled web of infantilization, rooted in the ways my disabilities were stigmatized. The idea that this ritual might just let me break free of even a few strands of that web—or even loosen it a little, giving me a little more room to breathe in the way that people saw me—was like a siren song. However, in short order, I was able to resist the pull. First the hours of drudgery—memorization and practice—involved. Then, the hours more I would have to spend in services on Shabbat mornings and the holidays, in order to satisfy the rules that my father had put in place, as rabbi of the synagogue in Gloucester. All told, the prospect served to sour the siren song into something of a banshee's cry.

My mother, though, engaged with me in a different way that was simply impossible to resist, let alone dismiss. Not really an argument but a picture my mother sat there painting over the next hours, drawing on a concept from sociology and that I wouldn't actually encounter until years later: the concept of "social scene." Even at age twelve, I had an understanding that most people had places, communities, activities, where they just fit, just belonged, were accepted, where they would be seen and valued and organically included as naturally as breathing.

In a sense, I'd found a more intimate sense of that aspect of human experience from art than from real life. As my mother talked with me, a hope began to take root inside me: if I undertook a bar mitzvah, the different groups of people I knew and cared about, who cared about and loved me, would come together in one place. I thought of scenes from novels and TV shows that showed how amazing it was to fit in—without having to try. My mother's picture resonated particularly because I'd already reached a conclusion in understanding my own social struggles. I just didn't tend to fit into pre-existing social structures that expected me to conform to social convention or "normal" behavior. I couldn't play normal social roles, read from normal social scripts in expected ways. But I came to realize that a bar mitzvah, as my parents were proposing, would offer me the chance to weave this as my own social scene from the ground up, designed to be perfect for me, exactly as I was, with no performance that was inauthentic or somehow counter to who I was or wanted to be. Even realizing this, I recognized a downside: that this social scene would be temporary, certain to unravel at the end of this single weekend, a span so short that I might feel that I missed it by blinking.

And, I realized that this didn't matter. The important thing wouldn't be the span of this social scene; it would be the opportunity to show the self that I was slowly, volitionally beginning to build, to all the people who mattered to me in the world. That vision eclipsed everything else in importance because, at that point, I had spent years in what felt like a perpetual confrontation with my body's own fragility. A string of seemingly interminable medical diagnoses, trials, and interventions seemed to be necessary to my continued well-being—every few months. These experiences forced me to confront my own mortality.

This planted a corresponding craving for identity validation, a fundamental response of the human psyche to the recognition of mortality. I wanted to know that people would see the person I was actually, genuinely starting to choose to be. One thing I had learned, living with a liturgist father, was that ritual was a solid way to suss out deep and complex communal meanings.

Despite the need to overcome several challenges, ranging from my theological belief to far more practical concerns, like going into sensory overload from the noise and the crowds of people, or how to read Torah without being able to "read," I decided to do it. I would do what would be needed to weave this custom-made, validating social scene as my identity laboratory, scaffolded by the power of ritual, however transient it might be. Ultimately, I came to this decision because I recognized it as a once-in-a-lifetime chance to test my fledgling identity in the one context I could imagine that would help me understand whether I was on the right track. This would be the story of how my mother, my father, and an extraordinary community of teachers, mentors, peers, and friends, many of whom I didn't realize were my friends until the day itself, and I came together to make my social scene a reality. There, I was able to truly begin my life's journey of conscious, deliberate development as a human being.

* PART 2 *

Different Teaching

Part Two is offered for educators and clergy, focusing on specific types of children with disabilities, including those who are blind, deaf, and hard of hearing; those who are nonspeaking or minimally verbal; and those who have learning disabilities, mobility impairments, and mental health challenges. Chapters 11 to 18 offer many practical tools for hands-on instruction, including teaching Hebrew and reimagining the d'var torah (Torah teaching).

✱ VOICES ✱

What If I Bark on the Bimah?

Pamela Rae Schuller

Pamela Rae Schuller, a comedian, speaker, disability advocate, and inclusion specialist with Tourette's syndrome, shares the funny and painful story of her Jewish education and bat mitzvah experience.

The year I studied for my bat mitzvah included many nights of tears, screaming, and anger. I struggled so much during the day at school that the thought of coming home and studying more on top of the pain of homework felt like punishment. The synagogue told my family that we were required to sit through a certain number of Friday night services throughout the year. My temple was a space where it had been made abundantly clear that, while I was welcomed, Tourette's was not. And we came as a pair.

I have Tourette's syndrome, a neurological disorder. It means that I make involuntary movements and noises. The media likes people to think that Tourette's syndrome is people yelling words. The truth is that *most* people with Tourette's *don't* yell words—but I was one who did!

I yelled words, I also made noises, and I flailed. . . My tics were constantly changing. The hardest part is that, as a thirteen-year-old, I didn't always know what to expect, so no one else knew what to expect either. People often know a little about Tourette's, but they don't always have a full picture.

My journey to becoming a bat mitzvah was not about celebrating becoming a woman in the eyes of Judaism. It was only about hitting the benchmarks that my small Midwest congregation had set. It was about passing a test. Instead of celebrating me—who I was in that moment, and the fact that I wanted to be Jewish—we were stuck in a merry-go-round of "How can she have a bat mitzvah service? Is it even possible?" I wondered what would happen if I started barking at my bat mitzvah.

I was the one who pushed to have a bat mitzvah. Everyone else seemed hesitant. During sixth grade, my Tourette's went from mild to incredibly severe. My synagogue struggled with my disruptive presence. When we were initially considering my bat mitzvah, the rabbi with whom I had really connected told my mother that we should try again in a few years, when, hopefully, things would be easier for me. But I was adamant about moving forward with the bat mitzvah process on the same schedule as my peers. Thankfully, my mom was on my team as an advocate and protector.

The preparation year before my bat mitzvah became about my mother reminding me that I had said I wanted to do to it, and her insisting that now I had to do it. She didn't need for me to have a bat mitzvah, but when I said I wanted it, she pushed me to practice—while I was already struggling with regular homework.

The synagogue made it clear that they would make no exceptions to their expectations or requirements. The benchmarks expected of all *b'nai mitzvah* would also be expected of me.

The rabbi, however, did allow my bat mitzvah cohort to learn the material in creative, outside-the-box ways. He let us choose projects from a list of options. We still had to learn the Torah blessings and the other traditional parts—which I did by memorizing a tape recording. But I chose all of the creative projects, which I loved: getting to watch Jewish films and write about them, create a script based on my Torah portion, and form Shabbat candles out of clay. The projects taught me quite a bit about Judaism, but I also learned that my observance felt forced, that attending services was an obligation, and that, even when exhausted, I still had to "successfully" sit through services to be considered a woman in the eyes of Judaism.

During that time, I was also depressed and struggling. I didn't believe in myself, and I was being asked to try to sit quietly through services, which was impossible for me.

I couldn't learn sitting down. My body is always in motion. Learning when you can't control your body is a challenge. Some kids do learn by sitting in a chair at a desk. But some kids learn upside down, sideways, and backwards. I was the latter, and once I got it, I got it.

There were months of fighting and threats that the party would be canceled if I didn't do my bat mitzvah homework. To be honest, it wasn't even the party I was excited about. I wanted to be on the *bimah*, in the spotlight, proving something, accomplishing a goal, feeling Jewish. But I didn't have the language at the time to verbalize that.

In the end, I hit the benchmarks. I learned the prayers. I had a "successful" bat mitzvah when I was thirteen. I read the Torah and I had a lot of fun writing my remarks, my *d'var Torah* (teaching). Truthfully, the memories of the service and the party are wonderful, although I'd like to forget my memories leading up to that day.

In the days after my *bat mitzvah*, it was made clear by other congregants and the synagogue leadership that my tics were disruptive and that I wasn't welcome in the congregation. I continued showing up—although soon after my bat mitzvah they officially asked me to leave. The temple board said I was not to enter the synagogue while I was having outbursts.

In religious school, the teacher threatened to quit. She was so frustrated with my flailing and barking and making noises that she announced, "Either Pam leaves or I quit." My peers stood up for me. The leadership did not. My presence caused drama and disruption, and they had enough. My family and I left the synagogue.

After being "fired" from synagogue, it was a long journey before I could feel connected to Judaism. In high school, I used to say I had no religion. For a long time, my feeling was, "If Judaism doesn't want me, why would I want it?" I felt angry. I pulled away from the Jewish community.

Today I love Judaism and live it in a way that feels authentic. I am proud of being Jewish, and proud of the work I see when it comes to inclusion in the Jewish community.

In religious school and in my synagogue, I was made to feel stupid. I now know that I am smart, though I learn differently. I have a master's degree in child advocacy and policy, and, professionally, I tell my story through comedy and storytelling. I consult with synagogues that want to restructure the entire b'nai mitzvah process by looking at each young person, and partnering with them and their families to create b'nai mitzvah that empower each individual in a personalized way. Just like in improv, I help synagogues adopt a "yes, and" approach. "Yes his bar mitzvah may look different, AND let's get creative."

I worked with one community that was sure a certain teen who communicated without language could not have a bar mitzvah. I met with the family and discovered that this boy is an incredible artist. "Yes, and" means saying, "Okay, where are this person's strengths?" The boy painted on the bimah at his bar mitzvah, demonstrating knowledge in his unique way. He painted parts of his Torah portion. It was beautiful. The community looked at the kid and saw amazing parts of him. That is "yes, and-ing": demonstrating knowledge in a way that is authentic to each young person.

Now, I spend a lot of time speaking and teaching in synagogues. I have some jokes about b'nai mitzvah. After all, going onstage during puberty is brutal: the cracking voices, the mothers telling their daughters to close their legs on the bimah while in a dress (maybe that was just me).

I wish my bat mitzvah had been a "yes, and" experience. What if my synagogue had said, "Yes, here is where Pam is now. How do we celebrate that and allow her to have a bat mitzvah in a way that pushes her, but not to her breaking point? How do we allow her to explore her Judaism? How do we create a space where it's okay to bark during services?"

No two thirteen-year-olds are alike, and that's an incredible thing. Imagine if we accepted every thirteen-year-old into Jewish adulthood by celebrating them for who they are, in that moment. Imagine if we customized the b'nai mitzvah experience to each child, and celebrated not only their burgeoning adulthood, but what they each bring to the community.

* CHAPTER 11 *

New Ideas for Your Toolbox:

Being the Great Teacher You Already Are

Meredith Englander Polsky

Meredith Polsky is the founder and current senior director of programs and partnerships at Matan, an organization that provides resources, training, guidance, and support to reshape accessibility to Jewish life. Meredith argues that there is no one path to b'nai mitzvah. She explains how any educator can make differentiated instruction work for every student.

You are an educator. A new student is assigned to your class, one who has a disability. Any of the following may cross your mind:

- "I felt like a pretty good teacher until Jacob joined my class."
- "I end the day feeling exhausted and defeated—like nothing I planned today went the way I expected."
- "I know people talk about 'inclusion,' but I'm not sure what that has to do with me!"
- "With the addition of Arielle, my classroom culture became chaos."
- "But I'm not a special educator!"

Do any of these sentiments sound familiar? So, you're feeling stuck? Now what?

Sometimes, children enter our teaching spaces who seem to challenge the very ways in which we do things. We want to be open-minded and flexible, but it can be difficult in the moment. We start to question ourselves and our abilities and are likely to become frustrated with our students. We can probably all imagine how this scenario plays out!

Here's a secret: *you know more than you think you do.*

You have more strategies at your disposal than you think you have.

You are better equipped than you ever realized.

How can I be so sure? Because special education is just really good education. Your experience with "typical" students, your ability to engage with them, the power of your presence, and the value of your connection are the very things that all students need. And you are already doing all of those things. YOU are exactly what—and who—your students need.

Not a Fan of Special Education

When Rabbi Dr. Marty Schloss started working in the religious education department of the Maimonides Institute for Exceptional Children in 1969, there were almost no programs, organizations, or options for Jewish education for children with disabilities. Marty is one of the field's trailblazers and devoted his career to Jewish special education. Yet he says, "You're not going to find me a big fan of special education. You're going to find me a big fan of quality education that enables each individual child to realize their potential for being active, participating members in the Jewish community, and that governs what it is you teach."

—I.T. and H.B.

We have an obligation to make sure Jewish education is accessible to all children. Inclusive Jewish communities blur the lines between "us" and "them," between having a disability and not having a disability, between what it means to be a "Jewish educator" and what it means to be a "special educator." In doing so, we learn firsthand what researchers have been telling us for decades: inclusive learning environments benefit everyone.

In inclusive classrooms, typically developing peers come to embrace a deep respect for differences among individuals, an increased capacity for empathy, and a feeling of empowerment that they can make a difference in this world. Teachers learn how to recognize individual strengths, work collaboratively with one another, and acquire different ways of solving problems and creatively addressing challenges. Adult members of the community are likely to become promoters of the rights of all individuals and show their children the value of equality, building supportiveness and interdependence. That sounds like a Jewish community I want to join.

The Blessing of Diversity

While this chapter focuses on the classroom, work teams in every industry—from tech to healthcare—are realizing the benefits of assembling people with different complementary strengths and styles. We even have a blessing to acknowledge the diversity of God's creation—"Blessed are You, God, who makes us all different." A classroom is a wonderful place to encounter and learn to work with ALL of God's creations!

—H.B.

You, as a Jewish educator, have the opportunity to help your community live the value of inclusion by demanding access for students with varying educational and developmental needs. You do not need to have all the answers in order to live this value! Some key strategies, a positive mindset, and the knowledge of where to go when you have questions will set you on a clear path toward successful inclusion.

Equity Versus Equality

If you have ever been in a room with multiple children, you've probably heard the dreaded words, "But it's not fair!" As educators, we may also be concerned about fairness—not wanting there to be different rules for different students, or aspiring to treat everyone the same. This comes from a well-meaning place, but should this be our ultimate goal?

Equality vs. Equity

Consider the images above. In the first picture, each child—regardless of their height—is provided with the same size block. The tallest child doesn't need anything to see the ball game over the fence, but he gets a block anyway. The second child receives a block, and it is exactly what she needs. She would not have been able to see the game without that block. The third child—because we are trying to keep things equal—receives the same size block as the first two children. It doesn't really matter, though, because he cannot see the game any better than he could without a block at all.

In the second image, the same number of blocks are used. No extra resources are allocated from the first image to the second—the resources are just distributed differently. What happens here? Each child gets what they need to successfully watch the ball game. Was each child treated equally? Well, no. They didn't all need equal size boxes—one of them didn't even need a box at all! They just all needed to be able to see the game.

The third image is really something special. In this case, the architects of the field anticipated the fact that many different kinds of people like to watch games. They planned ahead and built a see-through fence, so that nobody would have to carry out blocks every time people of different heights (inevitably) came to watch a game.

Equity and Equality with Respect to B'nai Mitzvah

The concept of "Fair Is Not Always Equal" applies to b'nai mitzvah as well. I have worked with students who attended Jewish day schools since pre-K. They learned Hebrew decoding, speaking, and translating from an early age, and were comfortable with Hebrew texts. The expectation for many of these students to prepare the entire weekly Torah reading—anywhere from 50 to 154 verses—was reasonable and fair. On the other hand, I have worked with students with intellectual and developmental disabilities who worked for just as many months or years as the day school students. They were able to learn between 1 and 3 lines. They worked just as hard. The expectation for each student was totally fair and not at all equal.

Equity and equality come into play when determining an appropriate amount of material to publicly recite, and to selecting a day for the service. While the norm in Orthodox and Conservative synagogues may be to chant the Torah portion and *Haftarah* (reading from the Prophets), some students benefit from a non-Shabbat b'nai mitzvah, where less Torah is read or the event features such accommodations as microphones, augmented communication devices, shorter services, and fewer guests. *Fair* might mean exploring such options as Monday or Thursday morning services (when using electricity would not be considered a violation of Shabbat) or on Rosh Chodesh (new month). Reform and many Conservative synagogues allow for chanting selections from the weekly Torah and Haftarah portions. Offering a range of options to all families, regardless of ability, should be strongly encouraged.

—H.B.

Universal Design

Just as we can be certain that people of different sizes will go watch a baseball game, so, too, can we be 100 percent confident that students of varying abilities will enter our educational spaces. Designing our programs, classes, and lessons proactively—like the fence on the baseball field—saves us time and money, and allows us to circumvent the inevitable frustration that comes from not meeting the needs of all of our students. This is known as Universal Design (UD) and it's not just for infrastructure.

Sometimes called "differentiated instruction" in educational spaces, UD is based on the idea that a "one-size-fits-all" model is detrimental to every student. We know that everyone learns differently. When we help students access their greatest strengths, rather than focusing on their weaknesses, everyone benefits.

Seize on and Highlight Non-Academic Talents

Students who encounter academic challenges often feel frustrated and "stupid." Great teachers can enhance students' self-esteem by bringing out non-academic talents and other areas of strength—especially those valued by their peers. Much of my thinking about this comes from my years of overnight camping experience, where different kinds of talents and abilities are able to shine. A "typical" campers may look with wonder as a person with a disability is the fearless first climber up the alpine tower, or reads Torah beautifully, or has perfect pitch—or knows every camper's birthday. Showcasing strengths helps everyone understand that we all have gifts and challenges. I always think of Rivka, a young woman with physical and developmental disabilities. She also happened to be a gifted Hebrew teacher—and helped many young staff members learn to read Hebrew.

—H.B.

When we are open and honest with our students, and we make inclusive practices the norm in our classrooms, children are sensitized to the fact that different people need different things at different times. That notion of "It's not fair!" rarely comes up once students feel confident that they, too, will get what they need in order to be successful.

When we do hear it, though, we can be pretty succinct in our response: *"I will treat everyone fairly, but I won't treat everyone equally because you don't all have the same needs."*

Tricks of the Trade

At Matan, through our many years of working with religious school educators, tutors, and other Jewish professionals, we have developed our top ten tips for successful inclusion.

1. Post the Plan

If you only take one thing from this chapter, I hope it's this: We all do better when we know what to expect, and this is especially true of children. By posting the schedule of events for the class or tutoring session, you are giving students a concrete idea of what will happen first, next, and last (key words to help students organize themselves and what they need to accomplish). For younger students, or those challenged by reading or processing language, include an image with each part of the plan. Example:

Flashcards: 10 minutes (3:05–3:15 p.m.)

Paired Reading: 20 minutes (3:15–3:35 p.m.)

Game: 10 minutes (3:35–3:45 p.m.)

Spelling Out the Whole Textual Plan

B'nai mitzvah students benefit by knowing the whole plan. At the first meeting, I make sure the student knows where in the Torah their portion is found and what it is about. I explain how the portion fits into the larger context of the Torah. For example, if their portion is *T'tzaveh*, I explain that it's the eighth portion in the Book of Exodus (27:20-30:10), which deals with the clothes of the priests. I make sure they understand that the Israelites have left Egypt, received the Torah at Mount Sinai, and are wandering toward Israel. I then use a pretend Torah scroll and a Tikkun (facsimile book of the Torah) to show the exact layout of the portion and the length of the entire portion. While some may think this makes a child anxious, I find it has precisely the opposite effect—it helps demystify the experience.

For example, Michael, a very bright student with language-based learning disabilities, was determined to learn the entire portion of *Emor*—all 124 verses. During each lesson, he checked his progress against the number of verses found in each *aliyah* (call to the Torah). Each month, when we finished learning an aliyah, he placed a colored check mark next to the breakdown chart—and smiled!

—H.B.

2. Wait for It

Have you ever heard of the five-second rule? No, not the one about eating food off the floor—the one about giving students five to seven seconds to answer a question. Many students need time to process your question and to formulate their answer. This patience is helpful for children with processing challenges and anxiety, among other things. Trying a five-second rule also helps the "quick-to-answer" students practice impulse control and patience. (Consider suggesting that these students jot down their answer on a paper next to them while they wait, or put their finger on their forehead to let you know they have an answer.)

3. Use Introductory Activities

Children have to navigate many different expectations and requirements throughout their day. Transitioning from one thing to the next can cause difficulty for many students, and it is important to help them switch gears to focus on the task at hand. One effective way of accomplishing this is by providing an introductory activity that can be linked to the topics you are planning to teach. Spending a few minutes at the beginning of class time to ease the transition will save many more minutes of distracting behavior during class time. Examples of introductory activities include:

- Crossword puzzle/word search
- Legos
- Play-Doh (great for students who benefit from some sensory input to help them focus)
- Drawing prompt
- Writing prompt
- Music-listening station

4. Do Social-Emotional Check-ins

There's a story from a Chasidic dynasty that goes like this:

> Once the Gerrer Rebbe decided to question one of his disciples: "How is Mosheh Ya'akov doing?"
> The disciple did not know.
> "What?!?!" shouted the Rebbe. "You don't know? You pray under the same roof, you study the same texts, you serve the same God, you sing the same songs, and yet you dare tell me that you don't know whether Mosheh Ya'akov is in good health, whether he needs help, advice, or comforting?"

Indeed, students can truly learn only once their most basic needs are met. Most important of those basic needs is a sense of security and a belief in the idea that the adult in front of them truly cares about their well-being. Checking in with our students before attempting to get anything else done will (1) demonstrate that we care and (2) give us a sense of where they're at. Maybe they will tell you they didn't sleep well the night before—how will that affect their ability to learn? How can we change things up to accommodate this new information? Maybe they tell you that they're feeling sad because their parents are fighting. This, too, can affect their ability to learn, and maybe you want to switch gears to do something upbeat and physical, rather than, say, the planned lesson on Cain and Abel.

5. Use Visual Timers

Here's a not-so-well-kept secret: Children (and teens!) have little sense of time. Providing a way for students to manage their time grounds them. Let's say you are going to spend twenty minutes on Hebrew reading, and then move on to a game for ten minutes. If the child is struggling with the Hebrew, it can feel as if this lesson is going to last forever. If there is a visual timer they can reference, they will recognize that they only need to focus, or "keep it together," for X number of minutes before they can move on to a preferred activity.

6. Include Multiple Modes of Instruction

No two minds think alike. When you are planning your lessons, remember to:

- Convey information using visual, auditory, tactile, and kinesthetic (physical) cues
- Build in multiple ways to participate in an activity
- Consider learning stations, small groups, pairs, and other configurations of students

Keep in mind that many kids learn best through movement, so consider how you can incorporate active (gross motor) games to give students a movement break while also incorporating learning opportunities. For some, pacing or rocking will help them pay attention (and attempting to contain these movements will mean a child will focus less, not more). For others, building in movement will help them regain focus.

7. Be on the Lookout

The best way to address students' needs is to be proactive and catch potential difficulties before they become problems. Keep an eye out for how students are responding to different demands. Learn your students' signals for when they are becoming distressed, hungry, or overwhelmed, and adapt accordingly before these signs become challenges. Offer a "brain break," fidget tool (see below), or another accommodation *before* they feel the need to respond in the only way they can think of in that moment—such as running out of the room screaming or hitting a nearby student.

8. Offer Choices

Provide students with acceptable choices of how they can engage in or complete a particular task, lesson, or activity. You will accomplish your teaching agenda, and the students will feel like they have some control over their learning.

9. Allow Fidget Tools

We should not be afraid to allow students to use fidgets that support their learning. Fidgets should always be accessible to students and not used as rewards or punishments. At the same time, fidgets cannot be an excuse for students *not* to focus. If they are being used inappropriately, you can simply say, "It doesn't look like this is helping you focus on your work right now. We can try something else later," and just calmly take it away. Students don't instinctively know how to use fidgets or the benefits that they can provide, but older students who find them useful have likely already determined which are their favorite fidgets. They should absolutely be permissible to accommodate their learning.

10. Consider Room Setup

Many challenges can be addressed, or at least improved upon, by taking a critical look at how your room is set up and where a child is in that space. In religious schools, this can be difficult because of limited space or shared classrooms, but it is always possible to make some modifications. Consider covering nursery school toys or distracting artwork on the wall. Would varied seating options, like beanbag chairs and wobble cushions, or space for walking around, be helpful? Check the lighting in the room, as well as the volume level. Keep in mind that all our senses are taking in information *all* the time. Look at your classroom or tutoring space from the perspective of someone who might have difficulty processing different kinds of sensory input.

On Classroom Behavior

As someone who conducts professional development sessions on a regular basis, I am often asked to teach behavior management. I always encourage the hiring organization to change how they think about behavior. I recognize that inclusion is much simpler when children are behaving in ways that feel manageable or expected. When children are acting out, that disruptive behavior affects the entire class, or even an individual tutoring session. I also know, however, that *all behavior is communication.* Consciously or subconsciously, the child is trying to tell us something through their actions. When we seek to understand the function of the behavior, rather than just focusing on the behavior itself, we have a much better chance of supporting that child's needs so that the challenging behavior is no longer an issue.

When we make sure that children feel safe, seen, and heard, and when we create a culture of acceptance and understanding, we are laying the foundation for a positive learning experience in which children don't need to rely on negative behaviors to communicate with us. We learn to recognize their needs, anticipate what will work best for them in any given situation, and help them become their own advocates. In those ways, we create a partnership with our students, in which mutual trust becomes the backbone of solving problems. Children understand that their needs will be met, because we have spent time demonstrating that we take each student's unique abilities seriously.

Consider this: Years ago, the director of a congregational school came to me and described a child who was constantly looking out the window. The teacher found him difficult to engage; she could never tell if he was paying attention. When interacting with other children, he appeared resistant and defensive, disconnected from his peers. His parents reported that he did not like coming to religious school and felt that he wasn't "as good at Hebrew" as the other kids.

One day, the teacher sat down close to this child's desk in the classroom and looked out the window. When she did, she noticed that the synagogue garden was in this student's line of vision. When she reflected on that out loud, the child smiled. (The teacher realized in that moment, sadly, that she had never seen him smile before.) She understood that she might be on to something, and she asked him if he liked the garden. Suddenly, there was a flood of information coming from this boy! He told her about each vegetable that had been planted, what their status was, which ones needed more sun, which ones needed less water... He was a real expert.

The teacher had an idea. She asked the student if, during their class break, he would like to go out to the garden to get a closer look and report back to her when he returned. He said he would like that. Over time, the teacher asked him to report back to the whole class. The other kids were amazed by how much he knew, and they would ask him questions about the garden. They started talking about their favorite fruits and vegetables, finding similarities and differences in their tastes. The teacher was stunned. This friendless student who had spent all of his time looking out the window was becoming an integral part of the class. And this skilled teacher started using these reports to teach different Hebrew words related to the garden. This child's confidence in Hebrew skyrocketed because it was connected to his passion.

The child's parents reported that he was going to religious school willingly for the first time, and that he came home happy. The teacher observed that it only took two to three minutes a week for him to give the garden report and answer questions—but it changed everything.

Making Use of IEPs

Two underused gifts that many parents of students with disabilities can bring their *b'nai mitzvah* teachers are a knowledgeable, caring teacher and an Individualized Education Program (IEP).

A teacher—even one unfamiliar with Hebrew or the process and content of b'nai mitzvah preparation—will offer useful insight into the child's unique learning style, effective teaching strategies, and observations about behavior and temperament. With the parent's permission, reach out to the child's primary teacher. The knowledge gained will prove useful in the b'nai mitzvah teaching process. The IEP (or 504 Plan), while a bit more technical, provides a blueprint for a child's education experience at school that can be applied to the b'nai mitzvah learning setting. IEPs are federally mandated and tend to follow a predictable format, including parental concerns; the student's current level of performance; the student's areas of need; goals; accommodations, modifications, and other supports; services; and location of services.

Reading an IEP

Each state can decide what its IEP will look like. For most, the first three sections of an IEP provide an overall picture of how the student functions and behaves in school. Section one, "Academic Achievement and Functional Performance," covers academic and functional skills, abilities, strengths, and challenges; classroom behavior; attention, communication, social skills, habits, and mobility; and how the school team intends to help them achieve those goals. Section two, "Goals," follows the SMART acronym—Specific, Measurable, Attainable, Results-oriented, and Time-bound. Section three, "Accommodations," may provide clues as to which tools and strategies will be useful in the b'nai mitzvah learning process. Among the accommodations a student might use: assistive technology, a scribe or computer for note taking, speech to text (dictation), or a special type of desk or chair in class.

Request a copy of the IEP from the parents, and ask if they can explain it to you—or direct you to online or district-provided resources for better understanding the content. Better yet, see if they will arrange a meeting in person, by phone, or on Zoom with the teacher who truly knows the student.

—H.B.

Partnering with Parents: A Key to Success

Communication with parents is an incredibly important aspect of teaching that we don't talk about enough. It's a potentially delicate process and can have significant ramifications for whether a student's needs are met. To simplify a complicated process, I like to think about family communication as a DREAM. (Maybe this has not been your experience!) But with a few tips and language suggestions, I hope you will feel more comfortable with these potentially challenging conversations.

D: Describe with Data

- Think about what information you are bringing to parents.
- What is that information based on?
- Have you homed in on the student's challenges? If not, engage the parents in a conversation about those challenges and how the parents address them at home.
- Describe a clear example of what you are seeing.
- Provide parents with the opportunity to describe the child they see at home.
- Have you kept track of strategies you tried with their child and the success of those strategies? Share those with the parents.

R: Remember the Goals

- What do you want to get out of the meeting?
- What have the parents expressed as their goals for their child?
- How will this meeting further the parents' goals for their child?
- Are there gaps or differences between your goals and the parents' goals? If so, try to minimize those gaps.

E: Establish a Relationship

- Think about what needs to happen before a parent meeting.
- Have the parents had time to establish trust in the school and/or in you as a tutor?

A: Actively Listen

- Follow the five-second rule (this pertains to parents as well as to children!)
  - Repeating
  - When you're listening, pick out the thing they said that seems most important.
  - Repeat the salient issue in a question.
  - Wait five to seven seconds before you say anything else.
- Make a guess
  - Offer "or something else"—this makes it easier for parents to correct you.
  - For example, say, "I think you might be concerned about how he fits in with his peers. Is that right, or did you mean something else?"

M: Meet Families Where They Are

- Meet families where they are on their journey, not where you think they should be.
- Believe what they tell you.
- Be flexible. Keep the goals in mind: What will ultimately benefit the child?
- If you've taught children with a similar challenge, tell parents this.
- Don't present yourself as the ultimate authority on their kid.
- Do show that you've been willing and able to handle unusual situations before.
- Sometimes, it helps to have some key language "in your back pocket." So here are some ideas. Remember to consider the family's goals, and not only the goals that resonate with you as an educator.
  - "For some other kids, I have found that this works well. . ."
  - "In the past, I have tried. . ."
  - "Are there things that others have tried that haven't worked well?"

- "Do you know of accommodations or modifications that your child finds helpful?"
- "This is your child's way of communicating his needs—it's our job to figure out just what he's telling us."

Many years ago, I was approached by a teacher at a training for religious school teachers. She said, "My director did a training with you last year, and she bought into how crucial it is for the Jewish community to include all students. It is really important. But now my religious school class has sixteen students and eight of them have special needs. It's still just me in the classroom, and I am not even a trained teacher."

I told her what I will tell you: There is a difference between promoting inclusion and promoting *successful* inclusion. Nobody is advocating for you to make promises you can't keep, or to set up a situation where the needs far surpass the capacity to serve them. Inclusion must be thought out and intentional; we must allocate resources to ensure that we can support educators who are creating inclusive experiences for all students. It is okay to create short-term and long-term goals, increasing your capacity to serve diverse students over time.

Choose one thing you would like to try out. Spend some time with it; play around with that strategy; utilize it over time and see how it feels to you and to your students. Then add in one more thing. Get comfortable with that and then add in something else.

As we learn in *Pirkei Avot* 2:16, "It is not your duty to finish the work, but neither are you at liberty to neglect it."

✱ CHAPTER 12 ✱

Reading Challenges:

A Multisensory Approach to Teaching Hebrew

Rebecca Redner and Arlene Remz

Rebecca Redner, an educational specialist at Gateways: Access to Jewish Education, in Boston, and Arlene Remz, founding executive director of Gateways, are passionate advocates for the right of every child to participate in Jewish education. In this chapter, Rebecca and Arlene suggest that with proper strategies and supports, such as those they describe, students with diverse abilities can learn how to successfully decode Hebrew to read prayers and Torah.

Eric's Story

Eric couldn't read. This wasn't unusual for a student in the *b'nai mitzvah* class at Gateways: Access to Jewish Education in Boston. The b'nai mitzvah class was designed around the needs of students whose disabilities required a higher level of support and expertise than most synagogues can provide. Many of our students struggle to read English. Eric was diagnosed with an autism spectrum disorder and mostly spoke in single words. Much of his speech was echolalic, repeating words and phrases he enjoyed from his favorite TV shows and computer games.

Eric attended a program within his public school for students with significant disabilities. His parents told us that his teachers had tried to teach him English letter sounds and how to sound out words, but he didn't respond well to this phonetic approach. So, Eric was taught to identify sight words instead. Eric had an excellent visual memory and learned hundreds of sight words. By the time he had enrolled in the b'nai mitzvah program at age eleven, he was able to read English materials appropriate for students in kindergarten or first grade. However, he was not able to decode new words.

The Gateways staff was intrigued by something Eric's parents wrote on his intake form: "Until he starts the program, it is unknown what he will be capable of." After talking it over with Eric's parents, we decided to try the process Gateways uses to teach b'nai mitzvah students how to decode Hebrew. We would start with a few Hebrew letters. If he wasn't able to learn them, or if he became frustrated, we could always modify our approach.

At first it was not clear whether we had made the right choice. Although Eric learned the sounds of a few letters and vowels quickly, he struggled to blend those sounds together. But after a few weeks of practice, it clicked! Eric began to blend letters and vowels together to read short words. As the weeks went by, Eric learned more and more Hebrew letters slowly and methodically. By the end of the school year, he had mastered almost the entire Hebrew alphabet and could slowly sound out and read words with confidence.

We could end this account with the day of Eric's bar mitzvah, when he proudly read Hebrew prayers from his siddur (prayer book). And if that was the end of the story, *dayeinu*, it would have been enough. But that's not where Eric's story ends.

Rewinding to a few months before Eric's bar mitzvah, I sat down with him to read a booklet about his Torah portion. All of a sudden, I heard Eric's voice reading along with mine—in English. I stopped, and Eric continued to read until the end of the page. He was able to read the rest of the story to me, only needing a bit of help to decode longer words.

I told Eric's mother how surprised I was to see Eric read his Torah story to me. She explained that after seeing how he had learned to decode Hebrew, she went back to his regular school and told them: "If he can learn to read Hebrew, you sure as hell can teach him to read English!" In fact, given Eric's success in learning Hebrew with an intensive phonetic approach, she demanded that his IEP be changed and that his school take another stab at using a phonetic approach to reading English. As a result, Eric truly learned how to read: to decode any word, rather than relying on memorized sight words. This is a skill that will open countless doors to him throughout his life.

Eric's story is an exceptional example, but it exemplifies how capable these students can be when they are given the right tools, and Hebrew can become a key that unlocks even more doors.

A Bar Mitzvah, One Word at a Time

Daniel's mother, Shelly, had been teaching religious school in New Jersey for seventeen years. When reflecting on her son Daniel's developmental disability, she thought that teaching her own child would be way too difficult. She collaborated with a colleague to prepare Daniel for his Sunday bar mitzvah on Rosh Chodesh (new month). They figured out early on that Daniel would do best learning Torah blessings and his two lines of Torah by learning one word per day. For example, they wrote the word *vayidaber* (And he spoke) in Hebrew letters and a transliteration on an index card on day one. On day two, they reviewed that word and introduced *Adonai* (God). After he mastered Adonai, they strung the words *vayidaber Adonai* (and God spoke) together—all before introducing the short words *el Mosheh* (to Moses) on day three. To cover all bases, they wrote the words in Hebrew (which Daniel could decode) and in transliteration, and they sang it. When he came up to the Torah, he knew it. The combination of memorizing the word visually and auditorily/musically meant that Daniel was able to chant perfectly.

Daniel was the first person with a disability to celebrate a bar mitzvah at his synagogue in Bridgewater, New Jersey. Shelly reflected, "No one thought about what he didn't do, but what he did do—it demonstrated who he was."

—H.B.

Advantages of Hebrew

Some believe it is unrealistic to teach a child with a disability to read Hebrew. Often Jewish educators and clergy will automatically recommend alternative strategies, such as using transliteration, or memorizing blessings, Torah, or *Haftarah* (from the Prophets) readings from a recording. These alternatives may be the right choices for some students; however, we believe that students with a wider range of disabilities can successfully learn how to decode Hebrew with the right methods.

Learning to decode an entirely new alphabet in which many letters look similar is an enormous challenge, and learning how to read in a new direction can add to the confusion. Yet over the years, the parents of several b'nai mitzvah students have told us that after participating in the Gateways program, their child's ability to decode Hebrew surpassed their ability to read English. A primary reason is that each Hebrew letter and vowel, with rare exception, corresponds to only a single sound. For example, the Hebrew letter כ will almost always make a "k" sound, but the English letter "c" sounds different in the words "carrot," "celery," and "cheese." How bewildering for emerging readers!

Learning to decode Hebrew will not be the right choice for every child. Students need to have enough time before the b'nai mitzvah date to build a strong foundation in Hebrew decoding. Another factor is the child's feelings: if learning to decode Hebrew is such a frustrating or anxiety-ridden experience for the student that it becomes a stumbling block to a successful and positive experience, then it's worth considering changing course.

The Gateways Hebrew Program

Gateways: Access to Jewish Education's approach to teaching Hebrew decoding is a highly structured, multisensory approach based on English reading programs, such as Wilson Reading System and Orton-Gillingham.

We use a method based on creating a strong connection between the shape of a letter and the letter's sound, which could be easily learned and recalled. First, every letter is given a mnemonic cue based on its physical form that helps students make the connection between its sound and its shape.

For example, the letter ת has a toe. When students see the letter ת, they can spot the "toe" in the letter and remember that it makes a "T" sound. Therefore, the shape of the letter itself serves as an intuitive reminder of what sound the letter makes. The mnemonic cues are reinforced through multiple senses. They color in a flash card, illustrating the mnemonic and highlighting the distinctive features of the letter, a visual cue. For ת, the "body" of the letter is filled in with turquoise, while the "toe" is colored the same shade as the student's skin. Some students have embellished those "toes" by adding toenails and colorful nail polish. Students might also use clay or pipe cleaners to sculpt the shape of the letter and create a motion that reinforces the mnemonic cue. For the letter ת, they might bend over and touch their toes or tap their toes on the ground. The four modalities involved in these learning activities—sound, sight, touch, and movement—help students process and remember the information they are learning.

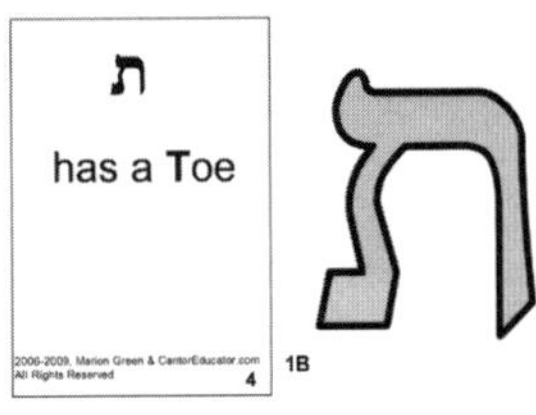

If a student hesitates or stumbles over the letter ת during a reading exercise, the instructor might draw an arrow pointing to the toe or use a highlighter to focus the student's attention on the toe of the letter. During virtual learning sessions, instructors have taken off their socks and wiggled their toes in front of the camera to remind students of the mnemonic cue. It's extremely valuable for teachers to use these simple tools to help their students arrive at the correct answer.

Embrace Shin Bet Taf Instead of Alef Bet Gimmel

The mnemonic cues and their accompanying illustrations are one piece of the puzzle. We teach the Hebrew letters in the order laid out in the *Z'man Likro* (Time to Read) series by Behrman House. The advantage to teaching the letters out of alphabetical order is that it splits up "problematic pairs" of letters that are often confused with each other. In a traditional system, students might learn the letters בּ (*bet*) and ב (*vet*) on the same day, or just one lesson apart. Learning similar letters at the same time often contributes to lasting confusion. But the order in which letters are taught in *Z'man Likro* gives students plenty of time to truly absorb בּ and become familiar with its features before being introduced to ב several lessons later. When students can already identify and read בּ with confidence, they are much less likely to mix it up. Additionally, the vowels are taught gradually, over many lessons, so students have time to learn each vowel well and practice combining them with different consonants.

By learning the letters out of alphabetical order, students can read a word many of them are already familiar with—שבת, *Shabbat*—by the end of the very first lesson. When students read words that have meaning to them, they become excited and motivated to read more. Each chapter of *Z'man Likro* focuses on key words, many of which are words that are already familiar, even to students without a background in Hebrew, such as *matzah* or *Purim*. Teachers can take this a step further and write out English words using Hebrew letters. When one student at Gateways was reluctant to practice Hebrew, we wrote out the names of different Pokémon characters (his favorite game) using Hebrew letters. Suddenly, Hebrew became his favorite activity because reading became rewarding.

Transliteration: To Use or Not to Use?

There is a standard system of transliterating Hebrew characters and words into English, which may be a useful tool for some students. Yet it is often more beneficial to use a system of "invented transliteration," where the teacher reads aloud each word in Hebrew and the student either writes or orally spells the word the way he or she hears it.

A standard transliteration may suggest *vay'dabeir* (and He spoke) or (saying), whereas the student may write "Vie yid dob bear" or "lay more." Students are more likely to remember the word if they write it the way they hear it. The words *lay* and *more* are common and familiar words he may know from English. While some might consider the use of transliteration to be "cheating," it is often the accommodation a student needs to read Hebrew.

—H.B.

Focus on Letter Sounds

We believe that it is not necessary to know the name of a Hebrew letter in order to read it. Learning letter names can be confusing because the name of the letter and the sound of the letter aren't always the same. While learning the letter names is useful for students who will learn to write Hebrew, this information is an easily removable obstacle for those who are only learning to decode.

The "Secret" of Sight Words

In English, "sight words" are commonly used words that don't follow the rules of spelling and therefore make decoding difficult or impossible. Examples include *does* and *who*. These words are therefore more easily memorized. Students are taught to recognize them by sight, so they can be quickly identified. There are famous word lists of several hundred words, dating back to the 1930s; the two most famous ones were created by Dr. Edward Dolch and Dr. Edward Fry.

The same philosophy applies to Hebrew reading. According to groundbreaking special educator Dr. Sarah Rubinow Simon, there are thirty-four need-to-know frequently used sight words in the prayerbook.

The following list of words includes one-third of the words found in the prayerbook; some examples include: *baruch* (blessed), *atah* (you), *natan* (gave), *kodesh* (holy), *shem* (name), and *eretz* (land). While Hebrew is a phonetic language, and learning Hebrew reading may be easier for some than English reading, this list of sight words might be a useful tool for many.

עם	לי	חסד	אתּה	אָב
עשָׂה	לעוֹלָם וָעד	טוֹב	בּית	אדוֹנָי
קדשׁ	לפנֵי	יוֹם	בּרוּך	אֵל
שׁם	מלך	ישראל	בּרך	אֱלֹהים
	נתן	כּי	הוּא	אָמר
	עוֹלָם	כּל	היא	ארץ
	על	לֹא	חיים	את

—*H.B.*

Individualized Instruction and Pacing

Although some synagogues use the Gateways system to teach Hebrew in large classes, within our building every student has their own tutor so they can learn at their own pace. This way no student ever needs to move on to the next lesson before they can read with accuracy. Some students might stay on a single lesson for a few weeks until they are ready to progress. Allowing students to learn at their own pace removes an enormous amount of pressure.

Our Hebrew program is highly structured and remains consistent from week to week. Many students with disabilities thrive on routine, and a clear, predictable structure can reduce anxiety because students know what they can expect and what will be expected of them. At the beginning of each session and after each activity, we refer to a schedule, where many students enjoy checking off the items they have already finished. Schedules also help students to realize that their learning time has an end point and helps them to budget their attention and energy.

Name: ____________ Date: ______

Hebrew Schedule

___ 1. Review the sounds and tricks for each letter and vowel

___ 2. Make words with the letters and vowel cards, and read each word

___ 3. Read _____ lines from the homework sheet

___ 4. Learn the sound and trick for the new letter(s) and vowel(s)

___ 5. Color the new: letter(s) and vowel(s)

___ 6. Make short words with the new letters and vowels

___ 7. Read____lines from the new homework sheet

___ 8. Put the letters and vowels into the pencil case

___ 9. If there is time: Play "tic tac toe"

gateways

The Importance of Review

Every Hebrew learning session begins with review: the instructors hold up the illustrated flash cards for the letters and vowels students have already learned, one by one, and students say the sounds, the mnemonic cue, and might also act out the associated motion. This activates their knowledge of previously learned letters and vowels before they're asked to do the more complex task of decoding. When the review of the flash cards is finished, the tutor then uses those same flash cards to spell out made-up words for the student to decode. Next, the student switches from reading words made from flash cards to reading printed words on a page of reading exercises.

These three review activities reinforce information and also allow the instructor to assess how well the student can read each letter. Every review session is an opportunity for informal assessment, helping the tutor determine whether to move on.

When a student is ready to progress to the next lesson, they are introduced to new letters and vowels the same way: first they learn the mnemonic clue, then they color in the flash card illustrating the cue, and finally they create a movement reinforcing the connection between the letter's shape and sound. New letters are paired with vowels students have already mastered. New vowels are paired with previously learned letters. This repeated practice of the new letter or vowel bolsters the student's memory, before proceeding with decoding exercises.

From Flash Card to Printed Page

Even students who can easily decode using their flash cards sometimes struggle to read Hebrew on the printed page. The transition from large flash cards with colorful illustrations to smaller black-and-white text is significant. One way we scaffold this transition is to place flash cards for the newest letters or vowel sounds above the reading page so a student can easily refer to them. If a student struggles with a certain letter or vowel, the tutor might illustrate every instance of the problematic letter or vowel on the page with a simple reminder of its mnemonic cue: the teacher might draw a small ball next to the ג that goes for the goal, or color the ו vowel orange. Students vary in how long they need that level of support.

Gamify the Learning

Learning to read Hebrew can be hard work, but teachers can make it fun by supplementing the structured exercises with games, such as those in the box. With a little creativity, some of these games can also be adapted for remote learning. We've found that turning reading into a simple game can transform students who are frustrated into students who are engaged and eager to read more.

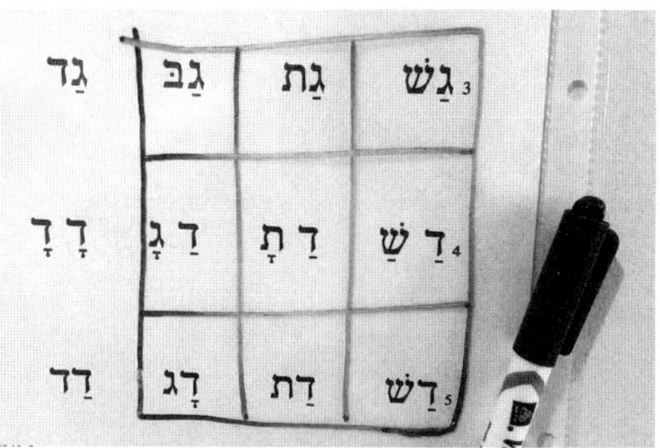

Games for One Student	Games for a Group
Beanbag Toss: Place letter and vowel flash cards in a grid on the floor, and give the student several beanbags. When you say a letter or vowel name, the student has to toss the beanbag onto the correct letter or vowel. If they miss, they have to say the sound of the letter or vowel the beanbag landed on.	**Flyswatter Game:** Place letter and vowel cards faceup on a large desk. Divide the class into two lines. Give the students at the head of each line a flyswatter. Call out a letter name, and the two students have to run forward and hit the correct letter with the flyswatter first in order to earn a point.
Hopscotch: Place several letter and vowel flash cards on the floor in a row at least one or two feet apart. Students have to hop from one card to the next while saying the letter or vowel sound.	**Kaboom!:** Place the letter and vowel flash cards in a paper bag, along with several cards of identical size with the word *kaboom*! written on them. Students take turns drawing a card from the bag. If a student draws a letter or vowel card, they have to say the sound and the mnemonic cue for the letter or vowel. If the student draws a '*kaboom!*' card, they have to put all their cards back in the bag. The student with the most cards at the end of the game wins.

Games for One Student	Games for a Group
Tic-Tac-Toe: Place a copy of the student's reading page in a clear plastic page protector. Use a dry-erase marker to draw a tic-tac-toe board on the reading page. The student and instructor must read the words in each box before making an X or an O.	**Four Corners:** Place the flash cards for the four most recent or most tricky letters and vowels in the four corners of the classroom. One student is chosen to be "it," and they stand in the center of the room with their eyes closed, counting to ten. While the student is counting, everybody else runs to a corner. The student then looks at one corner and says the name of the letter there. The students who were in that corner are out. This continues until there is only one student left, and that student will be "it" in the next round.
Spell It Out: Say a word, and ask the student to try to spell it out using their letter and vowel cards.	**Find It Fast:** Place flash cards on desks or on the floor around the room. One student, who is "it," says a letter or vowel sound, and the students have to run to that card and touch it. The last student to touch the card is "it" in the next round.

Make Text More Readable

Font, size, and spacing of Hebrew text can affect a student's reading, no matter what method is used to teach. Reading materials must be formatted to support learning, while they're learning to decode or over the long term. Many Gateways students read from personalized materials at their b'nai mitzvah. These materials are gathered into three-ring binders the students decorate and use proudly.

Just as in English, some Hebrew fonts are easier to read than others. At Gateways we print all of our materials using the font Frank Ruhl (the first line) which is used in many Israeli books, newspapers, and magazines. The Frank Ruhl font is clear, easy to read, and makes differences between similar letters more distinct.

ר ד כ ב ו ז ס ם

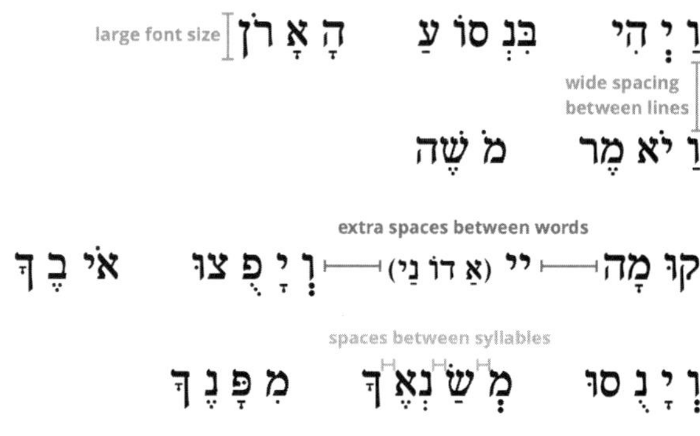

Bigger font size is often better! Most Gateways materials are printed in 32-point type, and materials for some students are double that size. Students tend to read more quickly and accurately, and are less likely to lose their place, when reading a larger font. Additionally, a student's ability to track, or move their eyes effortlessly from one word or one line to the next, is strengthened when there are larger spaces between words and lines. Our materials are generally formatted with extra spaces between syllables to help sound out multisyllabic words, five spaces between words, and at least three line breaks between each line of text. Large print and wide spacing help students feel less anxious by reducing the amount of material printed on a page. After learning how to decode using large-print materials with wide spacing, some students can make the transition to reading Hebrew from a typical siddur. Other students will continue to use these adapted materials, from their own binders at their b'nai mitzvah.

Support Tracking

Tracking, the ability to move the eyes across a page, is a challenge for many students, and many become distracted by all the words on a page. Beyond supporting with large font size, increased spacing, and syllabication, we can help these students by using blank sheets of paper to block out the lines above and below the line the student is reading. An arrow drawn on the sheets reminds students about which direction they should be reading. Some students might need a "word window" instead, created by cutting a small rectangle, the size of a printed Hebrew word, in the middle of a blank sheet of paper.. Another way to promote tracking is by encouraging students to point. We can get creative—one student used a toy car, another marked words in a clear plastic protector with a dry erase marker. Gateways b'nai mitzvah students make a *yad* (Torah pointer) from Sculpey during one of the first weeks of class. They are always proud of their creations, which makes the students eager to use their yad for pointing. Using a yad while learning how to read also helps to prepare students for eventually reading from the Torah.

Reading from the Torah

Learning to read from a Torah scroll introduces additional challenges. The Torah contains no formatting elements to help struggling readers. It uses a highly stylized font, words and lines are spaced closely together, and just a single column of Torah contains a large amount of text. We ease students into this challenge by degrees, beginning with an easy-to-read text that gradually morphs into the Torah script as the student gains fluency and confidence.

A Gateways student is assigned just a few words of their Torah portion at a time, no more than a single phrase. At first, the words of the portion are written out using all the modifications described earlier: large print, clear font, wide spacing, and syllabified words. When the student can read confidently and fluently, trope (biblical cantillation) is added. We use a type of intuitive musical notation instead of traditional cantillation markings, which can easily be confused for vowels by struggling readers.

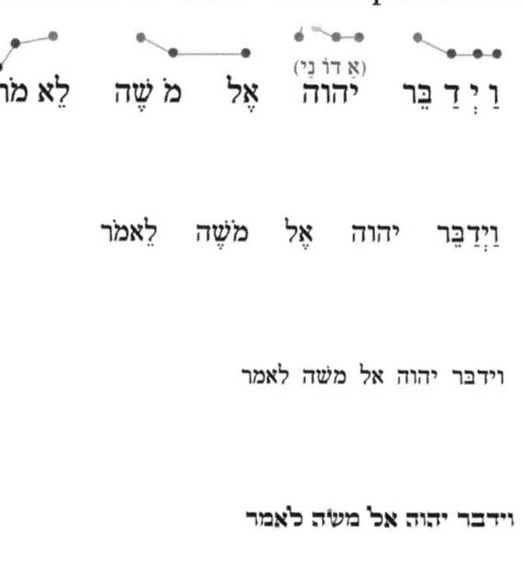

Learning to read Torah trope by associating single symbols with a series of musical notes is an enormous undertaking for a student who has already worked hard to learn Hebrew. Instead, we use a group of connected dots that show students what series of notes to sing based on their position and color. Often students point to the circles to "read" the music as they learn how to chant.

Once a student is able to chant a line of Hebrew fluently, the text is tweaked slightly: the dots illustrating the tune are removed, along with spaces between syllables, and the font size is reduced a little bit.

Hebrew Teaching at the Shefa School

I had the pleasure of preparing two bright twelve-year-old boys with learning disabilities for their *b'nai mitzvah*. Both were students at the Shefa School in Manhattan, a Jewish day school serving students in grades K–8 who benefit from a specialized educational environment. Shefa's founders observed many intelligent students with language-based learning disabilities floundering in traditional Jewish day schools. Shefa's policy is to wait to introduce Hebrew reading instruction until students are more comfortable with English.

When it came time to begin bar mitzvah preparation with these two Shefa students, my initial instinct was to use transliteration, along with their very good auditory memories. However, both boys were very clear—they wanted to master Hebrew decoding. Given their determination and their parents' support, I followed their lead. Manu and Mayer—classmates and friends—each learned to chant Torah, after rapidly progressing through the very straightforward book *Teach Yourself to Read Hebrew,* by Ethelyn Simon and Joseph Anderson.

Despite many years of experience preparing students with disabilities for bar mitzvah, Manu and Mayer taught me a very important lesson: I used to think that learning to decode Hebrew was tedious and laborious, especially compared to the rich stories of our tradition. With these two boys, I couldn't have been more wrong They enjoyed the repetition and were excited to master Hebrew decoding. On their bar mitzvah day, they chanted from the Torah scroll. They now have the skill to read from the siddur (prayer book), Torah, and any other Hebrew text they will encounter for the rest of their lives.

I now see just how empowering it can be simply to be able to read Hebrew.

—H.B

After students have mastered reading this line of text, it is modified again. This time the extra spaces between the words are removed, along with the vowels, and the letters are made smaller. Some students become anxious when they see that the vowels have disappeared; to them this appears to be a dramatic change. "No way am I reading that!" one student exclaimed as he pushed the sheet away his eyes wide. So, I pointed to the first word of the line that still had vowels and asked him to read that one word. Then I pointed to the same word without vowels and explained it said the same thing. I repeated this with the second word, and then something suddenly clicked for him. He flawlessly read the rest of the line without vowels and pushed the sheet away again, remarking, "That was too easy."

After a student can easily read and chant the line of text in a small font without vowels, we change the font to Tikkun text, the decorative style of printing in the Torah. However the script in each Torah looks a little different depending on the spacing and penmanship of the scribe, and the written text always looks different from a computer font. Therefore, we also ask clergy for a photograph of the section the student will read in the synagogue's Torah. Practicing from a photograph of the actual text in the Torah allows students to feel comfortable when they step up to the scroll for the first time.

Our students begin to learn their Torah portions using heavily modified text. But by taking small steps, they are eventually able to read from the Torah scroll with confidence.

Over the years we have been asked: Why make our students work so hard for so long to learn Hebrew, when they might simply learn the prayers and Torah portion from a recording or a transliteration? Couldn't our students do more if they didn't take all that time to learn to read Hebrew? It's true that they probably could. But a b'nai mitzvah isn't about the number of prayers a child leads or the amount of Torah they chant. When students prepare to become b'nai mitzvah, they have a unique opportunity to learn the skills they can continue to use as Jewish adults, skills that will help them participate in the Jewish community. A student who memorizes a Torah portion may rarely have the opportunity to chant that portion again. But students who learn to read Hebrew can continue to decode new prayers and words of Torah throughout their lives.

Consider Eric's story at the beginning of the chapter: Imagine how much more limited his life would be today if we had only taught him to memorize the prayers for his bar mitzvah. Learning to decode Hebrew is not the right choice for every child. But at Gateways we strongly believe that learning to decode Hebrew is not only possible, but beneficial for children with a wide range of abilities. As long as their teachers are equipped with the sufficient tools and training, we can expand the range of students for whom Hebrew decoding is accessible. When we teach Hebrew decoding, we hand our students a key they can use to unlock the gates of prayer, and so much more.

Adapting the Gateways Hebrew Approach to an Online Environment

We have learned that two elements are essential to success when working online with students who have disabilities. First, the materials must be even more engaging than those used in person for a student to stay motivated and focused. Students earn emojis as they say the sounds and mnemonic cues for each letter, they read words created by flash cards that rain down from a stormy sky, and instead of looking at a plain page of decoding exercises, students read words in undersea bubbles that float away.

Second, all learning is one-on-one: they have their tutor's undivided attention and care, and they often forge trusting relationships that enable students to take chances and try their hardest.

—Rebecca Redner, Gateways

✻ VOICES ✻

Reflections on My Anxiety-Filled Bat Mitzvah

Jennifer Fink

Jennifer Fink is a healthcare consultant with a strong interest in mental health awareness and disability advocacy.

In thinking about bat mitzvah and anxiety, let me begin by saying that I have the most loving, caring parents in the world, and that in 2005, when I was thirteen, we were not well-versed in anxiety and other mental health issues.

I grew up in an observant home with very high standards for accomplishment and performance. My brother and I were raised with the understanding that it is a privilege to have a *b'nai mitzvah* without sharing it with another student, and that one must read the whole Torah portion. For the learning, we never memorized, because we were taught that it is not legal [from the perspective of traditional Jewish law]. I went into b'nai mitzvah practice thinking, "My brother did this. I can do this."

My brother, who is two years older than me, was actually my bat mitzvah tutor. He is very smart, and school was always his strong suit. He's a well-respected doctor now.

When I started learning, we didn't know what we know now about anxiety, medication, and therapy. It wasn't until high school that I was diagnosed with attention deficit / hyperactivity disorder (ADHD). But really, ADHD wasn't the problem—that was a misdiagnosis. The truth was that my anxiety was so bad that I couldn't concentrate. It's been a theme all my life. My mother says that as a baby, I was even an anxious nurser.

When I was about to start learning for my bat mitzvah, my parents told me that I didn't have to do the whole portion. I thought that was just lip service. I knew that I had to do the whole thing to make them proud. I remember thinking that doing less was not an option, that I had to just plow through the whole thing, and memorize it, without a recording—this was the proper way.

It never dawned on me that there could be another way, other than to sit, study, and learn it. I would have benefited from a recording, and from not tackling the whole portion. My brain was not made for our traditional approach.

I look back on the actual bat mitzvah day and think it was terrible. My bat mitzvah scarred me; it was the worst experience ever. That day, I promised myself I would never read Torah again, and I would never go up on the *bimah* again, except maybe to open or close the Ark.

During my bat mitzvah, reading from the Torah scroll gave me so much anxiety because the trope symbols indicating musical phrases were not there. I just couldn't keep it straight. There were all of these different stimuli, and I kept losing my place. I was fighting back tears the entire time.

I would have preferred a smaller setting. Standing up on a bimah that was literally elevated, looking out at over six hundred people, added another layer of stress that I didn't need.

Many years later, after I married and had a child, I talked to my husband, Jason, about his bar mitzvah. He explained the relaxed way in which he learned. At times, he listened to a recording of the rabbi while he was skating on a hockey rink. He just breezed through it all.

I think the whole construct for how some families perceive b'nai mitzvah is wrong. In my family, b'nai mitzvah was a challenge that one needed to conquer. I felt I had to earn the party, because it was so expensive.

Jason and I talk all the time about what a bat mitzvah will look like for our daughter, years from now. Our highest value is to raise a well-adjusted child, with the tools and knowledge to navigate this milestone in a healthy way. That's important to both of us. We both care about instilling a work ethic, so we will be intentional with the message that "success metrics" are only measured by effort and hard work. If it's hard for her to study, we can decide together about the parts of the service that she wants to do, as long as she goes through the experience of learning. We want her to feel empowered by her bat mitzvah, not anxious.

✶ CHAPTER 13 ✶

Connecting the Dots:

A Bat Mitzvah for a Braille Reader

Batya Sperling-Milner and Rabbanit Aliza Sperling

Rabbanit Aliza Sperling and Batya Sperling-Milner are a mother-daughter team. Rabbanit Aliza is on the Talmud faculty at Yeshivat Maharat and is the director of education at Svivah, a Jewish women's community. Batya Sperling-Milner is a student at SAR High School in Riverdale, New York. Batya shares the story of using a braille text instead of a traditional Torah scroll at her bat mitzvah. Aliza explores the related halachic (Jewish law) considerations for using braille.

Batya's Narrative: A Personal Perspective

It was 2013, and four-year-old me was trying to figure out what made me different from my public school, pre-K classmates. As I sat on the classroom carpet pondering, it came to me in a moment of clarity I remember vividly to this day. I was blind, and I was Jewish, and those identities, combined, made me unique. As I grew up, I never viewed my differences as negative or alienating, thanks to the incredible support of my family, friends, and amazing braille teacher, Mary. Instead, my intersecting identities became the lens through which I viewed the world. With the help of my wonderful teachers at Milton Gottesman Jewish Day School, my love for Torah grew. I treasured my braille prayer books, their plastic bindings and worn pages feeling at once holy and familiar. The ways that I accessed Jewish ritual increased the love that I had for it.

So, when my bat mitzvah came around and suddenly my blindness seemed like an obstacle to entering the Jewish adult world, I was surprised. I didn't like to think that an identity that had accompanied me through my childhood was now becoming a burden or an impediment. Therefore, I decided that it wouldn't be. I worked together with my mom and dad, as well as a supremely kind cast of family, friends, and clergy, to create a bat mitzvah that exemplified the truth that I already knew: blindness and Judaism can build on each other to create something beautiful.

I was lucky in that I already knew Hebrew braille and could read and understand Hebrew. However, to read from the Torah I needed to learn the trope (biblical cantillation). This was a challenge. Practically, until my bat mitzvah, there was no braille trope system. This meant that if I wanted to chant the portion using the traditional tune, I would have to learn the melody only auditorily. It would be difficult to prepare my entire portion using this method. Also, I wanted to know trope so that I could use it to prepare Torah readings independently in the future. To solve this issue, Danny Sadinoff, a family friend who is a coding genius, created a beta version of a software program that converted trope into braille symbols. I used this to prepare my portion, and when the time came to actually read it, I used a version without trope, punctuation, or vowels, to mimic the Torah itself as closely as possible. Now, when I want to read from the Torah, I have a completely accessible Tikkun (facsimile book of the Torah) from which to practice.

At my bat mitzvah, I led the morning prayer using my braille siddur (prayer book). I then led the Torah service using routes to and from the Ark that I had practiced before. I read my Torah portion and *Haftarah* (reading from the Prophets) from braille texts. I didn't use a *yad* (Torah pointer) since I needed my fingers to read the text. A good friend instead painted a henna yad on my hand to show that my hands were in fact reading the Torah text. At the end of the service, I gave a *d'var Torah* (Torah teaching) to the congregation about the Torah portion and the power of empowering others.

My bat mitzvah was an amazing day that kick-started many other opportunities for synagogue involvement for me. Looking back on it, I am grateful for how it turned out because I was empowered to do what I wanted to do. I think everyone deserves the opportunities and accommodations so that they can do what they choose to mark their *b'nai mitzvah.*

My bat mitzvah got a lot of attention because the *Washington Post* reported on it. The admiration was both thrilling and bewildering; thrilling because of the impact I knew I was making for other blind and disabled kids, and bewildering because I was just a normal kid having my bat mitzvah. In an ideal world, it wouldn't be "inspirational" for a disabled person to engage in a typical rite of passage. Many blind people I had never met before showed up at the service. If you create an accessible space, people you never knew existed will come.

If you are reading this because you are a rabbi or a parent or a kid thinking about a b'nai mitzvah for a blind kid, you should know that there are ways to make anything you want to do accessible. Don't assume that anything is off-limits; you just need creativity, support, and a willingness to try. Through my bat mitzvah I learned that when we create access for individual members of the community, it both brings them in and improves the community as a whole. Access is not just a set of accommodations made for a single person. It is an ideology of openness that expands the spiritual capacities of everyone in the community.

The Rabbanit (Batya's Mother) Explains: Creating Accessible B'nai Mitzvah Rituals Using Braille

A blind person living today has opportunities that their predecessors could never have dreamed of. About two hundred years ago, fifteen-year-old Louis Braille invented a tactile reading code that gave blind people greater ability to read. Previously, books were created using raised print, which was laborious to produce, hard to read, and difficult for individuals to write. The invention of braille greatly expanded literacy for people who are blind or have significant vision loss. Today, braille is broadly accepted as a form of reading.

Braille is a system of raised dots that can be read by touch by people who are blind or who have low vision. It is not its own language; rather, it can be considered a transliteration of a print alphabet into a tactile code. Braille alphabets have been produced to support more than 133 languages. Research has found that blind people process reading braille in the same area of the brain that sighted people process reading print. Besides the braille reading code, braille codes in math and science have also been developed.

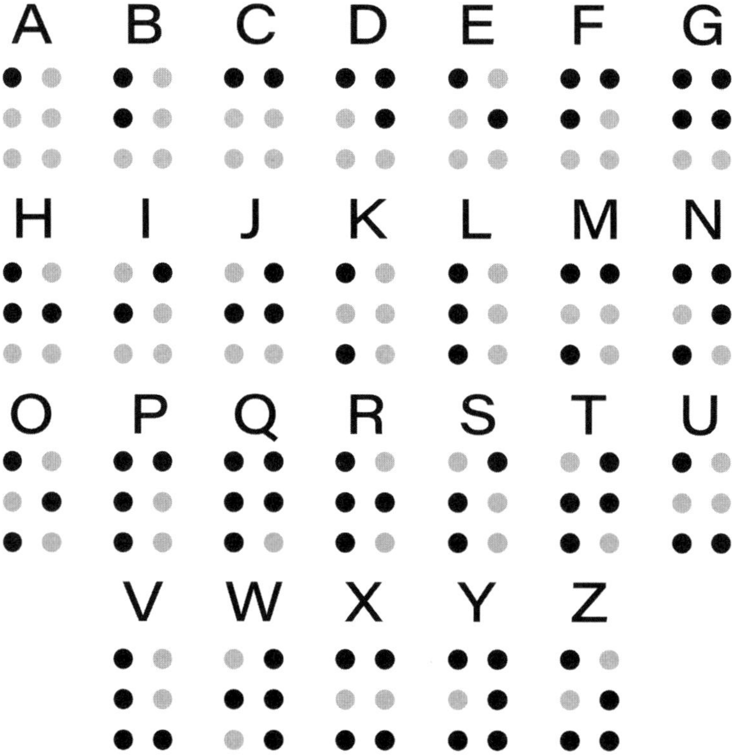

Braille system for the English language

The combination of braille use and technological advancement has led to incredible opportunities for individuals who are blind. They can read in braille, either through embossed books or through handheld electronic devices with refreshable braille displays. A blind reader who wants to read a book need only access a special Library of Congress website, download a braille book onto their braille display, and start reading immediately. A blind person who wishes to access the internet and computer applications can usually do so through connected braille displays or via computer screen readers.

In the 1930s, the braille revolution reached the Hebrew language, and Hebrew braille began to be developed, finally being completed in 1944. It is a tactile transliteration of the Hebrew alphabet based on international norms, with Braille symbols available for both consonants and vowels. A blind person can now read from a Torah printed in braille, similar to the way that a sighted person reads print. The only difference is that Hebrew braille replaces print letters with raised dots, so that the letter *alef* is a single dot, the letter *bet* is two dots, etc. Unlike print Hebrew, but in keeping with other braille alphabets, Hebrew braille is read from left to right. Today, Hebrew texts can easily be obtained in braille, and there are blind rabbis teaching in Jewish schools. Torah has become accessible to the blind community.

Obtaining Braille Texts for the Synagogue

It is important—even before a blind congregant has a b'nai mitzvah—to have braille prayer and Torah texts available in the synagogue, just as you have printed texts available for your other congregants. Even if you do not currently have blind congregants, consider having braille texts ready and available in case a blind person decides to attend or visit your synagogue. Make sure that staff knows where the braille texts are located, and that there is adequate signage, in print and braille, indicating that you have the braille texts and their location.

Reading from a Braille Text Instead of a Traditional Torah Scroll

While it might feel odd to perform a Torah service from a braille text rather than a traditional Torah scroll, we believe that the practice has a sound basis in *halachah* (Jewish law). The Talmud relates that the people of the Galilee in the third and fourth centuries did not have kosher Torah scrolls in their possession and asked whether it would be permissible to use a printed biblical text instead. The sages of the ancient house of study did not have a received tradition regarding the question and finally concluded that the printed biblical text may not be used because it would imply that the congregation was too poor to afford a Torah scroll, which would be a violation of *k'vod tzibur* (dignity of the congregation).

The medieval rabbis argued about the implications of this rabbinic text. Maimonides wrote that this means that a kosher Torah scroll is not required for Torah reading, and that one may read from a printed biblical text, a disqualified Torah scroll, or even from memory. However, many others argue that the Talmud only meant to permit kosher Torah scrolls that contain only one book of the Torah, and not codices or other texts that are not written according to the requirements of a kosher Torah scroll. Maimonides's view would imply that a braille Torah scroll could be used by a congregation. There is no concern for the Jewish concept of k'vod tzibur, since it would be clear that if the congregation owns Torah scrolls it is using a braille text to *enhance* its dignity by expanding access to congregants with visual impairments.

At Batya's bat mitzvah, we took out the kosher Torah scroll from the ark, and when participants received an *aliyah* (call to the Torah), they would find the place and follow along in the kosher Torah scroll. There was therefore no concern for k'vod tzibur since the congregation clearly owned—and was using!—a kosher Torah scroll.

The halachic questions concerning reading Torah for the congregation from a braille text are new and exciting. This summary has only referenced a few of the halachic arguments.

A blind child who reaches the age of b'nai mitzvah should have every opportunity to ritually celebrate this important milestone. There are resources available to acquire prayer and Torah texts in Hebrew braille, to learn Hebrew braille and braille trope, and even to borrow a braille Torah scroll. Although it might feel "strange" or "atypical" to conduct a service with these accommodations, it is precisely this willingness to expand our sense of possibilities of what the service can look like that defines us a *k'hilah k'doshah* (a holy community).

✻ CHAPTER 14 ✻

Opening Channels:

Working with Deaf and Hard of Hearing Students

Rabbi Darby Jared Leigh and Serena Leigh Krombach

Rabbi Darby Jared Leigh, a rabbi who is Deaf, and his hearing sister, Serena Leigh Krombach, a publisher turned educator, offer an introduction to Deafness in Jewish tradition, the experiences of Deafness, and the diverse ways Deaf people communicate. They share best practices for identifying and accommodating students' individual communication preferences. They also offer guidance for setting b'nai mitzvah learning goals and expectations and present a variety of strategies for achieving them.

Capital-D Deaf

Spelling *Deaf* with a capital *D* identifies Deafness as an integral aspect of identity, as it is for many Deaf people. Deafness is its own culture: people in the "Deaf world" share the experience of being a member of a minority group, a collective history, social norms, and a language, American Sign Language (ASL). The Deaf community is broad and diverse. We use *Deaf* to be inclusive of those who identify as "hard of hearing" or "person with a hearing loss," for example. We occasionally use the lowercase *d* to indicate deafness when it is referred to as a medical condition or as deafness in ancient times.

We have mostly fond memories of becoming *b'nai mitzvah* in the 1980s, but some still sting. At the time of Serena's bat mitzvah, our synagogue refused to locate, hire, or fund sign language interpreters to make the service accessible to family members and friends. When Darby began his bar mitzvah study, he was discouraged from chanting Torah, despite his skill in oral communication and eagerness to learn.

We have heard downright painful stories. For example, Dina, who also became bat mitzvah in the 1980s, remembers:

> *Correct pronunciation was the only goal, and the cantor was only trying to get his job done. To me, it all seemed to be simply speech therapy. . . . I felt ignorant. Something was wrong.*
>
> *[During the service,] I couldn't even read the words on his mouth. . . . My mind was trying to bail me out by trying to hear better, but my ears wouldn't cooperate. All decoding attempts failed. . . . I stood there feeling foolish, betrayed. This was the holy ritual in which I was to become a woman in the eyes of Jewish tradition. But I didn't feel the joy I was entitled to. After twelve months of speech therapy with the cantor, I felt the rabbi and the cantor stole the show.*

The lived experience of Deaf individuals (and their families) has improved considerably in recent decades because of several factors: the passage of the Americans with Disabilities Act in 1990, requiring communication access for deaf individuals in most public spaces; advances in technology, such as texting; and greater representation of Deaf people and culture in the media. A more recent bat mitzvah student, Shira, benefited from this progress. Her mother shared the following experience, which was altogether different from ours:

> *[Being tutored by a Deaf rabbi] completely shifted her framework as a Jewish person . . . We felt very prepared and truly embraced by our community and by the rabbi—she was able to really push our community to support our daughter more fully. Shira now has an interpreter at religious school and is truly a part of the Jewish community. This was an incredible experience for our family.*

Each individual, Deaf or not, who joins with Deaf students on their learning journeys should be guiding them toward a future in which they feel Judaism belongs to them, and they belong in the Jewish community. Sensitive clergy and educators will already know that, as the Talmud says, it's "better to be . . . a reed than . . . a cedar tree" (*Ta'anit* 20a). That is, flexibility is key. Deaf people are not all alike. One b'nai mitzvah that succeeds in being deeply meaningful and joyful to a Deaf person and family and community will not look the same as another. Build the vision for the ritual with each individual student and family, and make the journey toward it together.

Deafness in Torah and Tradition

Two Torah verses explicitly mention deafness. In Exodus 4:10, God charges Moses with rescuing the people of Israel from slavery; in response, Moses protests that he is "slow of speech and slow of tongue." God replies, "Who gives humans speech? Who makes them dumb or deaf, seeing or blind? Is it not I, Adonai?" (Exodus 4:11). God reminds Moses that all people, including those with disabilities, are created in God's image, so Moses must rise to lead. His identity as a person with a "disability"—being "slow of speech"— does not excuse him from this obligation.

"You shall not insult the deaf, or place a stumbling block before the blind" appears in Leviticus 19:14, among the verses that form the "Holiness Code." According to the influential Middle Ages biblical commentator Rashi, "the deaf" are mentioned to emphasize a general statement: you shouldn't insult anyone, even those who can't hear you insult them!

You might read these verses as a rationale for encouraging and supporting Deaf people's inclusion in Jewish community and leadership. Nonetheless, the ancient rabbis categorically excluded deaf people from full participation in Jewish ritual life. In ancient times, and centuries after—even not so long ago—deaf people were assumed to lack intellectual ability. "Deaf and dumb," a term that arose in English in the nineteenth century, may have meant "deaf-mute" to some, but Deaf people have throughout the generations generally been treated as if they were unable to learn and succeed as well as those who can hear.

Today, many Jewish denominations and synagogues affirm, in statement and practice, the full inclusion of all people. For example, in a statement "Regarding Deaf Jews," the Conservative movement's Committee on Jewish Law and Standards of the Rabbinical Assembly explored the Talmudic proscriptions and, using the same Jewish legal framework and approach, concluded that they should be discarded.

Ways to Communicate

Building a relationship with a Deaf student and their family depends on effective communication, so even before you begin the journey, learn what you'll need to do to ensure that communication flows as easily as possible. Use the label the student prefers (for example, hard of hearing rather than Deaf), and discover, rather than assume, their communication preferences.

Oral Communication

Oralism gives a Deaf child as much access as possible to auditory information via assistive listening devices, such as hearing aids and cochlear implants, and as much access as possible to spoken communication. This approach requires auditory and speech therapy, hard work not only for the child but also for the family. Ninety percent of deaf children are born to hearing parents, and most are likely to be raised to communicate orally, although Deaf children are increasingly learning language through both speech and sign.

Manual Communication

Manualism means raising children with signed language from birth. Deaf children who are native sign language users learn and develop language in the same way all children do, by exposure. ASL is its own language, with its own grammatical structure and syntax; it's a common misconception that ASL is a one-to-one correspondence of spoken word to manual sign. Moreover, sign language is not universal, and many regions have their own sign language dialects!

Assistive Technology

Whether ASL is their primary language or not, many Deaf people use hearing aids or cochlear implants. Hearing aids amplify sounds but may not make them intelligible or identifiable. Cochlear implants can improve listening ability considerably, but they don't "cure" deafness.

Lipreading

When navigating a world of English speakers, many Deaf people rely heavily on lipreading—a misnomer, because much of the useful information comes from other sources. Context tells you whether the word is *pear* or *bear*, for example, and facial expression and body language supply other clues to meaning. Lipreading requires intense concentration, and it's a lot of work! A teen who comes to b'nai mitzvah study from a school with hearing teachers and peers has been working hard to communicate all day and will probably be exhausted from the effort.

Creating the Environment for Effective Communication

For a Deaf person to maximize their communication abilities, they need to see your face and mouth clearly. Other adjustments to the environment and considerations to keep in mind:

- Position yourself close enough, but not too close. With more than one person in the room, everyone should be able to see each other. Move chairs into a circle; if you must sit at a rectangular table, pull out chairs so no one person is blocking another's face. Before you start a meeting, confirm that what you've set up works for everyone.
- Establish clear sight lines around all physical barriers.
- Make sure there's plenty of light, and that it's in the right place: if you are sitting or standing in front of a window or a lamp, your face and body will be dark and you'll be impossible to understand.
- Make sure nothing is blocking your mouth—your hand on your chin, a folder, a tall object on a desk. Understanding someone with a lot of facial hair can be challenging; the person should be sure to articulate clearly or consider getting an interpreter.
- Eliminate background noise. If more than one person is in the room, only one person should be speaking at a time. The Deaf person should always know who's doing the talking. Wait to make sure that the question or statement has been understood before responding.
- Speak clearly. There's no need to overenunciate or speak more loudly unless you're asked to.

* Be patient. You may have to repeat yourself, maybe more than once.
* Expect to expend some effort yourself in understanding the Deaf person. Deaf speech comes in many forms, and some voices are easier to understand than others.
* Use assistive technology, like the tried-and-true pen and paper, or a speech-to-text App MyEar, to create text for the Deaf person to read.

Hiring and Working with an Interpreter

Whether the Deaf person communicates mostly orally or mostly manually, they may prefer having an ASL interpreter to facilitate interactions. Ask the student or family right away if they would like to have an interpreter, and supply one, at no cost to the family. (Even hinting at the burden of cost implies that a Deaf member and their family are not welcome in your community.)

The family may have a preferred interpreter. If not, or if the interpreter isn't available, reach out to a local referral agency. Search the national Registry of Interpreters for the Deaf (RID; rid.org); you can narrow your search by location, particular certification, and specialty, such as "religious." The Jewish Deaf Resource Center (jdrc.org), the Jewish Deaf Congress (jewishdeafcongress.org), and the Washington Society of the Jewish Deaf (wsjdeaf.com) are good resources for finding interpreters familiar with Judaism, as well as for information about the Jewish Deaf community.

Look for the interpreter to be certified by RID, meaning they have had training and assessments. A well-intentioned member of the congregation who has learned some ASL but not met RID's standards does not qualify as acceptable, especially because of confidentiality concerns; neither does a hearing member of the Deaf student's family. Moreover, and most important, RID-certified interpreters adhere to a broad and strict code of ethics.

When you are communicating with a Deaf person with an ASL interpreter present:

* Defer to the student and interpreter as to where they will position themselves to maximize their sight lines.
* Direct your attention to the student, rather than to the interpreter, and speak directly to the student.

* Give the interpreter copies of all materials you give to your student/family. The more information an interpreter has in advance, the more fluid the interpretation.

Virtual Meetings

Zoom or other virtual meeting platforms may work for some Deaf people. Skilled lip-readers may be comfortable on Zoom. The platform has a speech-to-text function that transcribes spoken English in real time to on-screen captions, but the technology isn't perfect, so your words may be transcribed incorrectly. Keep in mind that the technology can't capture Hebrew at all, so any meeting involving Hebrew may, depending on the student's comprehension, need to occur in person.

Beginning the Learning Journey: Setting Goals and Expectations

Many synagogue communities, wary of the extra effort it might require to prepare a Deaf student for b'nai mitzvah, have steered prospective students elsewhere on religious grounds, saying, for example, "Our b'nai mitzvah students must chant Torah in Hebrew; if this doesn't work for you, we're not the best fit." Students have also had the experience of *wanting* to take on the challenge of Hebrew but being discouraged. Implicit bias about the capabilities of Deaf people leads to lowered expectations, which can make students feel "less than."

Instead, welcome the Deaf prospective b'nai mitzvah and family into your community as you would any other, consistent with your synagogue's policies—whether requiring that they become members, complete a certain number of years of religious school, or become b'nai mitzvah alongside another student. Set a date far enough ahead so the student can meet your shared goals. The service should not have to be modified. Plan for the learning journey by presenting your requirements to the student and family as they are: how much liturgy to lead, how much Torah and/or Haftarah to chant or read. Set the bar high. Begin from the assumption that the Deaf student can meet your community's b'nai mitzvah norms, but express your willingness to be flexible on as many of these as possible. Better to bend like a reed than stand unyielding like a cedar tree!

Language(s) for Liturgy and Torah

Prayer can come in all forms, in all sounds (and, of course, in silence). Darby often tells a variation of a Chasidic story. (*Note: another variation of this story appears in Chapter 8.*) A boy who wants to pray the High Holiday liturgy doesn't know how to pray, and he can't read from the *siddur* (prayer book), so, in tears, he just starts reciting the *alef-bet*. The rabbi hears him and stops the service to point out to the congregation that the most authentic prayer in shul that day is that child's expression from the heart. In Judaism, the most important aspect of prayer is intention.

Note that Jewish law does not require chanting in fulfillment of the mitzvah to read Torah (*Shulchan Aruch*, Orach Chayim 142). It's also permitted according to halachah (Jewish law)—and fully sanctioned by the Conservative and more liberal movements—to declaim Torah in a signed language. Your community may already allow for b'nai mitzvah to read, rather than chant, Torah or read an English translation, but if your custom is to chant and your student feels capable and interested in learning, give them every chance to do so.

A Deaf student may speak with a Deaf accent; that's no reason for them not to lead. The same goes for singing: some Deaf people have learned to hear well enough with hearing aids or cochlear implants that they can sing quite well; some may sing despite not being able to carry a melody at all. Darby admits that his "Deaf singing voice" might not be aesthetically pleasing, but prayer shouldn't have to be!

Your student's expressions from the heart may come in ASL. Be open to that! Using sign language to pray and teach Torah is authentic and permitted by halachah. Determine early on what sections will be signed, and use thoughtful translations, deferring to your student or seeking input from native or fluent ASL users.

Creating original translations as a part of your and your student's work together can add depth of meaning to the learning journey. But be careful and respectful of the language: remember that ASL has its own sentence structure, so rendering every Hebrew word in a sign in English word order would not be an ASL translation. Gestures or other "creative movement," which some communities create to go along with blessings or songs, are not ASL and wouldn't make sense to an ASL user.

Best Practices for Tutoring a Deaf B'nai Mitzvah Student

* Keep individual tutoring sessions at their typical length. Be sensitive to the communication efforts your student may have already expended during the school day, and set realistic goals for each session. (A longer timeline for preparation will allow for the extra time it might take to communicate with your student.)
* One-on-one tutoring typically works best. Trying to follow a conversation and lip-read more than one speaker increases the student's communication challenges.
* While many tutoring sessions occur with the educator and student sitting side by side—sharing a text—this might or might not work for your student. Consider other seating options, such as sitting across from each other, and always defer to the student's preferences.
* Text study involves a lot of looking up and down—remember to wait for your student to look up before you speak!
* Rather than expecting the student to take notes, which requires looking away from the speaker, prepare notes and/or a summary of what you cover in each session.
* If the service includes your student signing liturgy or Torah, build in time for the student to practice the translations.
* If you're lucky enough to have more than one Deaf b'nai mitzvah student, see if they'd like to learn together, or at least be in touch. You'll be supporting the Deaf student in their identity development in more ways than one!

As you would with any student, assess progress throughout the process. Be open and communicative with the student and family early on if you sense that you'll need to make adjustments. No student likes someone else making decisions for them about what they can and can't do, but Deaf people (children and adults alike) have confronted this particular form of discrimination for far too long. Rather than reducing the workload because the b'nai mitzvah date is quickly approaching, allow plenty of time to set goals thoughtfully, together, and for the student to achieve them.

The Service: Ensuring Communication Access for All

Your community may already use methods of communication access such as microphones and speakers, but note that these are all accommodations for the hearing people in the congregation.

You'll need to consider how the Deaf b'nai mitzvah, whether they are on the *bimah* or in the congregation, will know exactly what's going on at all points in the service. All the guidance listed above for creating the ideal environment for communication applies here. For example, consider lighting: Is your prayer space brightly lit enough for visual communication access (ASL or lipreading?) Are there windows in front of which a speaker or interpreter would be in silhouette? Be mindful of your community's practice when it comes to ritual choreography: What might you do if the b'nai mitzvah needs to lip-read the prayer leader(s) as they face the ark? Consider if others on the bimah can shift positions or if objects can be moved for clear sight lines. And, as in all circumstances, let the student express their needs and meet them as best you can.

ASL Interpreters

For anyone at the service who communicates in ASL, you'll need interpreters. If the service incorporates ASL, you'll need interpreters for those who communicate in spoken English—think about interpreters as ensuring equal access for all. You might want to have an interpreter who has been present for all of the tutoring sessions to interpret the service; regardless, book your interpreters as far in advance as possible, preferably as soon as you have a date. Note that the RID *Code of Ethics* and best practices require two interpreters for any job lasting longer than two hours, to reduce fatigue. You'll likely need two, and possibly even three; they'll switch places every twenty minutes or so.

The number of interpreters will depend not only on the length of the service, but also on where those who need to see the interpreters are sitting. For ASL-using members of the congregation, the interpreters should be stationed in the front of the room. If the ASL-using b'nai mitzvah can't also see them, you'll need an additional interpreter. Think through and plan the location of the interpreters well ahead of time, so that no one is scrambling to move chairs and people the day of the event! Find out how many Deaf family members and friends (and their families) will be coming and block off seats in the front row(s), so that they can easily move back and forth between watching the action on the bimah (and maybe even reading lips) and the interpreter. This will allow them to participate in the service, rather than just observe.

Interpreters do not need to know Hebrew to effectively interpret b'nai mitzvah. (However, if you are lucky enough to secure the rare one who also knows Hebrew, they may, with advance preparation, interpret directly from Hebrew into ASL.) When Hebrew is used, interpreters generally do one of the following: sign "Someone is speaking Hebrew now," fingerspell the transliteration of a short section (for instance, *s, h, m, a*), or sign an English translation.

The more materials you can provide an interpreter in advance, the better. In addition to translations, give them an outline of the service, a copy of the *d'var Torah* (Torah teaching), any other English text, and any notes. The interpreter will likely bring these in a binder—so have a music stand available to hold the binder during the service. Depending on the space's acoustics (and your community's permitted use of technology), the interpreter may need a microphone for voice translations of ASL. Invite an interpreter to the rehearsal to discuss any details and potential issues; however, these can also be addressed when the interpreter arrives, usually about half an hour before the start of the event.

A Final Word

Dina, the Deaf woman we quoted at the start of this chapter, told us that because her clergy and tutors did not break down the barriers to communication she faced, "I knew I could never make peace with God in the hearing world." But the imperative to do so comes from Torah itself. Exodus 20:15 says that every member of the community received Torah as Moses revealed it at Sinai, and "All the people saw the sounds." Maybe this was literally so—in that moment, people who used their eyes to communicate accessed Torah in the same way as those who used their ears. Or, as Rabbi Yochanan taught, "When God's voice came forth at Mount Sinai, it divided itself into seventy human languages, so that the whole world might understand it, and every nation heard it in their own language" (*Shemot Rabbah* 5:9).

The word *hear* appears not just in the retelling of the Revelation of Torah, but in fact in the central prayer of our tradition. As you prepare for and embark on the b'nai mitzvah journey with a Deaf student, think about how those who cannot hear can nonetheless find meaning in *Sh'ma Yisrael*, "Hear, O Israel." Our central prayer continues, *Adonai Eloheinu*, "Adonai is our God." Deaf b'nai mitzvah should indeed feel that Adonai is theirs, and, especially at this moment in their lives, that the Torah they read from belongs to them.

✻ CHAPTER 15 ✻

A Perfect Storm:

B'nai Mitzvah, Mental Health Challenges, and Being Thirteen

Audra Kaplan, PhD

Audra Kaplan, a clinical psychologist and adjunct professor, has worked in many leadership roles in disabilities inclusion organizations, including Camp Ramah and Keshet. She outlines different kinds of mental health challenges and provides recommendations for parents, educators, and clergy to help the b'nai mitzvah process become an opportunity to foster positive self-esteem and connection.

A child's mental health directly affects their physical health, ability to learn, and social relationships. Unfortunately, according to the US Centers for Disease Control and Prevention, over the past few decades, youth mental health has declined, with increasing rates of depression, anxiety, and suicidal thoughts. Add exposure to a barrage of social media and its endless flow of world news, violence, sexual content, peer pressure, and conflicting information, and many adolescents feel hopeless and filled with anxiety about their future.

Today, the most prevalent mental health concerns in the United States include depression, anxiety, ADHD, and behavior disorders.

The Role of Parents

Research shows that parents and caregivers can positively shape their children's mental health, and caregivers and educational systems can help youth feel connected, learn coping skills for emotional stressors, and provide early intervention when needed. Supporting a child's biological and social needs, including a need for strong relationships and connection to parents, friends, teachers, and other community members, will significantly contribute to their wellness.

The Jewish life-cycle event of *b'nai mitzvah* offers an opportunity for rabbis, cantors, educators, and other Jewish community members to positively shape a young adult's mental health and support teens with depression and anxiety. These lessons can be applied to *all* teens to build emotional resilience through the b'nai mitzvah process.

From the Parents' Perspective

They all struggle at this time of their life; seventh grade is the worst time to add on the stress of a bat mitzvah for any kid. But for children with anxiety, like my daughter, it is the perfect storm. We worked together to make it work, a team of me, my husband, my daughter, and her tutor.

— Carolyn

Modeling Self-Reflection and Living Jewish Values

B'nai mitzvah is a logical time for parents to talk to their teenagers about values and why Judaism is important to them. Parental attitudes toward b'nai mitzvah will directly affect the teen's motivation and commitment to the b'nai mitzvah experience.

Parents often bring emotions and memories of their own experiences to their child's b'nai mitzvah. For example, a parent whose own parents did not have the financial means for a large celebration may plan one, even though their child would prefer a quieter celebration, such as a *tikun olam* (social action) project with a small group of friends. This type of mismatch between parental expectations and a child's interests and needs can lead to an increase in anxiety.

Parents may also unwittingly put pressure on their child, feeling that the child's performance will reflect upon them as a parent, or become overly focused on comparing their child's performance to that of others.

Parents who approach the b'nai mitzvah process in an open, curious manner can listen—without judgment—to their child's concerns and priorities at this pivotal time. After all, the intention of the b'nai mitzvah is a coming-of-age within the community, a chance to feel competent in the expression of the b'nai mitzvah's new commitments, and an opportunity to feel joy in their growth and accomplishments.

From the Parents' Perspective

My child has extreme anxiety. While my husband and I wanted him to do as much of the service as possible and read Torah and *Haftarah* (reading from the Prophets), we stepped back, listened to, and observed our son. We made the decision that he would read one *aliyah* and the Haftarah at his bar mitzvah and would have other opportunities in the coming year to learn and lead other prayers in the service.

–*Lisa*

The Role of the Synagogue Community

In addition to parental support, forging a connection between the family and the community also helps promote teen mental health and wellness. The synagogue can provide a significant structure for a child to develop positive relationships with peers, receive constructive modeling from older teens, and gain the support of an extended "village." The b'nai mitzvah process allows young teens to develop a connection to Judaism and to feel a sense of purpose within the Jewish community.

B'nai mitzvah can be a key moment for teens to begin thinking about ways they can contribute to their community; in fact, many synagogues require the teen to use b'nai mitzvah as a kick-starter for giving back to their community, such as through volunteer work or donations. These activities can build self-esteem and relieve depressive symptoms.

Developing Emotional Resilience

In addition to being a meaningful Jewish rite of passage, b'nai mitzvah preparation affords opportunities to help teens build emotional resilience. Parents can bolster their children's emotional resilience through this process. Some examples, helpful for all children, include:

- **Self-advocacy:** Encourage teens to speak with the rabbi and tutor well in advance about any concerns; about their emotional, learning, and mental health needs; and to advocate for themselves.
- **Emotional toolbox:** Give teens insight into how mental health can affect their learning, and brainstorm together about what tools will help them weather times of stress.
- **Decision-making:** Involve teens in decision-making for their ceremony and celebration. A sense of control will help them build confidence and decrease anxiety.
- **Collaborative problem-solving:** Problem-solve how to handle difficult social moments leading up to the event, during their ceremony, and at the surrounding celebrations.
- **Meaning-making:** Help teens to find their own understanding of the meaning and importance of having a b'nai mitzvah. Linking the rite of passage to family and Jewish history can enable them to better connect to the greater community.
- **Emotional expression:** Offer opportunities to talk with your child in a relaxed, uninterrupted space (without phones or other distractions); this can show the teen how much you value their thoughts and opinions. The teen can share their concerns and excitement, and the parent can talk about their own b'nai mitzvah (if they had one). Often the teen will be surprised and relieved to hear that their parent also grappled with struggles and disappointments.

- **Healthy habits:** Stress the connection between healthy sleep, eating, and activity with emotional well-being. Keeping a regular schedule for your teen and family, and continuing regular activities are two concrete ways that parents/guardians can help their teen learn, maintain a healthy life balance, and alleviate nervousness. Remember to allow time for play and fun! A good laugh can be the best remedy for stress.

How B'nai Mitzvah Can Trigger Anxiety

The expectations of the b'nai mitzvah process can be daunting—reading in Hebrew (especially if it is not a teen's primary language) in front of a large crowd, writing and giving a *d'var Torah* (Torah teaching) or speech, and representing the family can all be anxiety-inducing. On top of that, it might be the first time a child has to complete a long-term project, one that can take months or years of planning and effort.

For people with social anxiety, everyday social interactions can trigger feelings of fear, self-consciousness, and embarrassment. Teens with social anxiety may have intense fears of peer interactions and exhibit heightened awareness of how they are different from others. They may put a lot of energy into avoiding conflict or not offending others, for fear of others seeing their inadequacies.

Some teens may even lash out at their parents. The teen's reactions might seem extreme and difficult for parents to understand. The b'nai mitzvah may spark inherent anxiety triggers, such as performing in front of others, talking with extended family and unfamiliar congregants, and dealing with the social demands of *kiddush* (social time after synagogue) and a celebration. A party that puts them at the center of attention may also prompt or aggravate anxiety.

Types of Anxiety

Teens with **generalized anxiety disorder** may have constant worry, restlessness, and trouble with concentration. Some teens might have physical symptoms, such as stomachache, headache, or a feeling of bodily jitters.

Obsessive-compulsive disorder (OCD) is characterized by unreasonable thoughts and fears (obsessions) that lead to compulsive behaviors. OCD often centers on themes such as a fear of germs or the need to arrange objects in a specific manner. The b'nai mitzvah, with requisite congratulatory hugging or handshakes, kissing of the Torah, sharing ceremonial objects, and a need to perform perfectly, might be especially challenging for teens with OCD. Some teens with OCD might also become upset if they make a mistake while reading Torah and are corrected in front of the congregation.

Performance anxiety happens when the pressure to perform becomes too intense. Performance anxiety can happen to athletes, public speakers, musicians, and of course, b'nai mitzvah students. Symptoms of performance anxiety might include a racing heartbeat, rapid breathing, trembling, sweaty or cold hands, dry mouth, nausea, or a need to use the bathroom.

Panic attacks may occur in some teens with anxiety. A panic attack is a brief episode of intense anxiety, which causes the physical sensations of fear: racing heartbeat, shortness of breath, dizziness, trembling, and muscle tension. Panic attacks can occur frequently and unexpectedly and are often not related to any specific trigger. They are more likely if a teen is overtired, has not eaten well, or is under excessive stress. If a teen has a history of panic attacks or panic disorder, it will be important for them to maintain their routine in the days leading up to the b'nai mitzvah, including their sleep schedule, regular exercise and activities, and downtime. Discuss the issue with the clergy and tutor early on in the process so that they can approach the teen with knowledge and empathy.

It is important to distinguish between worry and anxiety, as noted below:

Worry: situational moment of concern, fear, or nervousness	Anxiety: prolonged or intense worry that interferes with daily living
* Worry about an upcoming b'nai mitzvah * Nervous about trying something new. * Nervous about making friends * Feeling uncertain about attending your first b'nai mitzvah party. * Preoccupation with what to wear to a friend's b'nai mitzvah. * Worry that comes and goes	* Excessive worry about friendships, school, social situations, the health or safety of family members, or the future in general * Catastrophizing: thinking that the worst will happen * Repetitive and frequent thoughts about ________________ * Agitation, nervousness, rumination, repeatedly asking the same questions, talking quickly, fidgeting, withdrawing from activities or self-imposed isolation, change in eating or sleeping pattern * Crying or arguing before every tutoring session * Avoiding or refusing to attend a friend's b'nai mitzvah * Experiencing consistent physical symptoms every weekend that there is a b'nai mitzvah

How Parents and Guardians Can Support a Teen with Anxiety

While increased anxiety and emotional sensitivity go hand-in-hand with teen years for most people, parents can mitigate these feelings by using specific strategies.

Listen and Hear

Take the time to listen with open curiosity and without judgment. Don't anticipate the outcome of the conversation. Hearing the teen's thoughts and worries about their upcoming b'nai mitzvah will better position you to support and advocate for them.

Lay the Groundwork

Preparation for the special day should begin years in advance. A child's familiarity with the service, as well as their comfort with Hebrew or English prayers and their meaning, can help alleviate the unknown and decrease anxiety. Attending synagogue before they begin to prepare for the b'nai mitzvah will allow them to become familiar with the service, understand what's expected of them (that is, when to stand and sit), and build endurance long before the added emotional load of beginning their lessons. Parents should model the type of behavior that they would like to see from their child. Many synagogues now have an array of youth services, which are a wonderful way to encourage youngsters to feel comfortable in a service setting and learn prayers at an age-appropriate level.

Arrange for your child to have opportunities to be in front of the congregation at least a year before their b'nai mitzvah, doing things such as leading shorter prayers, perhaps Ein Keiloheinu or Adon Olam (the service-concluding prayer). If your synagogue does not have these opportunities, advocate for them with your clergy. They give the child the chance to stumble and learn from the experience, developing resilience in the process. Common prayers that pre–b'nai mitzvah children lead also include Ashrei and Anim Z'mirot, but your synagogue may have its own traditions. Once your child begins studying for their b'nai mitzvah, they will get a taste of the process and the reinforcement of how good it feels to succeed.

As the parent or guardian, you are the bridge between your child and their tutor, rabbi, and other educators, so you need to give them as much insight into your child as possible. Their understanding and knowledge of your child's learning needs will enable them to tailor your child's b'nai mitzvah preparation plan and give your child the greatest chance for success.

Leading up to B'nai Mitzvah

In the preparation time before their b'nai mitzvah, help your teen to:

4–6 months before:	* Develop a study routine * Learn relaxation techniques * Maintain healthy habits (eating and drinking, sleeping, exercising)
One month before:	* Encourage your teen to practice what they have learned and already mastered, rather than learning any new material. This will give them more time to build confidence and absorb the material. Get them to practice in the sanctuary and on the *bimah*. If they'll be reading Torah, ask to have them practice a few times from the Torah they will be reading from. * Practice breathing techniques and mindfulness with your teen. This will enable them to relax and move from negative to positive thoughts. * Talk through scenarios of how to manage the unexpected, from a cell phone ringing during chanting, to an unruly congregant, to needing a bathroom break. * Make sure they keep to their routine, especially exercise and sports. * Focus on the positive, and help the child visualize herself being successful.
Day of:	* Eat a good breakfast, but limit sugar and caffeine. * Keep a bottle of water on the bimah in case of dry mouth. * Focus on the positive, and help the child visualize herself being successful.

Extreme Shyness, Quiet Voices, and Performance Anxiety

There are students whose extreme shyness exceeds the typical bounds of nervousness. For these students, anxiety results in being unwilling or unable to be audible. We approach this gingerly, and creatively. Here are two strategies.

Avigail spoke and sang in the quietest voice imaginable. She was extremely nervous at the thought of anyone listening to her sing. Three months before her bat mitzvah, we moved lessons to the synagogue chapel on Sunday mornings. First, we met sitting down in the room; then, we stood up at the bimah; then we timed our lesson so early arrivals at minyan (quorum of ten Jewish adults) would overlap with us but not hear us; then we sang the smallest amount of Torah reading possible for people who came to the minyan to hear, until—slowly but surely—she was ready to sing on the big day.

Jonathan was a super-smart student and a member of the debate team, so he surprised me when he refused to sing alone. For many weeks, I compromised with him. I said, "I'll sing loud, you move your lips only." Eventually, I said, "I'll turn up my volume (pretend) and you turn yours down . . . "

We then gradually switched the balance of our volume controls. When it came time to practice with the rabbi in the main sanctuary, Jonathan refused to sing and shut down. The rabbi held his hand and slowly, slowly, he began to sing—and the congregation was able to hear his sweet voice on his bar mitzvah day.

—H.B.

Working with Teens with Anxiety: Guidance for Educators and Clergy

Clergy and Jewish educators can be sensitive to the needs of teens with anxiety in a variety of non–labor-intensive ways. This will benefit anyone going through the b'nai mitzvah process.

- Start early. Starting at least a year before the scheduled date will allow teens to pace their learning.
- Set clear and specific expectations of the teen. Make sure to provide clear explanations of what will happen at the b'nai mitzvah service.
- Create a study calendar leading up to the b'nai mitzvah, with clear goals and expectations. Have the parents share any academic tools and tricks that the teen uses at school to help ease the learning process. Provide mini-celebrations when the teen meets those goals.
- Teens with anxiety may take longer to form a connection with their tutor or clergy. Invest time in getting to know the teen before beginning lessons. Learn the teen's interests, style of learning, and their feelings about b'nai mitzvah.
- Understand that fears may inhibit the teen from trying new things, and being in front of a congregation might terrify them.
- Break down the learning process into small increments so that the teen feels success with each step of the process. Give positive feedback throughout.
- Reinforce that the at-home work is the teen's responsibility but encourage parents to provide positive reinforcement and to avoid power struggles.
- Be patient and flexible. Showing patience will go a long way in settling the teen's nerves. Being flexible will show the teen that they are more important to you than the service being perfect.
- Gradually give the teen additional opportunities to acclimate to b'nai mitzvah. For example, show the teen photos or short video clips of other teens performing parts of their b'nai mitzvah. Give the teen the opportunity to participate in youth or family services to build their comfort level. Have the teen learn and lead prayers with a small group from the congregation.

* Use a range of teaching styles and sensory modalities, such as visual, tactile, and musical.
* Practice, practice, practice, including the social aspects and choreography of the service. If the teen will be walking with the Torah, explain how this is done. If the teen will be sitting on the bimah, explain where and how to sit, and how to greet others who have honors. Fist bumps, high fives, or handshakes may be more socially comfortable for the teen than hugs and kisses.
* Show empathy for teens' worries, recognizing that these are very real concerns for a teen.
* Some teens with anxiety might have worries about physical reactions during the service, such as fainting, throwing up, or needing to use the bathroom. Be careful not to dismiss these fears or attempt to convince them that it will not happen. Problem-solve with them on what they can do if they have these urges during the service. Focus on concrete plans, such as where they can keep a bottle of water or some candy if they feel weak. Plan out the best times to take a break, if needed. Be sure to have a communication plan so that everyone on the bimah knows the teen's plan.

From the Parents' Perspective

Our son struggles with a mood disorder, as well as having anxiety and a learning disorder. For his bar mitzvah we worked with the rabbi to determine what were the essential things for our son to learn. He also learned his Torah portion phonetically (instead of reading Hebrew). It was more important to us that he have a positive experience, since he has his whole lifetime to learn and lead other prayers when he is ready. We filled the year with incremental, small special moments and celebrations. A year before his bar mitzvah date, we took him to buy his own tallit (prayer shawl). We wanted him to enjoy the process and not just the day.

–Amanda

Depression

Feeling sad is a healthy, normal part of life, especially for teenagers. For some teens the sadness comes out of nowhere, triggered by something as simple as a TV show or a song on the radio. Often sadness can be a reaction to a loss or disappointment, or a fight with a friend, or the end of a romantic relationship. Usually, the sadness passes quickly, and the teen moves on to something else.

For other teens, feelings of sadness do not go away, and the origin of the sadness is not always known. These depressive feelings and thoughts are persistent and present for most of the day. Teens with depression might lose interest in activities, or stop enjoying their preferred activities, have difficulty concentrating, or experience a decrease in energy levels. Others might not display sadness but have an increase in irritability or anger. A parent or teacher might assume that a teen has an anger-management or defiance problem, but another explanation for the behavior could be depression.

Sadness: situational or transient feelings	Depression: frequent, persistent, or intense sadness or despair
Age-appropriate and temporary reactions to school stress, losses, disappointments	Persistent feelings of sadness that last for two or more weeks and interfere with a teen's ability to eat, sleep, engage in activities, and maintain friendships
Upset and temporary reaction to a disagreement with a friend	Withdrawal from peers, frequent crying, mood swings, appears agitated or angry
Crying because of breakup of a friendship or romantic relationship	Inability to sleep or eat, or other noticeable change in daily functioning, because of a breakup of a friendship or romantic relationship
Melancholy at bedtime	Expression of hopelessness or helplessness
Generally happy and engaged in typical activities, including learning	Significant decrease in energy level and/or excessive agitation or argumentativeness

From the Parents' Perspective

Our son was resisting studying for his Haftarah. He would become teary-eyed when anyone asked him about his bar mitzvah. When we would remind him to study, he would whine and yell. My wife and I found ourselves getting frustrated and losing our patience with him. We decided to take a step back and give him space. Once we took the pressure off for a few days and then had an open conversation, our son was able to share that he was having trouble concentrating because of self-doubt. Instead of putting additional pressure on him, we worked with his tutor to break down the tasks and started checking in on his feelings more often.

—Joelle

Parent Support for a Teen with Depression

Many of the suggestions for parents supporting a teen with anxiety apply to teens with depression as well. But it is worth emphasizing several key points:

- **Lead with empathy and be curious.** A caring, trusting connection with parents or caregivers can make all the difference in how teens feel about themselves and how they cope with their emotions. Throughout the process, check in with your teen to see how they are feeling. Your teen may be more nervous about the celebration than being called to the Torah.
- **Consider emotional resources**. When planning the b'nai mitzvah weekend, consider your teen's and your family's emotional resources. Allow for downtime during the weekend to restore energy.
- **Praise and reinforce.** Learning for a b'nai mitzvah is a long process. Offering frequent and specific praise will help to keep teens motivated and build their confidence.
- **Be aware of social discomfort**. There is a fine line between encouraging teens to attend others' b'nai mitzvah and forcing them into social situations for which they are emotionally

unprepared. Offer them opportunities for building social connections, such as participation in Jewish camps, youth groups, sports, and school clubs.

* **Include them in the decision-making.** This will increase their sense of control.
* **Build in giving opportunities.** When teens are depressed, they are more likely to be overly inner-focused. Volunteerism can help teens build community connections and boost self-esteem.

From the Parents' Perspective

While we would have enjoyed having a Friday night dinner with our extended family during the b'nai mitzvah weekend, we knew that our son would be both physically and emotionally exhausted by a big event. Instead, we chose to have a quiet Shabbat dinner at home and let our son save his emotional energy for his Saturday morning service.

–Jeff

Working with Teens with Depression: Guidance for Jewish Educators and Clergy

* Get to know the teen and their family, their interests and motivations. Many families expressed the importance of having a rabbi or Jewish educator get to know their teen before b'nai mitzvah tutoring begins. Especially for a child with depression, a safe relationship can make a tremendous difference in learning.
* During lessons, focus solely on the teen. Turn off notifications on your phone and computer.
* Set up expectations for success. Determine what are the absolute expectations, such as reciting the blessings before and after Torah reading. As one parent shared, "Everything else is icing on the cake."
* Be open to alternatives to the standard b'nai mitzvah service. (See Chapters 5, 8, and 9 for specific ideas.)

- Give authentic and real praise and encouragement. Feedback that is as specific and concrete as possible will enhance the student's learning. For example, saying something as simple as "Nice job reading that Hebrew word, the sounds can be tricky and you pronounced it so well!" can make a huge difference in a teen's confidence.
- Provide ample time for processing. Allow breaks if the teen needs time to regroup or refuel.

From the Parents' Perspective

My daughter, who is introverted and struggles with self-confidence, expressed that she did not want to study with her bat mitzvah tutor. At first, I thought it was related to her depression and lack of motivation. But then when I sat and talked with her, she shared that her tutor would check his email and answer messages while she was learning her Haftarah. My daughter was too shy to say anything. I needed to step in and express to the tutor how their behavior would be hard for most students, but especially a student with low confidence. I chose to sit in on the next few sessions until he repaired the connection with my teen.

—Adam

Remember Why You're Doing This

For many children with anxiety or depression, the completion of the b'nai mitzvah experience can bring feelings of triumph, possibility, and pride. In many cases, this achievement is the biggest of the child's life thus far. Savor and celebrate this moment: the teen can now take their place in their community, and the parent and community have also triumphed in traveling with the teen to this new territory. Everyone will have learned a lot, so slow down and enjoy this special milestone.

✱ CHAPTER 16 ✱

Teaching *Their* Torah:

Beyond the Traditional B'nai Mitzvah Speech

Rabbi Rebecca Schatz

Rabbi Rebecca Schatz, associate rabbi at Temple Beth Am in Los Angeles, shares inspiration for alternatives to the traditional b'nai mitzvah speech. She strongly believes that every b'nai mitzvah has the ability to engage with Torah and share insights from it in a format that works best for them.

Too often, the *b'nai mitzvah* experience is cookie-cutter: the number of *aliyot* (calls to the Torah), what students should chant, what service they should lead, what the *d'var Torah* (Torah teaching) should sound like. However, no two teens are exactly the same; therefore, they should be treated as unique individuals on the day of their b'nai mitzvah. They are not up on the *bimah* at age twelve or thirteen to audition as a mini future-rabbi. They are standing up to lead their community as new Jewish adults taking on *mitzvot*, responsibility, and having learned skills to enhance their Jewish connection. The d'var Torah is an opportunity for a child to teach something they have learned from the process. So, it need not be a speech—it could be anything that reflects the way a child has learned and is interested in teaching their community.

At Camp Ramah in Ojai, California, I was often involved in creating programming and opportunities for all kinds of campers. There are campers who are interested in sports, or art, or movement, or singing, or writing, and so on. And, of course, there are campers who are neurotypical and campers who are neurodivergent. The Theory of Multiple Intelligences—posited by psychologist Howard Gardner—holds that no matter what is being taught, students should have the opportunity to explore learning in the way that they grasp information best. Based on this theory, any program that I created for Camp Ramah would have multiple ways "in" for comfort of participation and maximum acquisition of knowledge for all campers.

Tailor the Learning

I apply this theory to our b'nai mitzvah as well. I begin the process of sitting with a student who is learning their Torah portion by asking them, "Will you understand this information best by reading out loud, listening to it read to you, reading to yourself, listening while playing soccer, while standing up, sitting down, with a fidget, in person, over Zoom, using technology to read and understand, or is feeling the book in your hand and using a pen to take notes better for you?" Sometimes these questions take clarifying follow-ups, based on what I know about the student as their teacher. While "playing soccer" might be their preferred answer, what I really need to know is how they like to learn. From the beginning, the student knows that I am interested in their learning, comfort, and ability to retain information. Once I find a way into the learning, the fun can begin!

Tailor the Service

Part of d'var Torah-writing reflects culture. The first student to have a b'nai mitzvah and not give a traditional d'var Torah will be courageous, if giving a d'var Torah has been the community's norm. However, breaking that norm, to allow some students to give *divrei Torah* (Torah teachings) and others to teach in whatever way they prefer, will create additional questions about how the service may go. Allow the student, and their family, options and ownership over elements of the day that will enhance their learning and interest in this life-cycle event.

For example, I have seen families choose to sing a special rendition of the children's blessing that is their custom on Shabbat. I have witnessed others create bingo cards to allow those in attendance to follow the service. Some families create a program book, explaining certain elements of the rituals in case there are attendees who are not familiar with b'nai mitzvah.

Helping a Student Teach Their Torah

I often start a conversation with a b'nai mitzvah student with a question: "What is interesting to you about your Torah portion?" After hearing an answer, or helping the student arrive at an answer, my follow-up is this: "What would you like to teach the community about this?" When they can give me an informal thesis, I ask the final question of this trio: "How would you like to teach?" I suggest examples that I have seen before, or prompt them to explain the format of something they have taught or learned in the past. Most often I hear, "I want to give a speech like my friends." Sometimes that is exactly what the student should do. At other times, I know they will be more interested in learning Torah if they can do it through a favorite hobby or a medium. This cannot be forced, of course—most students will still write a d'var Torah—but for those who appreciate the joy of learning and teaching through creativity, the student and I consider options based on their interests.

Individualization Is Key

One child, Aliza, with elective mutism, had verbalized her studies with her tutors, but could not do it in a public setting. At her bat mitzvah, it was explained that Aliza had the knowledge to lead a service but lacked the confidence to do it in a public setting. At each point where she would have spoken, Aliza's best friend would say, "Aliza would like me to share" and she would say it for her. When it was Aliza's turn to read from Torah, she whispered into the cantor's ear, who would say, "Aliza just said X and Y," and then the cantor would verbalize the Hebrew.

—I.T. and H.B.

B'nai mitzvah students need to be encouraged to teach THEIR Torah, the piece of Jewish history and tradition that is guiding them in this moment, not THE Torah. Over the years, the majority of my students have given traditional b'nai mitzvah speeches, and that is totally fine. Again, a lot of that is grounded in culture.

However, those that have been outside the box not only needed differentiated learning, but created something memorable and unique to them. I had a student create a museum walk of her art, based on commentaries written about the Song of the Sea. I had a nonverbal student create a Jewish holidays video game that was sent out to the community in advance of and after his bar mitzvah so that he could share his learning with everyone. Another student created a graphic novel for her *Haftarah* (reading from the Prophets), giving a brief verbal introduction and leading everyone to follow along through their own copy of her book and more deeply understand the Song of Deborah. A student who celebrated her bat mitzvah at the evening service created art pieces that she shared as an interactive teaching.

Grant's Family History Video

Grant's family was intercultural and interfaith. Beyond the different religions, his grandparents were from different parts of the world and didn't get along. Looking to find common ground and heal the rift, Grant managed to honor both traditions with his untraditional bar mitzvah d'var Torah. While Judaism was his mother's family's religion, Grant wanted to involve his non-Jewish family as well. So, Grant, who has learning disabilities, decided to make a short film chronicling the one thing both sides had in common—coming to America through Ellis Island. The film served as a visual d'var Torah with a very clear message: We have more in common than we think, and we should embrace our similarities and celebrate our differences.

Using Zoom

During the pandemic, our world became the epitome of creativity. I saw students create videos and game shows to share, as well as musical performances or Torah dramatizations performed on Zoom. All of these expressions have the added potential to involve family and friends in the learning journey. While using Zoom as a platform for b'nai mitzvah may be problematic for a traditional community, the possibilities are endless if the service is held on Monday, Thursday, or Rosh Chodesh (new month)— that is, not on Shabbat.

A Bat Mitzvah and an Art Opening

Lisa was an extremely shy Modern Orthodox girl. For her bat mitzvah, she could have participated in a woman's prayer service, or learned a text and delivered a *d'var Torah* (Torah teaching), but she did not want to speak publicly. Instead, her family and teachers tapped into her artistic talents. Lisa created a series of paintings that served as illustrations and interpretations of biblical stories. They were mounted on artist's easels, and guests attended a "bat mitzvah art opening": an evening of special drinks, hors d'oeuvres, and other party foods. Family and friends walked around the room admiring and learning from Lisa's art—no speech required.

—H.B.

My goal as a rabbi is to find a way for the b'nai mitzvah student to become a teacher. Together we discover what moves them in this moment of their Jewish journey, and how to express it through a medium that is going to bring them comfort, joy, and some challenge. Most b'nai mitzvah do not become rabbis, but hopefully most gain confidence to stay Jewishly connected, proud, and engaged in their community. I am always honored by the opportunity to work with a growing student and their family. You can do this too: ask questions that create unique connections for the student. Help them demonstrate their learning in a way that is authentic to them as individuals. No matter what their developmental or neurological ability, there is always a way to connect learning and teaching that will enhance their Jewish life and feeling of belonging in the community.

✱ CHAPTER 17 ✱

Learning Disabilities:

The Diagnosis Does Not Define the Child

Sheldon H. Horowitz, PhD

Sheldon H. Horowitz, an expert in the field of learning disabilities, worked at the National Center for Learning Disabilities for twenty-six years. He applies the latest knowledge from the field to b'nai mitzvah learning and teaching, and reflects on his family's personal journey, supporting children with disorders of learning, language, attention, and behavior.

Understanding Specific Learning Disabilities

Of all the many possible categories and classifications of struggle a child can experience during their school years, learning disabilities (LDs) are the most frequently occurring and the least understood. Despite the prevalence of LDs, survey after survey demonstrates that some people still attribute LDs to things like poor vision, laziness, and even low intelligence—none of which is true and all of which can be incredibly hurtful, creating artificial barriers to success in all aspects of a child's life.

B'nai mitzvah preparation is no exception. Let's take a close look at LDs through the lens of this ritual, and challenge ourselves and our synagogue communities to truly understand LDs and celebrate the journey of children with LDs and their families.

Before delving into effective approaches to bar and bat mitzvah preparation, it is important to restate the obvious. Whether in schools or in synagogues, in families or in the outside community, there are still those who believe that LDs are "mild" or that LDs aren't even a "real" thing; that people with LDs are just "lazy" or "unmotivated" and that their struggles are a result of not trying hard enough. *NOT TRUE!* If anything, the opposite is the case. Individuals with LDs must exert *more* effort, *more* time, and *more* careful attention to accomplish tasks that place demands on their specific areas of weakness, rather than showcasing areas of strength. Shedding the shame and blame that all too often define the LD experience, especially during the middle school years, needs to be part of how we prepare children for a smooth, meaningful, and impactful transition into Jewish adulthood.

You Don't Look Like You Have a Disability

I can't count how many times I've heard parents and educators worry out loud about b'nai mitzvah preparation for children who have specific learning disabilities and attention disorders, such as attention deficit / hyperactivity disorder (ADHD). "He does not want to go to his lesson" or, "How is she supposed to learn so much Hebrew when reading in English is such a struggle?"

When I ask whether the teacher or tutor knows about the child's LD, all too often the answer is no, to which I immediately respond, "Well, why not?" No one *looks like* they have a learning disability unless they are required to perform tasks that relate to their specific areas of weakness. And unless you know, you can't explore opportunities to work around barriers and build on the child's strengths and interests.

LDs are sometimes referred to as "hidden or invisible disabilities" because they are indeed hidden in plain sight. For example, having a reading disability (sometimes called dyslexia) is not apparent until you look more closely and notice that the child is guessing at the sounds that letters make, focusing attention on the wrong line of text, or even looking at a different page. Very often, these children will try to memorize rather than sound out words and will go to great lengths not to expose their weakness. Needless to say, whether they struggle with reading, writing, spelling, math, or any other subject, trying to stay under the radar is not just hard work—it's exhausting.

Focus on Confidence Building

If a child's progress in learning and remembering b'nai mitzvah material from one lesson to the next is unexpectedly slow or uneven, or if they seem to be working on overdrive to keep up with the pace of teaching and practice, ask how they prefer to approach learning in school and whether there are techniques that they have found to be helpful. Do this whether or not they've been formally identified as having an LD. Don't jump to conclusions, keep expectations high, and make sure that every aspect of your work builds confidence, fuels enthusiasm, and supports perseverance and resilience.

There is no single set of characteristics that defines LDs. Even children whose LD leads them to struggle with reading are not poor readers all the time. When presented with reading tasks that include words they have memorized or seen and practiced many times, and when the subject they are reading about and the vocabulary presented is familiar or about a favorite topic, their performance may seem effortless, accurate, and flawless to the listener.

This is very much the case with b'nai mitzvah study. One of my adult students became increasingly upset at the start of her lessons, saying she wished she knew the meaning of the words she was learning to chant. I asked her to pick out a handful of words, and she immediately selected a dozen or so whose sound she especially liked. She used these words as anchors as she mastered more and more of the reading, and the smile on her face (not to mention her pride and confidence) when she reached each of those words in the text was priceless.

It's Hard to Predict for Whom This Will Be Tough or Easy

Parents of children who are gifted academically naturally assume that learning for *b'nai mitzvah* will be easy. Parents of children with learning disabilities (LDs) assume this process will be challenging if not outright torturous. I have found that torture or ease is often very unpredictable, since learning for b'nai mitzvah involves so many things and there are many tricks, strategies, and workarounds.

For example, Jesse's parents would have been delighted if he could chant three lines of Torah, given his language-based learning disability. Yet, his perfect pitch, amazing auditory memory, and guitar playing made learning to read Torah a snap—as long as the learning took place in transliteration and did not involve Hebrew decoding.

Max, another student with LDs, who attended a school for children with LDs, had supportive parents who would never push him to read the entire portion. Max's drive and determination to master chanting Torah enabled him to learn the *entire* Torah portion—all seven *aliyot* (calls to the Torah). It is important not to make assumptions, since so many factors are at work. Be ready to be surprised!

—H.B.

Stigma and Shame Are Not Welcome Here

Here's a challenge for the grown-ups in the room: Imagine a job where you have a great group of colleagues, and where you have areas of expertise that are recognized, even celebrated, by others. But there's one area that is your weak spot, your Achilles' heel, and you are constantly on the alert for ways to "hide" or "escape" attention. Then it happens: You need to step up and perform a task that plays to your weakness rather than your strengths.

* Is your heart pounding yet and do you sense your palms beginning to get sweaty?
* Can you feel your fight-or-flight-or-freeze instinct triggered?
* Are you suddenly sensing heightened self-awareness, finding it hard to concentrate and focus, and maybe feeling embarrassed?

Unfortunately, this is all too often the reality for children with LDs, and it doesn't go away after leaving school and entering the synagogue. The kinds of b'nai mitzvah–related things that can affect a child with LD include: sensitivity to certain types of clothing, auditory processing challenges when speaking into a microphone, or trouble figuring out where to look with all the shifting choreography and visual stimuli on the *bimah*.

LDs by Any Other Name Are Still LDs

There's an old baseball saying: "You can't tell the players without a scorecard." It may be helpful to think about LDs in the same way.

LDs pose particular challenges that do not stem from lack of effort, capacity to learn, or poor teaching. And LDs can manifest themselves in any language! Even children who have experienced success in (secular) school may struggle in tasks associated with b'nai mitzvah in unexpected ways. For example:

* Leading prayers (in English as well as in Hebrew) requires a level of comfort and facility with oral reading and public speaking.
* Reading from the Torah requires significant short-term memory skill as well as the ability to pronounce words in a non-native language.
* Reading both Torah and *Haftarah* (reading from the Prophets) portions require the precise integration of multiple "systems" (sounds/music; articulation of letter combinations into words; prosody of speech—intonation, stress pattern, loudness variations, pausing, and rhythm).
* Following the flow of the service requires significant attentional and executive functioning skills.
* Children with LD are likely to need targeted instruction, opportunities for practice, and ongoing support that is different from those of their peers.

LDs may not be visible in all situations. Since the vast majority of individuals with LDs struggle in the area of literacy, challenges can be anticipated when children are asked to engage in tasks that involve reading and writing (including spelling, organizing main ideas and details, and selecting vocabulary). Writing and delivering a *d'var Torah* (Torah teaching) could be especially difficult and would require extra time and support. And, some kids with LDs really shine with the support.

LDs happen along a continuum of severity. Some children may not meet their school district's threshold for LD classification, meaning that even though LDs are present, they remain undetected. So a personalized and individualized approach to b'nai mitzvah preparation for every child—with and without formal LD status—is of utmost importance.

It is important to remember that emotional and behavioral difficulties do not fall under the LD label. Think about this: You're going to school every day (or Hebrew school once or twice a week) and feeling unprepared, poorly equipped to participate, fearful of getting called on to read aloud or to repeat something that was taught. It's no surprise that children who have LDs may demonstrate characteristics such as low self-esteem, anxiety, depression, social isolation, and frustration, all of which could result in poor attention or disruptive behavior (none of which are part of the LD definition, but all of which can derail progress). Why the need to go into so much detail about the definition of LDs? Because knowledge is power when it comes to planning for success. Everyone who participates in b'nai mitzvah preparation should be sure that efforts have been made to provide adequate time, appropriate instruction, and support in Hebrew school and other synagogue settings.

Signs of LDs are often only evident when there is a mismatch between the child's inherent capabilities and the expectations of a particular situation or environment. For example, when a child who has a specific LD in reading is not expected to perform reading tasks, the "disability" seems to go away or at least not matter very much; that is, it doesn't impede their success.

How does this connect to b'nai mitzvah preparation? Maximize opportunities for the child to shape and engage in a set of experiences—from creating a tallit (prayer shawl) to Torah reading, from leading a service to delivering a d'var Torah to performing a mitzvah project that allows them to shine.

What Does the Brain Have to Do with It?

While no two brains are alike (not even in identical twins!) and the brain is constantly changing during early childhood through late adolescence, how a child learns best is as much a consequence of their neurological makeup as it is a response to their lived experience.

For b'nai mitzvah instruction, this means there are things that can—and, especially for children with LDs, should—be done during the years and months before beginning instruction. Among them:

- Begin to build a Hebrew vocabulary (listening as well as speaking), and consider music with Hebrew lyrics as a fun and effective way to do this.
- Introduce concepts, information, and skills using a variety of strategies and techniques (for instance, singing, drawing, even movement, such as hand tapping and dancing).
- Give b'nai mitzvah students opportunities to remember and create personal strategies with personal ways ("tricks") that work for them (you'll be amazed at the mnemonic devices—tricks for keeping track of the Hebrew letters, cues—they invent!).

A few other important things to keep in mind:

- Some children who struggle with b'nai mitzvah preparation may not have been formally identified as having LDs. These are often children who were "late talkers" and who may appear to have mild or intermittent language challenges that pop up from time to time.
- Lived experiences matter a lot. For example, a child who has musical training, or has been immersed in settings where Hebrew language is sung or spoken, may have an easier time learning a Torah or Haftarah portion. Networks in these children's brains have been primed to recognize, store, retrieve, and respond to these types of input and stimulation.
- Brain development is also influenced by the quality of a child's relationships and sense of safety, belonging, and self-confidence, so making sure that the b'nai mitzvah preparation process becomes a positive experience is not just a nice thing to do; it's supported by neuroscience!

* Each child with a learning disability has their own individual challenges. The key to success for these children is to personalize instruction and support to match who they are as unique students.

A Panda Named HaMivorach

Before I started working with Max for his bar mitzvah, his mother explained that Max didn't know how to decode in English, so learning to read Hebrew was out of the question. We would need to think creatively about how to teach Max the Torah blessings. We knew Max had a good auditory memory, that he was tactile, and that he loved technology and gadgets. We considered using a recording to learn the blessings by memory. Then Max's older brother Jake had the brilliant idea of giving each of his stuffed animals a name corresponding to a blessing like *HaMivorach* (the blessing before the Torah is read is *Baruch Adonai HaMivorach*). During tutoring sessions, I would point to each animal as their name came up in the respective blessing, and Max would know to sing it. (He simultaneously pounded out the rhythm of the blessing with drumsticks.) By the day of his bar mitzvah, Max knew everything, and the stuffed animals stayed home.

—H.B.

LDs in Families

Parents will sometimes confide that they have a learning disability—diagnosed or otherwise. This comes up frequently, though it is rarely explicit and requires some good detective work or sleuthing. I often ask parents to share the story of their *b'nai mitzvah* learning with their child. I ask what they did, how they learned, and what the experience was like. It opens a discussion between parent and child about process and expectation. I then assure them that there is no one right way to learn and that the only thing I am very rigid about is that we find the best way in for that student—be it auditory, visual, kinesthetic, or some combination.

—H.B.

Behaviors and Characteristics Associated with LDs

Some hurdles associated with LDs may be expected, such as staying focused (it's hard enough to maintain focus when dealing with the English language, no less Hebrew!), preparing a d'var Torah, and even writing thank-you notes for presents received. Some of these challenges are less predictable because they vary in how they affect learning from one person to another.

For many children who have an LD, language in general and reading in particular are incredibly challenging. For example:

- Even familiar words are often misheard (for example, Pulitzer Prize = "pullet surprise," Caesar salad = "seizure salad") or mispronounced (diagram = "dying gram").
- The speed and accuracy of reading is delayed, and rhythm intonation, stress pattern, loudness variations, and pausing, (sometimes referred to as prosody) are not quite right.
- Vocabulary is often fine, and comprehension skills may be age- and grade-appropriate, but organizing thoughts into coherent sentences and paragraphs can be challenging. Often, creativity is unexpectedly strong. Asking a child to develop a story to explain the Torah portion can work at times.

ADHD and Executive Functioning

Studies show that as many as 45 percent of kids with attention deficit / hyperactivity disorder (ADHD) also have a learning disability, according to Understood.org, a nonprofit dedicated to raising awareness and changing attitudes about learning and thinking differences. These students struggle with written expression (65 percent), reading (32 percent), or math (30 percent). Only about 5 percent of kids without ADHD have a learning disability.

LD and ADHD both have an impact on executive functioning, often referred to as the "management system of the brain," which lets us plan and get things done. Executive functioning involves such mental skills as working memory, flexible thinking, and self-control. Difficulties in these areas cause trouble focusing, staying on task, following direction, managing emotions, and more. Symptoms of ADHD (with or without a learning disability) may impact both the learning process and the celebration.

The student may require shorter learning sessions (thirty minutes as opposed to sixty), snack breaks, and special accommodations by the teacher. I once worked with a bar mitzvah student who sang as we swung on swings next to each other in his backyard. Other students enjoy doodling on their bat mitzvah sheets, and still others have learned their chanting while using a Hula-Hoop or dancing.

The student may also require accommodations at the service itself, including frequent breaks, walking around the sanctuary during parts of the service, not sitting on the *bimah* for extended (or possibly any) periods of time, or using fidget tools. Also helpful can be a party that includes facilitated games, shooting baskets, or using other ways of being active as opposed to more sedentary, speech-filled receptions.

—H.B.

Breaking Down Reading into Its Elements

Below is a list of building blocks of learning and development, common to most people, but which may require specific tailoring when teaching kids with LDs:

Building blocks of learning	Implications for children who have LDs during b'nai mitzvah preparation
Attention: Processing specific information in the environment while tuning out other details	* Make sure that the goals and expectations for each lesson are clear. * Create a cozy, quiet space without a lot of visual stimuli, so the child can focus. * Adjust the pace of instruction to avoid attention overload, which can trigger anxiety and frustration. (Remember: positive emotions support learning; negative ones undermine learning!)
Auditory Processing: How the brain recognizes and interprets speech as well as other sounds in the environment	* Watch for signs that the child might have difficulty discriminating between small differences in the sounds of letters/words (such as the Hebrew letters *bet* and *vet*/) or stringing unfamiliar sounds together (for instance, *le-heesh-tah-chah-vote*) * For children who have limited knowledge of Hebrew vocabulary, try teaching the meaning of words and phrases, or ask the child to pair unfamiliar Hebrew words with known words in English (and be ready to laugh—the things they come up with may seem random but are often hilarious).
Visual Processing: How the brain interprets visual information from the world around us	* Using a finger to point and follow along can be helpful, especially when tracking letters and words from right to left in Hebrew. Using a *yad* (Torah pointer) to point and follow along can also be a great motivator and elevates the Jewish aspect of the experience!) * Remembering the shape of a letter or a particular trope (biblical cantillation) notation can be hard. It may be helpful (and fun!) to let the child add their own markings (arrows or slash marks, for example) that remind them of how something is pronounced, the sequence of words, or the melody they want to use. Hebrew letter yoga can also be helpful.

Building blocks of learning	Implications for children who have LDs during b'nai mitzvah preparation
Cognitive Flexibility: Sometimes known as "cognitive shifting" or "flexible thinking," this is the ability to quickly adapt to new, changing, or unplanned events.	* Expect the unexpected! During lessons, think about how to practice what to do if the student loses their place while reading from the Torah or siddur (prayer book), or if someone reaches across the table and moves a microphone so it blocks their line of sight. * It also involves learning from mistakes, adjusting to changes in routines, trying new things, and switching from one task to another. For example, help create brief "rescue routines" that could involve steps like "stop, take a deep breath, smile, look up, look down, start again."
Working Memory: The ability to keep new information in mind for quick and easy use. It's sometimes called "short-term memory."	* There is a reason this is called "working" memory—it's hard work! The ability to hold on to information in your head develops with age and experience, and at age twelve or thirteen, children can look very different from each other in this ability area. * If children seem to be forgetful, struggle to follow instructions, have difficulty paying attention, or find it difficult to switch easily between tasks, working-memory weakness might be the reason. * Identifying patterns and building routines can be very helpful. Consider starting each lesson with a review of where you left off, making specific mention of something that elicited a positive emotional response.
Long-Term Memory: Nearly permanent storage of learned information and experiences. Some information is held explicitly (you know that you know it), and some is held unconsciously or implicitly (without realizing it).	* Over time, words, phrases, melodies, and even movements are "remembered" in what seems like an automatic and effortless way. This is how long-term memory works. The key is to model, practice, and repeat. But the secret sauce for success is making the stuff being learned meaningful and pleasurable.

Building blocks of learning	Implications for children who have LDs during b'nai mitzvah preparation
Metacognition: This literally means "thinking about your own thinking." This can encourage students to think about their preparation methods and whether those methods are appropriate or useful.	* Provide lots of opportunities for the student to self-check what they know, ask questions of themselves, and monitor what they have learned as a way to self-assess their level of comfort and confidence. * One terrific way to teach and enhance metacognitive skills is to ask the child to "teach back" what they have learned. * After reflection, encourage students to think about whether they would like to change something about the way they are learning so that the lessons and practice are more helpful and meaningful for them.
Speed of Processing: The time it takes to receive information (through any of our senses), make sense of it, and respond.	* Children who have LDs or related disorders like ADHD often struggle in this area. They may look confused when asked to perform an unfamiliar task, or take longer to respond, even when the task at hand is familiar. * Feeling anxious or under pressure can slow down processing speed, and, for some children, this is an area in which they experience significant struggle.

Strategies for Working with Children with LDs

There are a number of strategies that may be used to support b'nai mitzvah students with learning disabilities. They include scaffolding, advanced organizers, and peer-assisted learning.

Scaffolding

* This is an approach to systematically build upon students' experiences and knowledge as they are learning new skills.
* Begin by performing and modeling the more difficult steps of a task while letting students do the easier steps. Gradually, let students take responsibility for completing the more difficult steps.
* When children get "stuck," talk about what just happened, describe the problem, and model some language they can use to

come up with a fix that works for them. This type of self-talk and problem solving can be used over and over again and can be incredibly effective in helping children to persevere and keep from feeling defeated or discouraged.

This strategy also helps students learn that it's okay to make a mistake as long as they understand why they made it and determine how to correct it.

Tips for Teaching Torah Trope

Torah trope (biblical cantillation) is a very useful tool for people learning to chant Torah. There are twenty-seven trope symbols, divided into "families," which serve as a guide to singing. This brilliant system was developed somewhere between the sixth and tenth centuries CE by Jewish scholars and scribes known as Masoretes. Tropes provide three things at once—the musical notes, the punctuation, and the accent marks within a given word.

Many students learn and master the twenty-seven notes before they begin learning their actual portion. Others learn as they go along. Some thrive on the predictability and enjoy making up playful names. Some disregard the trope names and use numbers. Visual learners often like to color-code a given sequence. Some students make their own directional lines as the tune goes up or down or is extended for a certain number of beats. While these systems may or may not help all students, pointing them out to the student certainly can't hurt! Ultimately, most students will be looking at a Torah scroll, which is in a special font with no musical notes or punctuation. The tropes may help the student get to the point of readiness to read from the scroll when these "training wheels" are removed.

—H.B.

Scribing the D'var Torah

While organizing and writing may be difficult for some with learning disabilities, some children are "off the charts" when it comes to ideas. There are numerous ways to capture these ideas without having students write them down, a practice they are often desperate to avoid. I often say, "You talk. I'll be the scribe!" I write notes as fast as I can, then go home and transcribe them in an ongoing *d'var Torah* (Torah teaching) document. We then add to it each time, and over several weeks or months, it becomes the d'var Torah—and the actual writing does not feel painful for the student. One of my students, Dylan, and I often informally discussed the idea of a new month being a time for renewal and fresh starts, and how his bar mitzvah was five days before Shavuot, the holiday of the giving of the Torah. Each discussion over a two-month period became a different paragraph in what turned out to be a ten-minute d'var Torah, including thank-yous to his parents, brothers, and a dog.

—*H.B.*

Advanced Organizers

This can be a wonderful way to help children prepare a speech or write a d'var Torah.

* Use a graphic approach of their choosing (for example, a chart, boxes with connecting lines, diagrams using circles and shapes). This helps children to access their prior knowledge, come up with new questions, and jot down key words and any ideas they want to develop in their remarks. It also records any specific language they want to use once they begin to write.
* With ideas, key words, and phrases well-organized, the brainstorming and writing process can begin. (Note: More than a few of the children I've taught decided to use this advanced organizer approach to create a blueprint of sorts for themselves, making it easy to keep track of different activities throughout the bar and bat mitzvah preparation process.)

Peer-Assisted Learning

This approach was originally created and studied as a strategy to accelerate learning for middle school– and high school–aged children. Features of this strategy are easily and effectively applied to bar and bat mitzvah preparation.

- Reciprocal teaching: This is when students switch roles with a teacher/tutor. For example, the teacher recites lines of Hebrew text and the student monitors and offers corrections. (Spoiler alert: This can quickly become a favorite activity, and a way to build the child's confidence while honing skills.)
- Opportunities to capitalize on the powerful impact of social connectivity, especially during the middle school years, should not be missed. If possible, look for ways for children to engage with peers (or students who are slightly older) to practice what they've learned and receive encouragement and support. For example, the b'nai mitzvah student could do a short presentation in front of younger students as a practice run that has the added benefit of inspiring other students.

While it may be hard to escape the mindset of a b'nai mitzvah being orchestrated in a particular way, there is no best practice or preferred run of show, no list of must-dos when it comes to children who have special learning and behavioral challenges, including those with LDs. The goal is to create a rite of passage—not just a "day of" event—that is meaningful, empowering, and memorable.

Keep in mind that every child, and family, is different. One of my sons (who has ADHD and dyslexia) wanted to read from the Torah and give a speech from the bimah. My other son (who has a central auditory processing disorder) wanted family and friends to share the Torah reading, and instead of his offering a d'var Torah, he created a graphic depiction of the *parashah* (Torah portion) that served as the front cover of a program he designed to welcome guests to prayer. He was under no pressure to speak in front of the crowd, and at no time felt diminished by his having orchestrated a bar mitzvah experience that was different and memorable in a very personal way. Both boys, now with their own families, recall their becoming b'nai mitzvah with pride, and remember each other's celebrations as being perfect for who they are. It doesn't get better than that.

✻ VOICES ✻

Say Something

Daniella Bardack-Tarrab

Daniella Bardack-Tarrab was inspired by her own disabilities to work professionally in the human resources field. She tells the story of her bat mitzvah speech, which went viral before that was even a thing.

When I was a young teenager, I had several significant speech impediments. They were so significant, in fact, that I often couldn't be understood by others. Because of the way my mouth and throat were constructed, talking for more than a few minutes at a time was physically painful, as if a heavyweight fighter were punching my mouth and throat nonstop.

So talking was physically painful. And it was emotionally painful for me, too; I was bullied nonstop by classmates who made fun of me, year after year.

Regardless, when the time came for my bat mitzvah ceremony at my Conservative synagogue in Washington, DC, Tifereth Israel Congregation, I was determined to give a speech offering thoughts on my Torah reading. My two older brothers did it at their ceremonies. Why not me too? The night before the speech I started crying because my jaw and tongue hurt while practicing, so I was not sure if I would make it through the speech on the big day.

Here are some excerpts from my talk that day on January 18, 2003:

> We have a poster in my school, Julius West Middle School in Rockville, Maryland. It says: "Don't just talk...say something." Say something.
>
> I like this poster because it tells me that if someone is going to take the time to listen to me, then I must be honest in what I am

saying. And sometimes being honest means saying something that is painful to reveal.

Most of you have probably noticed by now that I cannot correctly pronounce certain words and sounds. For me, the simple act of speaking makes my jaw and tongue and brain feel like they are running a marathon or lifting a thousand pounds. It's pretty exhausting, both physically and mentally, for me to speak. You see, people think I'm shy but I'm really not; because I don't talk correctly, I just don't like being completely embarrassed when others hear me talk.

So, while everyone in my bat and bar mitzvah class says how nervous they are about their ceremonies—which I am—not everyone literally starts crying tears of anguish wondering if their jaw and tongue will be too tired to let them finish reciting what they studied for almost a year. I did, just last night.

There's a part of me that would rather be doing anything else in the world than what I'm doing right now: giving a speech moments after reciting some of the longest Torah and *Haftarah* [reading from the Prophets] portions of the year. But then I thought about the Torah portion that I just recited, B'shalach.

Perhaps the most famous segment of today's portion is the Song of the Sea. Moses and the Children of Israel have just escaped from Egypt. Terrified, the Israelites press forward through the Sea [of Reeds] that has parted for them, not knowing whether they will live or die—and, if they live, whether they will do so freely or as slaves. But they trust in God. They don't know what is on the other side of the just-parted sea, but they do know what is on the side from which they've come.

The side they are coming from is full of despair. The other side is full of hope. So, they make the leap from despair to hope, from slavery to freedom.

All of us, I think, have times in our life when we need to cross our own seas. We go into the water hoping, even praying, that we'll make it safely to the other side.

For Moses—who also had a speech impediment—and the Israelites, it was an actual sea that separated them from the life they knew to the unknown life they prayed would be better.

For my Orthodox saba, my grandfather, his sea was overcoming a lifelong belief that girls and women should not be called to the Torah and teaching me everything I chanted today.

For my other grandparents, their sea was moving from New York to Maryland in their seventies to start a totally new life.

For homeless people at the shelter near this synagogue, their sea is trying to be happy every day when they don't even have a home.

And, today, right now, by making a really hard decision to leave my fears behind and speak publicly to you, which I didn't have to do, I am crossing my own sea as well.

And it is both scary and exciting for me, just as it must have been for the Israelites after they finally reached dry land all those years ago.

[NOTE: At this point in my talk, some five or six minutes into it, the discomfort I felt within my head and throat from chanting lengthy portions of the Torah and Haftarah, and from then delivering this speech, was so overwhelming that tears were starting to roll down my cheeks as my body started to shake.]

I started my speech by telling you about the physical and emotional pain I have because of my speech problem. Yes, my mouth is very tired now and, yes, my jaw and tongue really, really hurt a lot.

But I still wanted to end by telling you how totally awesome it feels to be speaking in public like I'm doing now. I bet this feeling of "Oh, wow, I really did it" is probably the exact same feeling the Israelites must have had after they made their crossing.

So, in conclusion, I want to thank you for sharing the most scary and wonderful day of my life with me, the day I crossed my own sea by telling you the story of how the Children of Israel, led by a man who also had a speech problem, crossed theirs. For today is the day I consciously decided with God's help that the embarrassment and pain my speech problem has caused me all my life—it's gone! It's gone!

Shabbat shalom.

My congregation—like most Jewish congregations—usually does not applaud during services. Nonetheless, upon finishing my talk, with tears streaming down my face, I received a forty-five-second-long standing ovation from the hundreds of people in our sanctuary. I honestly did not see that coming.

Nor did I see coming what would become the aftermath of that speech. A few people in our congregation asked me for a copy of my talk, and I happily obliged by emailing it to them. What I didn't expect, however, was that they in turn would send it to people they knew.

And those people would send it to people they knew.

And those people would send it to even more people they knew.

And soon the speech was traversing the planet, again and again and again.

Within days, and over the coming months, on a regular basis, my parents and I were getting emails from total strangers around the world telling us, often in intimate detail, how much the speech inspired them to try to overcome their own inner demons.

"You inspired me to overcome my nerves and go back to school to finish my degree." "As a South African, thanks to you I'm going to work more publicly for racial reconciliation in our country." "Your speech helped me overcome my fear of driving on highways and I just signed up to take driving lessons." "I also have speech problems and I wanted you to know that I just enrolled in a public speaking course."

I can't count how many middle-aged people told me I inspired them to change careers. And even a five-year-old who had been in the audience when I spoke said my talk helped her overcome a fear of heights.

The talk transformed me as well. Almost immediately upon finishing it, my psychology changed from someone whose default was "I can't do it" to someone whose more confident default was "I can do it." It was as if an "off" switch in my soul had been turned to "on." I accelerated my speech therapy. The incessant bullying I had endured by those who made fun of the way I spoke no longer bothered me as much. And in college, I took two public speaking courses, earning A's and the praise of my professor.

There's a nice postscript to the story, by the way. Approximately twenty years later, I was married to a wonderful man at the same synagogue where I had celebrated becoming bat mitzvah. The rabbi who performed my wedding ceremony, Rabbi Ethan Seidel, was the same person who presided over my bat mitzvah ceremony decades earlier. In his blessing of my husband and me, he reminded the audience of my talk years earlier in the same room, and the extraordinary impact it had had on those in the audience that day, and subsequently on others worldwide.

And it wasn't lost on him, or on any of the family members and friends at my wedding who also had been present at my bat mitzvah ceremony, that earlier that day I had insisted upon giving a wedding *"tisch,"* a twenty-minute or so public teaching to those assembled at the wedding, something not traditionally done by women.

And why not? My life has changed now. Public speaking comes easily to me these days.

I already crossed that sea, after all, and I know I can cross other seas too.

CHAPTER 18

No Talking Required:

Preparing Nonspeaking Students

Rebecca Redner and Arlene Remz

Rebecca Redner, an educational specialist at Gateways: Access to Jewish Education, in Boston, and Arlene Remz, former executive director of Gateways, are passionate advocates for the right of every child to participate in Jewish education. Rebecca and Arlene believe that children who are nonspeaking or minimally speaking are capable of active, meaningful participation during their b'nai mitzvah. Through two case studies, they offer guidance, starting with the initial planning stages, educational strategies, and possibilities for working with and using assistive communication devices.

Ellie and Adina, two of the students in the *b'nai mitzvah* preparation class at Gateways: Access to Jewish Education, were typical tweens in many ways. Ellie loved taking horseback riding lessons, watching Boston Celtics games, and turning up the volume on Top 40 hits. Adina relished drawing, going shopping, and having her nails painted in bright colors.

As young women with disabilities, however, Ellie and Adina did not follow typical paths as they prepared for their b'nai mitzvah. Ellie had cerebral palsy; she zipped around her classroom in an electric wheelchair and used a touch-screen device—a Dynavox—to communicate. Adina was diagnosed with both an intellectual disability and autism spectrum disorder, and she expressed herself by speaking only two or three words at a time. When people see students like Ellie or Adina, they might make assumptions about what they are capable of. They might not be able to see past Ellie's wheelchair, or they might misunderstand Adina's silence.

Creating Initial Goals

Two years before Ellie's bat mitzvah, her parents met with the rabbi of their medium-sized Reform synagogue. The family went to services regularly, and Ellie's older siblings attended religious school. The meeting opened as the rabbi, his face beaming, recalled when Ellie was born and expressed his joy at watching her grow. He then became serious and conveyed how sincerely he wanted Ellie to have a bat mitzvah that was just right for her. "We will do anything to make this work," he concluded.

Ellie's parents then spoke about their hopes as the rabbi nodded his encouragement. They said that they weren't sure what Ellie's bat mitzvah service would look like, only that they knew the synagogue's typical service wouldn't work for her. When pressed about how they envisioned Ellie participating in the service, they said Ellie might use her Dynavox—her touchscreen communication device—to recite prayers and chant Torah. They also acknowledged that using the Dynavox was fatiguing for Ellie, and asked if the service could possibly be limited to forty-five minutes. The rabbi immediately flipped through his siddur (prayer book) and pointed out key prayers and readings to include in an abbreviated service.

Ellie's parents knew they wanted to keep it small and would only invite a few close family members and friends to the bat mitzvah because Ellie had had stage fright and had burst into tears during performances at school. They worried that Ellie might be overwhelmed on the *bimah* in the sanctuary. At this, the rabbi stood up and led an impromptu tour of the building, pointing out several different spaces he thought would accommodate a small service. They chose a cozy social hall with wide glass doors that led out to a lovely stone patio surrounded by woods. The rabbi explained that folding chairs could be set up on the patio so Ellie's early autumn bat mitzvah could be held outside if the weather was pleasant. Everyone looked at each other and grinned. It was the perfect setting for Ellie.

Back in the rabbi's study, they put their first goals for Ellie's bat mitzvah on paper: they identified several prayers that Ellie would lead on the day of her bat mitzvah using her Dynavox, as well as a single verse from her Torah portion. Ellie's parents, more confident now, expressed hope that Ellie would learn the meaning of her Torah portion and be able to glean a lesson from it. They tossed around ideas for teaching Ellie the story of her portion and helping her compose a *d'var Torah* (Torah teaching). Ellie's parents left the temple beaming, finally able to envision their daughter's bat mitzvah.

A few months later, Adina's parents met with the rabbi of their medium-sized Conservative synagogue, where the family attended Shabbat morning services every week. Unlike Ellie's family, Adina's parents had a clear vision of what they wanted their daughter to do and what her bat mitzvah could look like. They ticked off several goals: Adina would learn about the meaning of becoming a bat mitzvah, she would recite the Sh'ma prayer, chant the blessings before and after the Torah reading, and write a d'var Torah. Although Adina's parents felt that she was capable of doing more than this, they also believed that the bat mitzvah should be a low-pressure experience for her. Adina had lost her speech at a young age after experiencing seizures, and as her mother explained: "I don't want to have this bat mitzvah to show Adina off. I want to celebrate her hard work and recognize how far she has come."

When Adina's parents finished laying out their vision, the rabbi asked if he could add one more goal: that he and Adina would get to know each other better. Although he said hello to Adina every week at services, he wanted to build a deeper connection with her, and to learn more about her abilities. The team decided that, to achieve this goal, the rabbi could work with Adina to compose a d'var Torah, just as he did with other b'nai mitzvah students. The Gateways staff provided him with materials and gave him guidance about how to support her.

Adina's weekly routine included attending Saturday morning services in the sanctuary, so her family knew that she would feel most comfortable with a Saturday morning bat mitzvah service. Although Adina happily sat through the entire Saturday morning service each week, her parents wondered if the bat mitzvah service could be abbreviated slightly because several of Adina's classmates had trouble sitting still for long periods. Since the bulk of her participation would be during the Torah service, the team decided that the beginning of the service would be shortened to conserve her energy for that central piece of the service, and it would have the added effect of easing sitting time for classmates.

As it became clear that Adina would master the Sh'ma and Torah blessings with plenty of time to spare before her bat mitzvah, the bat mitzvah team expanded their initial goals for Adina. In addition to reciting the blessings over the Torah, Adina also learned to recite one verse of her Torah portion.

Learning Prayers

For both Ellie and Adina, Dynavox Picture Communication Symbols (PCS) were a vital part of teaching them to understand and recite prayers. But since their abilities and strengths were so different, the way symbols were used and the instructional strategies incorporating symbols varied.

Ellie was adept at using her Dynavox. For her, as a young woman with cerebral palsy, the Dynavox was essentially her voice; it was her primary way of communicating with others. The Dynavox displayed twenty virtual buttons on a screen, each illustrated with PCS. The display was dynamic, which meant that Ellie could tap a button labeled "Art," and a new page of buttons showing art supplies would come up. She could slowly but accurately tap the buttons she wanted to navigate through pages of vocabulary and find the words she wanted.

The Gateways staff created a page of symbols on her device labeled "Siddur [prayer book]," with the prayers illustrated by PCS. Symbols can bring the meaning of the prayer to life. The PCS used on Ellie's Dynavox either represented what would be happening at that moment in the service, such as an icon of an open Torah for Ellie's Torah reading, or an element of the prayer's meaning, such as an icon of a person holding their hand to their ear to illustrate the literal meaning of the word *sh'ma* (hear). Ellie learned the reason each symbol was chosen, which enhanced her understanding of the prayers she led. At first, the prayers in Ellie's Dynavox were added using the device's default method of text-to-speech. When Ellie tapped the button, an electronic voice spoke the typed message aloud, but it could neither pronounce Hebrew correctly, nor could it sing. Thankfully, Ellie's device was able to record voices, and eventually the electronic voice was replaced with that of her older sister's.

In the years since Ellie's bat mitzvah, the Gateways team has worked with many different students who use Dynavoxes or iPads to communicate. Each student uses their device in a different way, depending on their academic abilities and physical dexterity. The Gateways team believes it is important to have more than one button whenever possible so that there is an element of choice and intention. For example, one of Ellie's classmates with minimal dexterity used an iPad app that displayed just two large buttons on the screen at one time, making it easier for her to locate and tap the correct one.

Example of what a Dynavox screen could look like

Update on Communication Devices

Augmentative and Alternative Communication (AAC) devices are for children who have not started speaking, for those who have lost speech, or for those with a range of communication difficulties and speech disorders. They include systems, strategies, devices, and tools to support people with communication difficulties. These may range from sign language and pictures to letter boards or activating a voice programmed into the device.

Two widely used programs are Proloquo, an AAC app for Apples devices designed for nonspeaking children and adults that is completely customizable and designed for an array of fine motor and visual skills, and TouchChat, also for Apple devices, which transforms iPads, iPad minis, iPhones, and iPod Touch into powerful communication tools. New devices, programs, and apps are emerging all the time to assist nonspeaking children and adults. Ask around for the latest and most powerful communication tools.

Dynavox has continued to evolve and now offers additional devices, including the TD I-Series, an eye gaze-enabled speech-generating device.

–H.B.

Another student used an iPad with an app that could be controlled by a physical switch mounted on his wheelchair near his elbow. This student, who did not have a lot of control over his hands, triggered the switch and activated recordings of prayers and Torah by moving his upper arm. With this student, his instructors took particular care to ensure that he understood what each prayer meant. When he practiced using his device to say prayers in class, the teachers did not simply say: "Hit the switch." They would say: "It's time to say the Sh'ma and tell everyone that there is just one God," or "Let's say the blessing thanking God for giving us the Torah." By reinforcing this meaning over and over again, they tried to ensure that this student was praying with intention rather than just tapping a button.

Symbols also helped Adina, the student with an intellectual disability and autism spectrum disorder, learn prayers, but in a very different way. Adina was able to use her voice to recite the words of a prayer. Although she only used about two or three words at a time in conversation, she could string together more words by repeating after someone else or reading aloud. Adina had an excellent visual memory, and although she couldn't read by sounding out words, she was able to identify hundreds of sight words. We could use Adina's visual memory to teach her to read the prayers, and, by using PCS, we could help her understand them.

The first step of this process was to translate Adina's prayers into PCS. Oftentimes, when parents see the way we have written out prayers for their children with the help of symbols, they remark: "I've been saying these prayers my whole life, and this is the first time I've understood what the words mean!" For students who are not able to read, it can be easier to recognize picture symbols.

Dynavox's Boardmaker software, used by special educators around the country, was used to illustrate each word of the prayer with a symbol that represented its meaning. This software has a library of tens of thousands of simple symbols that clearly illustrate just about any concept. Whenever there was a word or phrase whose meaning couldn't be captured by an existing symbol, we used a graphics program to create new symbols in the style of PCS. Once the prayer was completely translated into symbols, the words and symbols were enlarged and printed out onto flash cards for Adina.

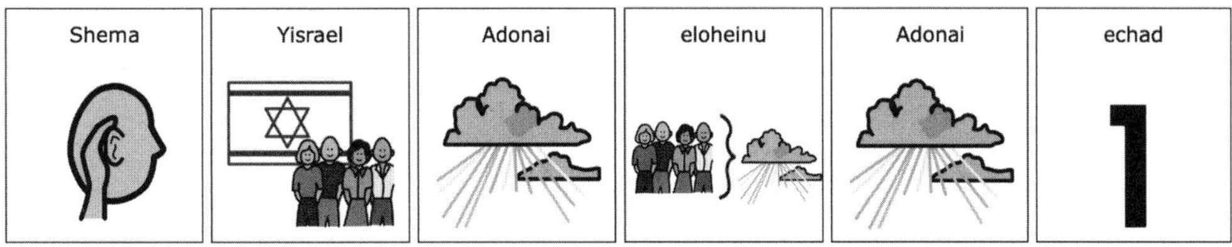

Adina's flash cards

When Adina was introduced to a flash card containing a transliterated Hebrew word and picture symbol, we showed her the card, said the name of the word, and asked her to repeat the word. To test Adina's mastery, we put two other flash cards on the table, and asked Adina to point to the word she had just learned.

Whenever Adina correctly pointed to the new word, she was also asked to say the word aloud. We repeated this exercise a few times, shuffling the cards around so the new card was always in a different place. As Adina grew more familiar with the new word, we increased the level of difficulty. As Adina's vocabulary grew, we began to put flash cards together in the order in which the words appeared in a prayer for Adina to read.

Adina also enjoyed playing many different games using the flash cards. We would lay out the flash cards on the floor and call out different words, while asking Adina to toss bean bags onto the correct words. Adina slowly mastered many new words, and over the course of several months learned to recite the Sh'ma, the blessings over wine and challah, and the blessings before and after the Torah reading.

Learning Torah: Understanding the Stories

Both Ellie's and Adina's parents told us that their daughters loved stories, and they hoped that their daughters would feel a connection with the stories from the Torah. They also wanted their daughters to go beyond simply enjoying the story and learn a lesson from the story or think about the story in a more critical way.

At first, members of the Gateways team working with Adina and Ellie read them simple illustrated stories of their Torah portions as part of their weekly lessons. Both Adina and Ellie slowly became familiar with the stories, and enjoyed the repetition of hearing them over and over again.

Ellie's Torah portion was *Ki Tisa*, which told the story of the Jewish people creating the Golden Calf while Moses received the Ten Commandments on Mount Sinai. As Ellie became familiar with her illustrated version of the story, Rebecca challenged Ellie to demonstrate how much she understood. At first, Rebecca simply asked Ellie to point to specific parts of the illustrations: "Show me the Ten Commandments. Where is Mount Sinai?" After several weeks, Rebecca asked Ellie multiple-choice reading comprehension questions and showed her three possible answers illustrated by PCS. Ellie was asked questions such as: "Who climbed up Mount Sinai? How did the Jewish people feel when Moses was on Mount Sinai? What did the Jewish people make while Moses was gone?" Ellie pointed to PCS symbols to respond and answered every question correctly, showing us that she fully understood the story.

When Moses saw the Jews worshipping the Golden Calf, what did he do?

Multiple choice options to test Ellie's comprehension

Ellie was able to use the communication boards on her device so effectively that Rebecca decided to push her a little further. For *Ki Tisa* we created a paper communication board, which can be either a physical or digital page of pictures or symbols that a person can point to in order to communicate with others, containing all of the people, actions, objects, and feelings in the story.

For a few weeks we modeled pointing to the symbols on the communication board as she read the story. A few weeks later, we gave Ellie a copy of the story packet containing only the illustrations without words. We asked Ellie to write her own version of the story using the paper communication board. Over the course of two tutoring sessions, Ellie slowly picked out symbols, eventually writing out the entire story in her own words. From this point on, every week we reviewed

with Ellie the version that she had written. Seeing the cover of the booklet, *The Story of the Golden Calf, by Ellie,* would make her grin at receiving the author's credit.

Ellie was also pushed a little further with questions that drew out her opinions about the story: "Why do you think Moses broke the tablets? If you were Moses, would you have broken the tablets? What would you have done instead?" Just as with the reading comprehension questions, she was provided choices among three different answers that she could point to. Ellie's responses to these questions, along with her retelling of the story, eventually became the basis of her d'var Torah.

If you were Moses, what would you do if you saw the Jews worshipping the Golden Calf?

How do you think God felt when Moses broke the tablets?

Adina learned the story of her Torah portion in a similar way to Ellie. Adina's portion was more difficult to teach because her portion didn't tell a story. In her portion, *Acharei Mot-K'doshim*, God gave the Jewish people laws on topics as varied as sacrifices, sexual immorality, honesty, and treating others with respect. We decided the best way to make it appropriate, understandable, and meaningful for Adina would be to focus on the issues that were relevant and important to her. Among the rules we focused on were: do not take things without asking, help people with disabilities, respect your parents and people who are elderly, love other people, be fair, tell the truth, and be kind to people—even those you don't know. For Adina, the law about being honest with weights and measures was interpreted as: tell the truth. And the laws of gleaning became: help make sure everybody has enough to eat. Since Adina and her family volunteered at a local food pantry, this value had meaning for her.

We illustrated these rules in a booklet for Adina. The booklet of Adina's Torah portion contained repetition in order to help her absorb the information on each page. A new rule was presented on each page with an illustration. As Adina grew more familiar with this story, we created an activity in which she sorted cards with pictures of actions that Jewish people had to do to be holy, such as being kind and telling the truth, from other actions such as stealing and lying. Like Ellie, Adina also completed a packet of questions about her story. Each question had three possible answers, represented in symbols that she could point to.

Who speaks to the Jews in your Torah portion?

In this way, Adina showed us that she understood the story of her Torah portion. And, like Ellie, these questions later became the basis of her d'var Torah.

God told the Jewish people: "If you have extra food, give it to people who are hungry and don't have enough food to eat. Follow my rules to be good people."

So the Jewish people listened to God and followed God's rules. They tried to be good people by giving extra food to people who were hungry.

I can listen to God and follow God's rules. I can try to be a good person by giving extra food to people who are hungry.

Learning Torah: Reciting a Portion

Both Ellie and Adina learned to read a single verse of Torah instead of an entire portion. Since it took Adina at least a week to learn a single word, we knew that learning a full reading would take more time than we had. It was decided that Adina would share the chanting of the portion with the rabbi or another Torah reader her family wanted. Adina would recite either the first or the last verse of a reading, and the other reader would recite the rest.

Adina learned these words in the same way that she learned the words of her prayers. She was introduced to the words and their meanings using flash cards. Adina then learned to recognize and read the flash cards through structured exercises, games, and reading practice.

After Adina learned all the words in her Torah portion, they were written out on a single sheet of paper. Adina's rabbi allowed us to place this sheet of paper on the open Torah scroll on the day of Adina's bat mitzvah so that she could fluently read these words of Torah in front of the open Torah scroll.

Ellie also recited a single verse of Torah instead of a complete portion. However, Ellie's rabbi stated that this verse could make up the entirety of Ellie's *aliyah* (call to the Torah). She said the blessing before the Torah reading, and then instead of having another person chant the rest of the portion, Ellie would recite her line and then finish by saying the blessing after the Torah reading.

When Ellie recited the prayers using her Dynavox, she could tap a single symbol to sing an entire prayer. But Ellie's Torah portion was the centerpiece of her service and of her bat mitzvah learning experience, and we wanted to emphasize the meaning of the words she would chant. After consulting with Ellie's parents, as well as her speech and language pathologist, we decided that the portion (Exodus 34:1) should be split into somewhere between five and eight phrases, each represented by a single symbol.

Before programming the Torah portion into Ellie's device, we taught her the meaning of the phrases she was to recite. The symbols representing each phrase were put into a small booklet, accompanied by an English translation of the Hebrew words, so Ellie would understand what she would be saying. We read the new booklet to her every week. Once Ellie was familiar with the meaning of the words of her Torah portion, we programmed the symbols into Ellie's device and again enlisted her older sister to lend her voice.

Each week, we read the story packet with the translation of the Torah portion to Ellie. After each page, we asked Ellie, "How do you say that in Hebrew?" Ellie would then tap the corresponding button on her Dynavox. This repeated exercise helped Ellie understand the meaning of the Hebrew words. After that, Ellie would recite her portion all the way through, practicing the process of tapping the buttons one after the other until she could do it smoothly.

The B'nai Mitzvah

On a sunny September morning Ellie's family and friends gathered on the patio outside of her temple's social hall. Ellie, wearing an apricot-colored dress covered in flowers, eagerly led the assembled group in prayer. After reciting each prayer, she tapped the button on her Dynavox labeled *Yasher Koach*, a Hebrew phrase of congratulations. She had been accustomed to using this button for congratulating her peers when they led prayers during class, but on the day of her bat mitzvah she spontaneously used it to express her pride in her own accomplishments. Afterward, her rabbi remarked: "I am truly awed by Ellie and the effort she expends to express herself." As he reflected on the importance of this day in Ellie's life, he said, "I am deeply thankful and proud that Ellie knows that she is a part of a congregational family—a place where she was, and will always be, welcomed."

Several months later it was time for Adina to celebrate her bat mitzvah. The sanctuary was packed with friends, family, aides, former babysitters, teachers, therapists, and Gateways staff and volunteers. Adina's mother wanted not only to celebrate Adina on this occasion, but to celebrate all the people who had helped Adina reach this milestone in her life. Adina stood confidently on the bimah and joyfully recited all the prayers she had learned. Afterward, Adina's mother wrote about the day: "It was all amazing, but hearing my daughter, who had once lost her words, say the blessing for her first aliyah was the highlight!"

Adina is now twenty-one, and her mother said, "All these years after her bat mitzvah, [Adina] still is wearing her tallit and kippah (head covering) when she goes to Saturday morning services. She still enjoys going and I have noticed over time that she has started to stand right before everyone else does at an appropriate time or say some random words from a prayer during it. Clearly, she is paying attention. The work you did with her for her bat mitzvah (and in Gateways) has lasted well beyond her bat mitzvah."

Final Thoughts

Young adults who are nonspeaking or minimally speaking can become b'nai mitzvah and can be valuable participants in Jewish communal life. Ellie's and Adina's stories illustrate what is possible when synagogues, families, and educators are determined to ensure that every child is fully welcomed into the Jewish community. Regardless of type and degree of disability, it is possible to customize the learning and service for each student. The key is willingness. It is true that not every synagogue or family has access to the special education expertise and experience that Gateways brings to the Boston Jewish community. But you do not need that expertise in order to be welcoming, to embrace each child as they are, and to be open to trying new things. This is the obligation of Jewish educators, who are charged to "teach each child according to their own way."

About the Editors

Howard Blas

Howard worked for the Ramah camping movement in disabilities inclusion for forty years as director of the National Ramah Tikvah Network of the National Ramah Commission and director of the Tikvah Program at Camp Ramah in New England. Howard has led numerous Ramah and Birthright Israel Shorashim Asperger's Syndrome trips to Israel. He has spent several summers traveling across the United States, visiting innovative jobs sites and training programs for people with disabilities. In February 2019, he climbed Mount Kilimanjaro as part of a Friends of Access Israel delegation, which included four climbers with paraplegia.

Howard, a social worker and special education teacher by training, has prepared students with a range of disabilities and "special circumstances" for b'nai mitzvah for more than thirty-five years. Howard writes regularly for many Jewish publications, including the *Jerusalem Post*, Chabad.org, JNS (Jewish News Syndicate), ejewishphilanthropy, Jewish Disability Inclusion News, and *Sight Line* (Covenant Foundation). Howard received the S'fatai Tiftakh Award from Boston's Hebrew College Jewish Special Education Program in 2012 and the 2013 Covenant Award for excellence in Jewish education. A longtime resident of Connecticut, Howard moved to Israel in 2025. Learn more at howardblas.com.

Ilana Trachtman

Ilana is an Emmy Award–winning documentary filmmaker and has produced and directed critically acclaimed non-fiction programs for more than thirty years for PBS, HBO Family, ABC, Showtime, Lifetime, Discovery, A&E, and The Sundance Channel. Ilana's films strive to reveal human stories hidden in plain sight, and to provoke the viewer to discover immediate, irresistible recognition of themselves in the films' subjects, inspiring social change.

Ilana has created character-driven films about a diverse array of topics, including champion high school mariachi musicians (*Mariachi High*, PBS), the legacy of slavery in Peru and Mexico (*Black in Latin America*, PBS), a girls' empowerment program run by a reformed gang leader, (*Our Heroes, Ourselves*, Lifetime), glassblowing apprenticeships for kids in juvie (*The Arts Advantage*, ABC-TV), and the heroic original LGBTQ activists (*The Pursuit: 50 Years in the Fight for LGBT Rights,* WHYY). Ilana's theatrically-released feature documentary, *Praying with Lior,* about the spiritual gift of a boy with Down syndrome, won six Audience Awards for Best Documentary and the Grand Prix at the International Disability Film Festival, was a critic's pick of the *New York Times*, inspired Special Olympics Chairman of the Board Timothy Shriver to write an Op-Ed in the *Washington Post*, and was screened on Capitol Hill. Her film *Ain't No Back to a Merry-Go-Round* is about the first organized interracial civil rights protest in America. Ilana lives in Philadelphia with her husband and two daughters.

About the Contributors

Jacob Artson

Jacob Artson is an adult with autism who communicates by typing with support. He lives in his own home in Los Angeles with the help of his wonderful aides. He is completing his high school diploma and loves his synagogue, Ikar. In his free time he enjoys hiking, basketball, and hanging out with family and friends

Daniella Bardack-Tarrab

Daniella Bardack-Tarrab works as a human resources professional and has also worked as a barista, a full-time dedicated aide to a boy with autism, and a Hebrew school teacher. When she's not inspiring others to pursue their dreams, you might find her sailing on the Potomac or watching YouTube videos of her favorite dog breed, the bichon frise. She and her husband are members of a local Conservative congregation in Virginia.

Meir Yishai Barth

Meir Yishai Barth, who goes by Yishai, holds a master's degree in Health, Medicine and Society from the University of Cambridge department of history and philosophy of science. As a Gates Cambridge Scholar, he is currently pursuing a PhD in the sociology of rehabilitative medicine. He was diagnosed with cerebral palsy shortly after birth and was later diagnosed with a cortical visual impairment that keeps him from reading or writing by visual means. Barth has been involved with Jewish disability activism since the age of eight, through public speaking, writing, Jewish youth leadership, and political advocacy. He aspires to dedicate his life to the study of the relationship between ability diversity and aspects of core identity, including spiritual practice and belief.

Rabbi Allison L. Berry

Rabbi Allison L. Berry is the director of the Betty Ann Greenbaum Miller Center for Jewish Healing at Jewish Family and Children's Service in Waltham, Massachusetts. She is honored to lead the center's work, offering pastoral care to individuals in the Jewish community and beyond, guiding them through the many stages of grief and healing. She also serves as a trusted resource for colleagues and professionals seeking consultation in the areas of pastoral care, mental health, and building caring communities. She previously served as a congregational rabbi at Temple Shalom in Newton, Massachusetts.

Shelly Christensen

Shelly Christensen is a pioneer in the faith community disability inclusion movement and an international speaker, author, and consultant. She is the author of *From Longing to Belonging—A Practical Guide to Including People with Disabilities and Mental Health Conditions in Your Faith Community.* Christensen cofounded Jewish Disability Awareness, Acceptance, and Inclusion Month (JDAIM) in 2009. She directed the award-winning Minneapolis Jewish Community Inclusion Program for People with Disabilities before founding her consulting group, Inclusion Innovations. She is the senior director of faith inclusion and belonging at Disability Belongs (formerly known as RespectAbility).

Rabbi Menachem Creditor

Rabbi Menachem Creditor serves as the Pearl and Ira Meyer Scholar-in-Residence at UJA-Federation of New York and is the founder of Rabbis Against Gun Violence. He is an acclaimed author, scholar, and speaker with more than two million views of his online videos and essays; thirty-one published books, including the COVID-era, two-volume anthology *When We Turned Within*; and six albums of original music, including the global anthem "Olam Chesed Yibaneh." He and his wife, Neshama Carlebach, live in New York, where they are raising their five children.

Wendy Elliott-Vandivier

Wendy Elliott-Vandivier is a certified senior professional in human resources with a diverse background in government civil rights enforcement, managing human resources in private industry, and community advocacy. She has worked for the US Department of Education Office of Civil Rights. Elliott-Vandivier has been a leader in the disability civil rights community for more than thirty years. She is a former chair of the Philadelphia Mayor's Commission on People with Disabilities. Her paintings and cartoons explore issues of family, memory, and experiences as a disabled woman.

Jennifer Fink

Jennifer Fink is a healthcare consultant at Chartis with more than a decade of experience in healthcare consulting, nonprofit leadership, and organizational transformation. Prior to Chartis, she launched a nonprofit organization that provided support and comfort to military-connected children and their families. Fink is a member of the MedStar National Rehabilitation Hospital Community Health Advisory Task Force; she previously served on the University of Maryland (UMD) School of Public Health Alumni Board, UMD Hillel Board of Directors, and the UMD Jewish Leadership Council. Fink holds a bachelor of science in behavioral and community health from the University of Maryland.

Elaine Hall

Elaine Hall, "Coach E," is an internationally recognized leader in inclusion and belonging. Her groundbreaking organization, the Miracle Project, was profiled in the Emmy–winning HBO documentary *Autism: The Musical.* Hall codeveloped Nes Gadol, an award winning *b'nai mitzvah* program for neurodivergent and disabled children. She consults for TV and film production companies, including Netflix, Amazon, Disney, Hulu, and Sony; has appeared on CNN, CBS, and NPR, and in the *New York Times,* the *Wall Street Journal, Haaretz,* and the *Jewish Journal*; and has appeared in *Love on the Spectrum* and *As We See It,* among other shows. Her memoir, *Now I See the Moon: A Mother, A Son, and the Miracle of Autism,* was an official selection for Jewish Disability Awareness, Acceptance, and Inclusion Month and by the UN for World Autism Awareness Day.

Sheldon H. Horowitz, PhD

Sheldon H. Horowitz is an educational consultant who served as the director of professional services and then as senior advisor, strategic innovation, research, and insights at the National Center for Learning Disabilities (NCLD) for more than twenty-five years. Prior to his role at NCLD, he directed outpatient hospital-based evaluation and treatment programs in psychiatry and developmental and behavioral pediatrics, and taught at primary, secondary, and college levels. He provided leadership on many of NCLD's key projects and programs, including hosting national summits, the creation of an LD Checklist and a suite of early learning and literacy screening tools, the creation of transitioning-to-kindergarten content for at-risk students, and an early learning observation and rating scales program.

Audra Kaplan, PhD

Audra Kaplan is a psychologist and educator specializing in mental health and disability inclusion. She supports children and adults navigating emotional, developmental, and relationship challenges, and partners with families, schools, and communities to create thoughtful and supportive environments. She is also a longtime leader in disability inclusion and program development in Jewish spaces, including Camp Ramah and Keshet.

Gabrielle Kaplan-Mayer

Gabrielle Kaplan-Mayer is an author and Jewish educator whose work focuses on disability and creativity. She is the proud recipient of the 2022 Covenant Award and currently edits the Jewish Disability Inclusion News. She also is the director of virtual content and programs for Ritualwell. Kaplan-Mayer leads Feed Your Spirit Writing, facilitating expressive writing workshops focused on spiritual curiosity, and also writes a Substack called *Journey with the Seasons*, a weekly practice of meditative reading, expressive writing prompts, and deepening practices. She and her family live in Elkins Park, Pennsylvania. Find her books, personal essays, plays, and more at www.gabriellekaplanmayer.com.

Matan A. Koch

Matan A. Koch is former senior policy advisor at RespectAbility, a national disability organization. With a Senate-confirmed appointment by President Barack Obama to the National Council on Disability, for a term that ended in 2014, Koch is a national leader in disability advocacy. A graduate of Yale College and Harvard Law School, he oversaw expansions in RespectAbility's workforce engagement, education, faith inclusion, and leadership programming as the organization doubled in size. Considered one of the nation's leading Jewish inclusion experts, Koch has developed training and materials for many Jewish organizations, including Hillel International, the Union for Reform Judaism, and Combined Jewish Philanthropies.

Serena Leigh Krombach

Serena Leigh Krombach, MA, MSEd, grew up as the only hearing member of her immediate family. She is an early childhood special education teacher. As a freelance writer and editor, Krombach has worked with university presses and nonprofit organizations, including Gallaudet University Press, the Conference of Interpreter Trainers' *International Journal of Interpreter Education,* and the American Speech-Language-Hearing Association. Her two (hearing) sons became b'nai mitzvah at Congregation Beth Elohim in Brooklyn, New York, with interpreters at the service for Deaf family and friends.

Rabbi Darby Jared Leigh

Rabbi Darby Jared Leigh is rabbi of Congregation Kerem Shalom in Concord, Massachusetts. He was ordained by the Reconstructionist Rabbinical College. Leigh was born deaf, educated through an oral/auditory approach, and mainstreamed among hearing peers. He acted with the National Theater of the Deaf and worked as a counselor with the New York Society for the Deaf. At home in both the Deaf and hearing worlds, he works to bridge them, introducing ASL translations of songs and blessings to his congregation, forming an ASL choir, and serving as rabbinic advisor to the Jewish Deaf Congress.

David Neufeld, PhD

After a five-year stint as a professional actor, David Neufeld earned his joint doctorate in special education from University of California, Berkeley, and San Francisco State University. He has worked at the intersection of Judaism and disabilities since the early 2000s. He currently serves as the dean of learning support at Jewish Community High School of the Bay in San Francisco; before that he spent ten years as the director of inclusion at Jewish LearningWorks, supporting Jewish educators, schools, and families across the Bay Area around special needs inclusion. In addition to this role, he has a private practice as an inclusion coach and consultant for families, schools, and organizations. He lives in Berkeley with his wife and two daughters. Find him at www.drdavidneufeld.com.

Meredith Englander Polsky

Meredith Englander Polsky founded Matan (www.matankids.org) in 2000 and serves as Matan's senior director of programs and partnerships, as well as a selective mutism specialist at a private clinical social work practice. She is a nationally sought-after speaker on Jewish disability inclusion. She holds a master's degree in special education from Bank Street College, a master's degree in clinical social work from Columbia University, and a graduate certificate in early intervention from Georgetown University. Polsky is a 2017 Covenant Award recipient and co-author of the award-winning I Have a Question About children's book series (Jessica Kingsley Publishers), helping children with special needs (and all children!) grapple with difficult topics.

Rebecca Redner

Rebecca Redner is an educational specialist at Gateways: Access to Jewish Education in Boston, where she strives to make Jewish education accessible, meaningful, and joyful for students of all abilities. In this role, she designed the Gateways b'nai mitzvah curriculum, and creates accessible materials for students, trains and supervises tutors, and coordinates with parents and clergy to develop and implement a vision for each child's b'nai-mitzvah experience. Redner is also the author of the *Gateways Haggadah* and the *Gateways Shabbat Family Companion*. She graduated from Boston University with a bachelor's degree in special education and holds a master's of Jewish education with a certificate in special education from Hebrew College.

Arlene Remz

Arlene Remz retired as the founding executive director of Gateways: Access to Jewish Education and is recognized as a national leader in the field of Jewish special education and inclusion. She holds an MEd from Columbia University in technology in education and an MA in special education from New York University. Remz spent her early career as a special education teacher in Massachusetts and New York, before leading research, curriculum development, and dissemination projects funded by the US Department of Education's Office of Special Education Programs. Arlene founded the Gateways b'nai mitzvah program as a unique, Boston-based model helping students with a wide range of learning challenges from across the community and across the religious spectrum.

Rabbi Rebecca Schatz

Rabbi Rebecca Schatz is the associate rabbi at Temple Beth Am in Los Angeles. During rabbinical school she developed programming around life-cycle events, such as b'nai mitzvah, and created new opportunities for celebrating traditional holidays. Schatz has directed experiential religious schools, facilitated mother-daughter b'not mitzvah programs, engaged women in Torah study, and continued to pursue her passion for musical prayer with students of all ages.

Pamela Rae Schuller

Pamela Rae Schuller holds a BA in psychology and youth outreach through the arts and an MA in child advocacy and policy, and is an internationally recognized advocate and performer, known for her ability to weave together comedy, storytelling, and a compelling narrative on disability inclusion and mental health. She works with companies and leaders worldwide to inspire a new understanding of inclusion; has been featured on Netflix, the Doctor Mike channel, and in the *New York Times*; and is working on a novel about all of the time she spent in detention at boarding school. Learn more at www.PamelaComedy.com.

Stephen Shore, PhD

Stephen Shore is a full-time professor at Adelphi University, as well as an adjunct at New York University Steinhardt School of Culture, Education, and Human Development and Hofstra University, focusing on aligning best practice in supporting autistic people to lead fulfilling and productive lives. His most recent book, *College for Students with Disabilities*, combines personal stories and research for promoting success in higher education. Shore is a current board member of Autism Speaks, the Organization for Autism Research, and the American Occupational Therapy Foundation; president emeritus of the Asperger/Autism Network; and advisory board member of the Autism Society.

Jessica Leving Siegel

Jessica Leving Siegel is the founder and executive director of the Center for Siblings of People with Disabilities (www.siblingcenter.org). Based on her own experience, she published *Billy's Sister: Life When Your Sibling Has a Disability*, a picture book to help kids understand the emotions they might grapple with having a sibling with a disability, and the companion workbook, *My Sibling Story*. Siegel hosts "The Special Siblings Podcast" (available on Apple Podcasts, Spotify, and SoundCloud). She is a seasoned Jewish communal professional who has worked in various roles for BBYO, the Jewish United Fund of Chicago, and Spertus Institute for Jewish Learning and Leadership. Her writing has appeared in the *Jerusalem Post*, the *Boston Globe*, *USA Today*, and more.

Rabbanit Aliza Sperling

Rabbanit Aliza Sperling serves on the Talmud faculty at Yeshivat Maharat and directs its Halakha in Action fellowship program. She is the director of SVIVAH's HerTorah, a pluralistic women's learning community dedicated to expanding women's Torah, and a faculty member of the Wexner Foundation. She received her ordination from Yeshivat Maharat and a JD from New York University Law School. She lives with her to help kids in Riverdale, New York.

Batya Sperling-Milner

Batya Sperling-Milner is a blind Jewish teen who is passionate about fostering accessibility and inclusion in her community. She enjoys learning how disability and *halachah* intersect, educating others about ways to be more inclusive, and mentoring other blind and disabled youth. She lives in Riverdale, New York.

Gila Vogel, PhD

Gila Vogel has a long career in special education, directing the special education program at the Bureau of Jewish Education of Southern New Jersey before moving to Israel, and teaching in the special education department at Beit Berl College for thirty-five years. Vogel received her doctorate from Haifa University, with a dissertation about the significance of a b'nai mitzvah ceremony for children with developmental disabilities and their parents. She cofounded the B'nai Mitzvah Program for Children with Special Needs of the Masorti Movement in Israel, and serves on the board of directors of Chimes, Israel, an organization that works to improve the quality of life of people with special needs.

Rebecca Wanatick

Rebecca Wanatick received a BA in both elementary and special education from the University of Hartford and her EdM in special education from Boston University. She is the director of disability inclusion and belonging at the Jewish Federation of Greater MetroWest NJ, serving as a facilitator between families and community agencies, making connections and raising the level of inclusive programming community-wide. Wanatick provides family and educator workshops, teen advocate training, synagogue inclusion committee support, and outreach and advocacy for individuals with disabilities and their families. She lives with her family in New Jersey.

Glossary of Hebrew Terms

Adon Olam:	The prayer that concludes most Shabbat morning services.
aliyah (*aliyot*, plural):	A call to the Torah to recite blessings before and after a selection of the Torah *parashah* is read.
beit midrash:	A place of Jewish learning or study.
bimah:	Platform or podium in a synagogue.
d'var Torah (*divrei Torah*, plural):	A short speech teaching a lesson from the weekly Torah portion.
Haftarah:	A selection from the biblical books of the Prophets, traditionally chanted by b'nai mitzvah following the Shabbat Torah reading.
halachah:	Jewish law (halachic, halachically: referring to Jewish law).
kavanah:	The intentionality one brings to each prayer.
keva:	The parts of prayer that are fixed and part of each prayer service.
Kiddush:	Prayer recited over wine.
kiddush:	Social time after synagogue service, which may include recitation of Kiddush and food.
kippah (*kippot*, plural):	Head covering or yarmulke.
Masorti:	Term used in Israel for the Conservative Movement.
mezuzah (*mezuzot*, plural):	Parchment of the central Jewish prayer, the Sh'ma, affixed to a doorframe in a decorative case.
minyan:	A quorum of ten Jews over age thirteen needed for public prayer, including the reading of the Torah and the recitation of the Kaddish (mourners' prayer).

na'aseh v'nishmah:	This phrase means "We will do and we will hear," which the Israelites responded at Mount Sinai when the Torah was given to them. The word order highlights their faith and willingness to serve God.
parashah:	Torah portion; the Torah is divided into fifty-four portions.
Rosh Chodesh:	New month—the first day or two days of each Hebrew month, which is observed as a one- or two-day mini-festival on which Torah is read.
Sh'ma	Central prayer of the Jewish religion recited in the morning, evening, and at bedtime. It is the declaration of belief in one God.
siddur:	Jewish prayer book.
simchah:	Celebration or happy occasion.
tallit (*tallitot*, plural):	Prayer shawl with fringes on each of the four corners.
tefillin:	Phylacteries. These leather straps hold boxes with biblical verses inside. They are wrapped around the arm and placed on the forehead during weekday morning prayers.
Tikkun:	A book used as one prepares to read from the Torah scroll. It contains a facsimile of the Torah layout in one column, and the text including vowels, punctuation, and musical notes in the other column.
tikun olam:	The Jewish concept of repairing the world or social action, often an important part of the b'nai mitzvah preparation process.
trope:	System of biblical cantillation.
tzitzit:	Ritual fringes on the four corners of the tallit (see above).
yad:	The pointer used as one chants from the Torah scroll

Index